HER… HIRE
Village Book

Compiled by the Herefordshire Federation of Women's Institutes from notes and illustrations sent by Institutes in the County

Published jointly by
Countryside Books, Newbury
and the HFWI, Hereford

First published 1989
New expanded edition 1999

COUNTRYSIDE BOOKS
3 Catherine Road
Newbury, Berkshire

ISBN 1 85306 578 1

Designed by Graham Whiteman

Front cover photo of Eardisland
and back cover photo of Lower Brockhampton
supplied by Derek Forss

Produced through MRM Associates Ltd., Reading

Printed by J.W. Arrowsmith Ltd., Bristol

Foreword

I am delighted to write the foreword to this new edition of *The Herefordshire Village Book*. Herefordshire is one of the most beautiful counties in England with its gentle undulating countryside. The rivers Wye, Lugg, Frome and Arrow thread their way through the county, joining together its market towns with the cathedral city at its heart.

But its villages, with their unique parish churches, are Herefordshire's chief delight. Tourists follow the black and white trail, the ancient half-timbered houses, now made into desirable residences whilst retaining their charm. There is much to explore in Herefordshire, a feast for the eyes with so many beautiful views and a voyage of discovery to find its history and its people.

We are very grateful to the WIs for their contributions to this new book, each one revealing a knowledge and love of the county that is their home.

Audrey Popple
Federation Chairman

Acknowledgements

The Herefordshire Federation of Women's Institutes is grateful to all members and friends for their hard work in providing the information, amendments, additions and drawings for this new edition of the Village Book. Thanks also to the co-ordinators, Evelyn Hatcher and Ann Wood and their team Paddy Ariss and Dorothy Rock.

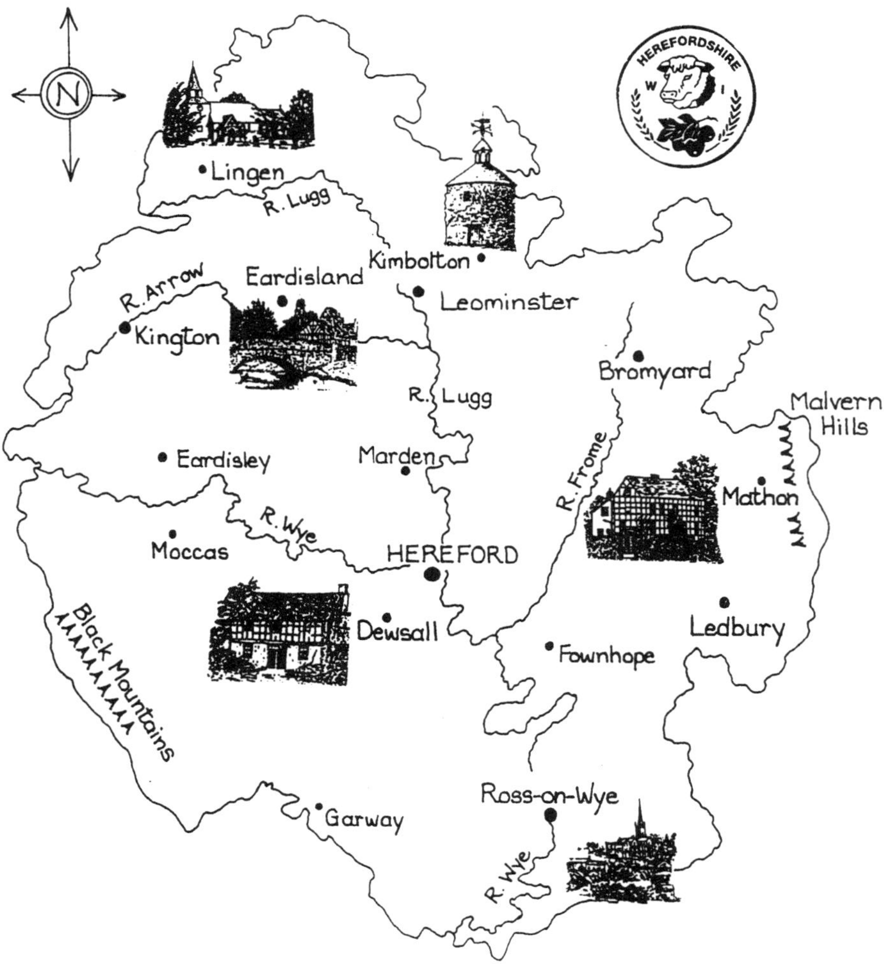
N
HEREFORDSHIRE
W
I
Lingen
R. Lugg
Kimbolton
R. Arrow
Eardisland
Leominster
Kington
Bromyard
R. Lugg
Malvern
Hills
Eardisley
Marden
R. Frome
Mathon
R. Wye
Moccas
HEREFORD
Black Mountains
Dewsall
Ledbury
Fownhope
Ross-on-Wye
Garway
R. Wye

ABBEYDORE

At the beginning of the Golden Valley is the scattered parish of Abbeydore. It is easy to find by turning off the Hereford to Abergavenny road at Pontrilas and passing through the neighbouring parish of Ewyas Harold, following the Peterchurch road.

On the parish boundary stands the Neville Arms where lunch is served every day and there is a caravan and camping site. The present building is dated 1907 but there has been an inn on the site for many years. Two hundred yards further along the road is the Old Vicarage where antique furniture is sold and restored.

Next door is the remains of a 12th century Cistercian monastery. French monks and their followers lived here until the Dissolution of the Monasteries in the 16th century. A hundred years later a member of the Scudamore family restored what can be seen today, a building one third of its original size. From that time on it has been used as a parish church and services are still held regularly. It is an impressive place where the high vaulted ceiling gives an uplifting feeling which has to be experienced to be believed.

On leaving the churchyard through the west lychgate the path passes through a farmyard which was once the village green. At the end of the path is the old village school, which is now the village hall.

From the old school the road forks to the right towards Kingstone and passes Abbeydore Court Gardens. Here on the banks of the river Dore tea is served in the idyllic setting of an English country garden.

A pleasant walk along the bank of the river passing west through the 'kissing gates' opposite the Court brings the visitor to Riverdale, a former Victorian workhouse. Now converted into private houses its grey brick facade still dominates this part of the valley.

There are no shops in Abbeydore and the nearest post office is at Bacton, a small village on the hill opposite Riverdale.

ALLENSMORE

Though its hamlets, including Cobhall and Winnal, are described in the Domesday Book, Allensmore itself did not appear on the landscape of Herefordshire until late in the 13th century, when Alan de Plokenet (or Plugenet) inherited Kilpeck Castle, and extended his lands by draining a large tract of marsh to the south of Haywood forest, which came to be called 'Alan's-moor'.

Today you can drive down the A465 south from Hereford without really being aware that you are passing through Allensmore and its scattered hamlets tucked away down narrow lanes on either side. There are and always have been farms dotted over this homely landscape, but it was originally desperate poverty which gave Allensmore its characteristic linear development of single houses strung out along the little lanes between these farms. In the 16th and 17th centuries Allensmore and its hamlets of Cobhall, Winnal, Hungerstone, Mawfield and Webtree were largely squatters' villages where people built what shelter they could along the roadside, appropriating a strip of land for cabbages, hens, and the odd pig. Though these villagers apparently earned their living as flax and hemp spinners they actually mostly begged, gleaned fields, and raided orchards and gardens.

From these unpromising and impoverished circumstances came Allensmore's greatest notoriety, when the villagers initiated and inspired a six week uprising which came to be called 'The Herefordshire Commotion'. In May 1605 Alice Wellington, a Catholic, died excommunicate from the Church of England, and was refused burial in the churchyard by the vicar, Richard Heyns. He was woken at dawn the next morning by a funeral procession of around 50 people, and by the time he could reach the churchyard Alice had been laid to rest there. Mr Heyns' outrage was met with rude responses and threats to his person, so he rushed off to report the scandal to the Bishop. As Allensmore had an absentee Catholic landlord and, like much of south-west Herefordshire, was then a staunchly Catholic area, the Bishop could not have been too surprised. But a stern response was necessary, and the High

Constable of Webtree Hundred came that same day with warrants and a posse. They attempted to arrest three ringleaders, who responded so violently that the Constable ended up with one prisoner and several damaged officers. He then lost his solitary captive on the way back to Hereford when he encountered nearly 50 men armed to the teeth with assorted weapons. The Constable sensibly decided to hand back his prisoner.

But for the next six weeks there were raids and arrests involving gentry, farmers and villagers over an ever wider area. These punitive expeditions were countered by resistance, attempted ambushes, or empty homes whose occupants had fled to the safety of Wales. By August however the rebels found themselves leaderless and priestless, and the 'Commotion' subsided as swiftly as it had begun.

The church of St Andrew, where the 'Commotion' began, is typical of many churches in south Herefordshire, with its massive square tower with a peal of six bells. But only the Norman south doorway is older than medieval times. The east window contains beautiful fragments of ancient glass, said to be from the cathedral, and on the south wall is a large early 14th century window with three trefoiled lights, one of only two in the county. Outside, to the right of the porch, is an unusual tombstone carved with a blacksmith working at his forge.

Nearby is one of several attractive half-timbered houses scattered through the parish, of which the oldest is the cruck-framed Little Cobhall Farm. Examples of many types of domestic architecture, including Georgian and Victorian, can be found along the lanes. But Allensmore Court, home of the Pateshalls who became lords of the manor in 1725, was demolished in 1957 some years after the death of the last lady of the manor. The family were generous local benefactors and contributed much of the £1,000 needed for restoring the church in 1880. The village school which opened in 1870 was built on a site given by Evan Pateshall. Unfortunately the school closed in 1957 and now local children are bussed three miles to Kingstone. Happily the old school is now the village hall and is in regular use by the local people and their organisations.

Trains no longer stop at Tram Inn station, but frequent buses run the five miles to Hereford where many locals work. The flax and hemp spinners have long disappeared, but employment is now provided locally by the farms, two plant nurseries, a grain mill, a stud farm and the well known all-in-one garage, petrol station, post office and comprehensive general stores.

In 1871 there were 147 houses in Allensmore parish; today there are only 156. And future development must be very strictly limited, as it is now, by the perennial drainage problems caused by a huge impervious clay barrier just below the land surface.

ALMELEY

Almeley village is 400 feet above sea level, with views across to the Wye valley, the Black Mountains, and in the distance the Brecon Beacons.

There are many 17th and 18th century half-timbered buildings of interest. St Mary's church is 13th to 14th century with massive tower walls. It is a beautiful church and well worth a visit.

Castle Frome is 17th century with an adjoining 15th century barn, now part of the house. Three cruck timbers rise in a curve from the ground to the roof ridge. This building was an open hall; two thirds of the crucks and roof are soot marked, while one third was partly enclosed and is unstained.

Almeley Manor or Court House is of medieval origin, timber-framed with brick. In about the 15th century, the two-storeyed porch was added. The outer entrance has a moulded lintel, possibly Norman.

The Friends Meeting House was built by the first Quaker to live at Almeley, Roger Pritchard, who bought Summer House Farm in 1669. He converted a cottage into the Quaker Meeting House in 1672, and meetings are still held there every Sunday morning.

Nieuport estate had many owners and it was finally sold in 1909. Half the farms were bought by tenants, the rest by Mr Collet Mason, who sold it in 1919 to the Herefordshire County Council. Farms were divided into smallholdings (as today). Nieuport House became a sanatorium, closing in 1951. The Latvian Society took it in 1953 as a home for elderly Latvian refugees. This closed in 1997, and the house has been sold again.

Almeley has a post office, and The Bells inn incorporating the village shop, as well as The Lyon Inn at Ferney Common. The recreation hall built in 1926 is the social centre for all village activities, and has recently been refurbished.

Agriculture is the chief occupation in Almeley. There are no factories, and some residents find work in Hereford or Kington. The parish acreage is 3,550. Some cider orchards have been planted, a few farmers having given up milk production, and there are beekeepers in the parish. One misses the old country words and dialects, like 'unts' and 'untytumps' (moles and molehills).

In 1988 a conservation order was placed on part of the village, along a footpath to the Batch, past where two streams meet. High above this spot is a 'Twt' or 'Toot' of the Saxon period, a military lookout on the end of a flat plateau stretching from Woonton on past Summer House, Malt House and the Friends Meeting House, all listed buildings. A private conservation area has been developed at Batch Cottage.

There is an old story of The Buck Inn, Woonton, when a farming wizard from Preston came for a meal. When asked what he should pay, the landlady said, 'Fourpence to eat, four to drink, eight pence in all.' The farmer considered this too much and, placing the money on paper in the middle of the table, he drew a circle round it. When the landlady tried to take the money she began to run round the table unable to stop, saying, 'Four to eat, four to drink, eight on the whole.' A servant tried to stop her, but she too ran round after her mistress. The ostler came to help, and he too went round the table. Another servant went after the farmer who told him, 'You take the money with a pair of tongs, that'll stop 'em.' It did.

In 1994 mains drainage came to the village, and in 1998 some new houses were built. However, a proposal for street lighting was rejected, and Almeley remains a peaceful, beautiful and friendly village.

ASHPERTON

Ashperton stands on an old Roman way between the Hereford/Worcester and Hereford/Ledbury roads. It is now the main

Gloucester/Leominster route and although the modern road goes through Canon Frome and Stretton Grandison, it deviates somewhat from the original. The histories of these three villages are very much entwined.

When John de Monmouth died in 1270 the land at Ashperton became the property of William de Grandison who built a manor and later converted it to a castle and moat. His wife Sibille, while her husband was away crusading, was afraid of walking over the swamps of the Frome to their church at Stretton Grandison and had a chapel of ease built at Ashperton. In the early 14th century this chapel was entirely rebuilt and became the forerunner of the present church. In the early 1840s a tower was added to the west end and later was re-roofed with slates. The story is told of a later vicar who, when his own house roof leaked, used to take the slates off the church roof to repair it.

In 1375 the Grandison family became extinct. A map of the early 18th century shows the castle mound with trees growing on it and the moat, but no castle. That is how it is today and it is fished by local anglers who belong to the Ledbury Angling Society. It is all now owned by a local farmer who inherited it from his father.

Several gentlemen left money to be invested and used for a variety of purposes: ten women in the village had a loaf of bread supplied each week delivered from Hereford, which caused consternation to the Hereford baker as these women had their bread from local bakers during the rest of the week; coats were to be provided for four men each year; and crown pieces were to be given to eight women in need, perhaps widows. Apprenticeships were also paid for. The charity is now called 'Consolidated Charities' and two trustees distribute money from land rents and invested money. This takes place on 21st December each year.

The Hereford/Gloucester Canal which runs through Ashperton, Canon Frome and Stretton Grandison to carry coal, cheese, timber etc was begun in the 1790s. In 1861 the opening of Ashperton railway line to Hereford killed all the canal trade and it fell into disuse. Unfortunately the railway station fell victim to the Beeching cuts in the early 1960s and closed down.

Eventually much of the land at Ashperton and Canon Frome

came to be owned by the Hopton family. Then in the 1950s most of the estate was sold off to the farmers and workers on the estate. To this day there are few rented properties and only two council houses.

Until 1988 there was one village pub – The Box Bush – but it closed down, having been in the licensee's family for over 80 years. During the Second World War this pub ran the 'corner' shop and at one time dealt with 1,000 ration books – many of these belonging to gypsies who were working for local farmers. This shop closed in the 1960s and since then there has not been one. Sadly there is now no pub but the Hopton Arms, just further down the road, although just over the border into Munsley village, is considered the 'local'.

In the early 1970s Sun Valley built a factory farm in Woodsend, Ashperton which at the time was regretted by most villagers. The site is on the edge of Ashperton Park, an area of ancient woodland. Now the factory is hardly noticed as it is surrounded by trees.

Ashperton is now a mixture of newcomers and locals, happily blending together. In the 1850s the population was about 600, a far cry from the original 50 or so in the 11th century, but nowadays it has fallen back to approximately 140–150.

There are still many farms in the village but most workers commute to nearby towns. There is a proportion of new property in the village, mostly built in the late 1970s but it blends in well with the old.

ASHTON, MORETON & EYE

The Luston group of parishes is situated in the north of Herefordshire within two miles of the Shropshire border, the parish boundary joining the out-parish of the market town of Leominster. Ashton, Moreton and Eye were a close-knit community with the majority of their residents being dependent for their livelihood on the estate around the mansion of Berrington Hall. All the land in these three hamlets was owned by the Berrington estate, most of which was let as tenanted farms.

During the Second World War, Berrington Hall was a hospital, mainly for convalescent servicemen. Six thousand American soldiers 'invaded' the peaceful countryside, and huts were built for them in the parkland of Berrington Hall and Ashton. Prisoners of war, Italian and German, followed the Americans into the parkland huts. They travelled daily to work on farms in the area. Several married local girls and didn't return home after the war. After the war in 1946 'squatters' occupied the huts. Some were soldiers returning from the war, marrying and setting up home in them because there was nowhere else to live. The huts were finally demolished in 1954.

In 1957 the 3rd Lord Cawley surrendered to the Treasury the house, park and 'pool' in part payment of estate duty as a consequence of his father's death. The property came into the ownership of the National Trust. The death of Dowager Lady Cawley in 1978 at 100 years of age marked the end of the mansion as a home providing the livelihood of many workers.

Tourists have started to be important to the area, several farmers' wives provide bed and breakfast accommodation and changing fortunes in farming have seen the conversion of one farmer's buildings into self-catering accommodation and more recently rural workshops. A thriving craft business with candlemaking as its main enterprise offers an interesting visitor centre and coffee shop in an old barn on another one-time smallholding.

Seven farms owned by Lord Cawley were rented out to other farmers. Now only two are tenanted and one has been sold off. The remainder, as the tenants retired, have been amalgamated into the Berrington Hall estate which employs only seven full time agricultural workers to farm almost 2,000 acres of land.

In the 1920s three farms grew hops in Ashton village to supply the many small breweries in and around Leominster. The last hopyard was dismantled in 1988. Sadly the 'hop flavour' for beer can now be produced synthetically.

Moreton and Eye have as their centre the village church of St Peter and St Paul dating back to 1170. Eye Manor built in 1680, famous for its 17th century plaster ceilings, stands adjacent to the church and became the vicarage in 1817 until 1912. The Rev Wilfred Buckle (1890) employed a curate, farmed two farms and had an enterprising daughter who turned the house into an academy for young gentlewomen in about 1900.

The derelict canal that passes through Moreton was part of the Kington, Leominster and Stourport Canal projected in 1790 to bring coal from the Shropshire coalfields. Only two parts remain in the area - a stagnant area near the road by the vet's surgery with a hump-backed bridge over it called the cutting bridge, and a lane from Ashton to Orleton called Tunnel Lane which passes the remains of an old canal tunnel.

The railway played an important part in the village until 1950, being used for transporting coal, fertilizer and farm machinery and used by children attending secondary school in Leominster and several people who worked there. The stationmaster retired in 1950 and passenger traffic ceased in 1967.

The villages of Ashton, Eye and Moreton retain their agricultural link, many still being employed in farming, although most of the children are leaving the area to take up other professions. Cottages are being sold off the Berrington Hall estate as they become vacant. Five new dwellings have been built in Ashton and Moreton since 1970, two of them for agricultural workers, until then the last new house was built in 1934. Three council-owned smallholdings are still farmed as mixed farms in a traditional way but with modern machinery.

ASTON & ELTON

Aston and Elton, surrounded by hills, are in the north of the county, tending to look to Wigmore as well as Ludlow for facilities, and part of a group parish council since 1973.

Aston's parish church of St Giles is of Norman foundation and built of sandstone. The north doorway has some decorative carving. The chancel was rebuilt in the 13th century. Just to the north-east of the church is a mound which was perhaps the remnants of an ancient castle or fortification.

Elton has the 18th century Elton Hall, where Thomas Andrew Knight lived till 1809 and where he experimented with new varieties of cherries. The parish church is close by and is of Norman origin, although it was rebuilt in 1876. The royal arms of Queen Elizabeth I can be seen inside, carved in wood.

In the mid 19th century Aston had a public house but it appears that Elton never had one. In both of these settlements farm buildings are being converted into dwellings.

ASTON INGHAM

Aston Ingham is not so much a village as a parish of scattered dwellings collected into tiny hamlets. These are set in rolling fields and orchards against a backdrop of hills and woodland.

Aston Ingham is mentioned in the Domesday Book where it appears as Estune. The Romans established a look-out post on Cwm (or Coombe) Hill, and further evidence of the Roman occupation was discovered in 1855 when a Mr Irving reported the finding of two buried chests containing Roman bronze and copper coins, on Cwm Hill. They are dated the end of the 4th century. However, it is believed that Aston Ingham's history could go even further back as it lies in a direct line or ley from the camp on May Hill to that on Aconbury. It is thought that a tumulus or long barrow could lie beneath the church.

At the time of the Norman Conquest, the living was given to the Abbey de Cormeilles in Normandy. However, after about a century it was sold to a wealthy family – the Ingayns. Thus, Estune Ingayn through the centuries has become Aston Ingham.

The church was largely rebuilt in 1891 but there still remain small evidences of the very ancient church which once stood here. It has a very fine lead font, dated 1689 and inscribed with the letters W.M., W.R., commemorating the reign of William and Mary. There are believed to be only 38 such fonts in the country. There are also two carved, stone coffin lids believed to date from the 12th century, possibly those of Sir Thomas de Eston, one time lord of the manor, and his wife.

The church is well known for having the lightest ring of bells in the county. The six bells have a total weight of only 18cwt 2qrs 18lbs. It also has an almost unique record created by the Whatley family. A Charles Whatley was appointed to the living as rector in

St John the Baptist church at Aston Ingham

1785 and began an unbroken line of Whatleys at the rectory until 1964. There are still members of the family living in the village today.

There has been only a very limited amount of new building permitted in Aston Ingham but virtually all the old cottages and farmhouses have been modernized and extended. There are still several very old houses in use. The oldest, Springfield Grange, dates from the mid 12th century, although recent boundary changes now put it outside the parish. Babylon Farm dates from the beginning of the 15th century and Upper Coldridge (now derelict) from the early 16th century although the west barn to this farm is dated a century earlier. Warren Farm, Knightshill Farm and the now derelict Old Oaks Farm are all mid 16th century and Coldwell Cottage, now The Moate, and Blakemoor Farm, now derelict, are early 17th century.

Like many villages which can trace their history through the centuries, Aston Ingham acquired several charities and customs, some of which are still in existence today.

The school was founded from an annuity of £10 in the will of a Christopher Stocke – this annuity 'For and toward the setting up, keeping and maintaining of a free school in the parish of Aston Ingham for the teaching and instructing of ten poor boys of the parish forever.' There is also a field which is owned by the parish, although it lies outside the boundary, which is known as the Stockings Field (Stock Ings) and which has recently been brought back into use for the village as a recreational ground with a cricket pitch, tennis courts and space for sports and fetes.

The Booth charity, set up by Stephen Booth, dates from 1889. From it, part provided each child in the school with a new one shilling piece annually and the rest went first to a clothing and coal club. Later the money provided book prizes at the school.

A third bequest which is still carried out annually is that known as the Garrold Bread. Richard Garrold, who died in 1859, left money 'to buy a loaf of bread for each poor family in the parish, to be distributed at Candlemas (2nd February) for ever.' The bread is still blessed in church and handed out to parishioners on the Sunday nearest to 2nd February.

Two other customs which sadly have fallen into disuse are the celebration, on 11th August, of the reopening of the restored church and the harvesting of the cherry crop, the former with a service followed by a tea party and sports, the latter wlth a feast at the local inns. Today, village cricket, Scout sports and church bazaars are all equally well supported and enjoyed.

Many local people still have a soft Hereford dialect and use names and words peculiar to the district. In addition, the strange use of pronouns and tenses makes the brogue fascinating listening.

At one time, practically everyone living in Aston Ingham would have worked on the land, or have been connected with it in some way. It is still an agricultural parish although the actual numbers employed on the land are in a minority nowadays. There is both livestock and arable farming and apple orchards abound, albeit of the commercial type, not the cider apples for which the area was once famous. There are also enterprises growing mushrooms and chicory and a gunsmith has replaced the blacksmith. Most people in employment, however, must travel to the surrounding towns to find work.

AYLTON

To the east of Putley lies the parish of Aylton. The population is small and scattered amongst 27 houses. The church dates from the 12th century and stands on a mound. Its dedication has been lost in the mists of time, as have all the early deeds and papers relating to the parish. These were probably burned along with those of Putley and other parishes in Herefordshire at the time of the Civil War of the 17th century.

Adjacent to the church is Court Farm, once famous for its cider which was sold as far off as Wales. It was also a hop growing area, but this has largely been given over to other methods of farming. About a mile distant is Aylton Court, where in the 1850s the daughter of the family was accidentally shot by her brother upon his return from a shooting expedition. He tripped on the doorstep and the gun went off, killing her instantly. According to the parish register she was buried in the churchyard, but soon after her burial bodysnatchers desecrated the tomb and her body was stolen, probably for medical research. The grave remains empty. It is said that her ghost can be encountered upon the staircase at the house.

Changing patterns in agriculture have brought about the fragmentation of most of the farms and a large number of the farm buildings are now given over to housing. The church has recently been repaired, restored and decorated and remains open for regular worship.

AYMESTREY

Aymestrey lies some 20 miles north of Hereford in an area typical of the lovely countryside which borders Wales. The A4110, which is part of the old Roman Watling Street, goes through the village and narrow lanes network the area joining the outlying farms and houses and the hamlets of Yatton, Leinthall Earles, Covenhope and Upper Lye. Hills, woods, pastures, the river Lugg and the abundance of footpaths make it a popular place for walkers and a pleasant place to live. Topography has made the village a ribbon development and it has a church, shop with post office, village hall, garden centre and a pub, the Riverside Inn.

The Battle of Mortimer's Cross took place during the Wars of the Roses in 1461 and was a victory for Edward, Duke of York, later King Edward IV, who was trying to prevent the Lancastrians reaching his castles at Ludlow and at Wigmore (held by his mother Ann Mortimer). The day of the battle was Candlemas Day when snow lay on the ground and the prevailing atmospheric conditions produced three separate images of the sun, which Edward interpreted as an omen in his favour. Some 4,000 men were killed and it is thought that some of them are buried in a mass grave in Aymestrey churchyard. An inscribed tablet (dated 1799) to commemorate the event may be seen at the junction of the A4110 and the B4630 north-west of Kingsland.

The church, dedicated to St John the Baptist and St Alkmund, dates from Norman times, with alterations and additions made during its long history. The beautiful rood and parclose screens are a notable feature. There are six bells in the tower, one of which can be rung from the porch. This was rung every evening to guide travellers bewitched or tempted out of their way in Poke House Wood. The bellringer was paid from the rent from a piece of land which had been set aside by one of the unfortunates who had been plagued by 'Poke' (Puck). The present clock (1875) replaced a much older one which was an exhibit in the Science Museum at Kensington until 1952. It is now in Leominster Museum.

Quarrying of sand and gravel on a commercial scale has been carried out at Aymestrey since the 1950s. In 1987 a Bronze Age burial tomb or cist containing the skeleton of a child of about eight years old was found during excavation work.

There are two old mills – Aymestrey Mill and Mortimer's Cross Mill. The original mill at Aymestrey was mentioned in the Domesday Book and the present mill dates back to the early 1800s and was producing flour until the mid 1960s. Today it is in a good state of repair and in working condition. The old stables adjoining have been converted into a print-making studio producing hand-printed lithographic limited editions for artists. The flat-bed lithographic press is driven by gears, belts and pulley wheels powered by the water wheel, and the present owner has installed a water turbine which generates electricity for heating and lighting. The mill at Mortimer's Cross was in operation until 1940 when it was run single-handed by a 20 year old miller. The mill dates from the 18th century and is driven from underneath instead of water falling onto the wheel from above. This mill is open to the public.

As this is a rural area about half the population are farmers or in some way connected with agriculture. these are mainly 'local' families, often inter-related. Nearby Gatley Park is the home of Sir Thomas Dunne who is the Lord Lieutenant of Hereford and Worcester.

BALLINGHAM

The small scattered village of Ballingham is situated on the river Wye, approximately nine miles from Hereford and nine from Ross-on-Wye. The village boasts lovely walks along the river bank and country footpaths with panoramic views. There is a great deal of privately owned salmon fishing in the area.

The school has been closed for many years but the building still stands, dating back to 1827. It serves as a village hall but is due for renovation. This attractive hall stands by the village green and pond which was reclaimed in 1977 (the Queen's Silver Jubilee year) by the endeavours of Ballingham & District WI. A bench is provided there, from which to savour the peaceful atmosphere.

The local railway disappeared in the 1960s, and the small station remains as a private dwelling. The ferry across to Fownhope had ceased many years earlier – it was used mainly to ferry parishioners across to see the doctor.

The parish church, dedicated to St Dubricius, was restored in 1883 but the porch still survives from the 11th century. Opposite the church is Ballingham Hall which dates from 1642. There was a beautiful red brick barn but it was blown down in a gale.

Part of Ballingham Wood has been felled and replanted, but until the trees mature the area provides panoramic views hitherto unseen.

BARONS CROSS

Not long ago, Barons Cross was essentially farms and orchards, but in recent years much of this has been razed to the ground. Now there are around a thousand houses.

Today Barons Cross is part of Leominster even if at arms-length and consequently facilities like school, post office and shops are about a mile away.

BARTESTREE

The parish of Bartestree consists of 421 acres and it starts at the crossroads on the A438 Ledbury road. The old village of Bartestree lay around the chapel dedicated to St James but today's main road bypasses the narrow chapel lane. The present chapel is the third on the site, the first being of Norman origin. Until 1928 the chapel was under the jurisdiction of Dormington and the Bartestree children were expected to walk four miles each way to school at Tarrington. Bartestree Court is a 17th century timber-framed building, enlarged and partly faced with brick in the 19th century.

There are two large farms, Lower Bartestree and Pomona Farm. Pomona lies in the north-east of the parish, on the south side of the line of the old Roman road. Near the lane to Pomona a hop field can be seen by the old railway bridge. Mr Godwin built his tile works here near to good clay beds in 1868. The site was chosen for its convenience to the now redundant canal and railway station.

There is evidence of an early settlement in the field opposite the lower end of the chapel lane, where it joins the Ledbury road. From this point the building most worthy of note is visible. One cannot fail to observe the Victorian Gothic pile of buildings, the Roman Catholic convent of the order of Our Lady of Charity and Refuge.

Elizabeth, the eldest daughter of Robert Biddulph Phillips MP of Longworth Hall, had entered the mother convent of the order in Caen, Normandy. After her mother's death she returned home and her father founded the convent in 1863, a year before his death. The convent was a refuge for the reformation and employment of 'fallen' women. At the turn of the 20th century there was a thriving laundry business and underwear was manufactured. The standard of work was so high that linen was sent from all parts of the kingdom. There are some beautifully embroidered altar cloths to be seen. Today, St Michael's Hospice has been built in the convent grounds on land given by the nuns. It exudes a very peaceful atmosphere.

There is a spacious Roman Catholic chapel attached to the convent. However, Mr Phillips wished that the chapel of about 1330 at Old Longworth should be removed and rebuilt at the convent. This wish was carried out after his death and it is in regular use.

The roads are greatly improved today, but the *Hereford Times* of 13th November 1852 reports that the Gloucester mail coach bound for Aberystwyth hit disaster in bad floods. There were three passengers, the coachman and a guard, as well as mail and parcels. At half past five the coach approached the bridge between Dormington and Bartestree, over the river Frome, commonly known as Five Bridges, through a considerable depth of water. Suddenly the coachman was heard to utter a cry of 'Good God' and in an instant the coach was deep in the water. Although it was dark, help arrived and everyone was rescued. Mr Hardwick, a Hereford solicitor and one of the passengers, was taken to one of the Longworth lodges where sadly he died. The remnants of the bridge can still be seen upstream from the present road and bridge near Moor mills.

There is no shop or public house at Bartestree and the inhabitants have to go into new Bartestree for their recreation. In the late 1980s, the Council erected a Bartestree village sign on the road where it had previously been known as Hagley, as shown on the Ordnance Survey map. The post office situated in Hagley had nevertheless been known as Bartestree PO to prevent confusion with Hagley in Birmingham! The old village hall and the New Inn public house were in Hagley – however, the former was demolished in 1995 and the site redeveloped with housing, taking the name of St James Close. In 1997 a new village hall was erected, complete with extensive playing fields, and is now much used by the community.

BELMONT

Belmont first came into being when a wealthy landowner, Mr Wegg Prosser, built Belmont House and the abbey. He was a recent convert and offered the abbey to the Benedictines. After some discussion, because the original site of their abbey had been at Newport they decided to settle in the English/Welsh border country and in 1854 Belmont Abbey was founded. On 21st November 1859, the monastery was officially opened with the title of St Michael's, Belmont which became the Common Noviciate for Benedictine Congregation; a house of studies for Juniors of the Brotherhood.

The house is now Belmont Golf Club. Belmont also consisted of five farms starting with Pool Farm at the city end of Belmont Road, five cottages and a post office.

Today Belmont is a rapidly growing housing area extending from the city of Hereford as far as the river.

BISHOPS FROME

The approach to Bishops Frome from the west, on the main Hereford–Worcester road, crosses the built up embankment over the flood plain of the little river Frome which gives its name to the village. The ecclesiastical part comes from the fact that the valley of the Frome belonged to the Church at the time of the Domesday Book in 1086. From any other direction, a traveller will usually come down one of the three steep hills leading to the village – Stanley Hill from Ledbury, Fromes Hill from Worcester, or Summerpool Hill from Bromyard.

The church, in the centre of the village, sits firmly and comfortably on the raised mound which may well indicate a previous Saxon stronghold before the Normans built on the site. Little remains of their 12th century church except the round arch of the south door and the beautiful chancel arch. But a visitor should not miss the massive lead-lined Norman font, or the effigy of the Knight Templar.

There is ample evidence of the Civil War in the area. With Royalists garrisoned at nearby Canon Frome, and Parliamentarians in the next village of Bosbury, the soldiers may well have spent their free time in the Green Dragon, which is a pub of great antiquity. Cannonballs have been found locally and an elderly resident remembers that a field on the slopes of Ward Hill, the highest point in the village (550 ft), was called 'The Bloody Verlands'! He spent much of his boyhood playing war games on the site.

There are now six public houses in the village, since the Holly Bush has closed down. The Chase is actually next door to The Green Dragon, The Major's Arms is in the middle of a steeply winding road called Snails' Bank and a little further up on the brow of Fromes Hill is The Wheatsheaf. Down at river level are The Five Bridges and The Fir Tree on opposite sides of the main road. Several explanations can be given for this cluster of pubs, the most likely being the nature of farming over the last 300 years. Until recently, when agricultural practice has changed rapidly, nearly the whole of the Frome valley was planted with hops which involved a lot of casual labour during September and October, especially when the picking was done by hand.

In the 1920s, the heyday of the hop-picking era, the population of Bishops Frome would rise from about 700 to as many as 5,000. At that time there was in the village a farmer and successful businessman called Farmer Pudge who particularly liked pickers who brought their own accommodation, such as the true Romanies, who set their beautiful horse-drawn caravans on the fields on one side of the road, and the 'hedge crawlers', as they were called, who had their untidy camps on the opposite side. Other farmers had their pickers from South Wales and the Black Country. It was a wild and exciting time for the village and money flowed in and there was a great need for places to quench the thirst and for conviviality in the evenings.

But what of the Courts in the village? There are seven of these too, all within a mile of the church. On a hill to the north is Hall Court, in the valley Broadfield Court, Kingstone Court, and Paunton Court by the mill. On the slopes of Summerpool Hill is Instone Court. Sadly, Court Farm, in the centre of the village, has been demolished, but the retirement bungalows built near the site still bear the name of Farm Court. But the oldest and most interesting was Cheyney Court. Unfortunately the beautiful Elizabethan manor house, which seems to have been built on a much earlier foundation, was burnt down in 1888. So the present Cheyney Court is of the 20th century, but there are some ruins of the old building and especially of the chapel which adjoined it and traces of the moat can still be found.

BISHOPSWOOD

Bishopswood lies on the banks of the river Wye about four miles south-east of Ross-on-Wye. It is a very scattered village and the adjacent scenery has romantic beauty and loveliness not surpassed anywhere on the Wye. Part of Bishopswood is in Gloucestershire, the dividing line being a brook which goes underground just above the site of an old mansion, reappearing at the riverside.

The name Bishopswood is derived from it being part of the Bishop of Hereford's estate in the Ross area, and in 1442 the Bishop promoted one of his valets, Alexander Jordan, to the office of 'Keeper of the Woods'. The woods were used for hunting and timber felling.

In 1590 iron smelting was started when the Earl of Essex became owner of the land. However, there is evidence of Roman ironworks in the area! Blast furnaces for casting pig iron were erected in the reign of Charles II by the Foleys. After several changes of hands they were purchased in 1801 by the brothers John and William Partridge who during a long and prosperous career were regarded as two of the most prominent and successful ironmasters of the period in the Forest of Dean and South Wales areas. Imported bar iron was brought up river in barges and remelted at Bishopswood. Coal was also brought from the Forest of Dean and dispatched down river from Bishopswood wharf, now more usually known as Pebbley Beach.

Further evidence of Roman occupation came in 1895 when on a wooded hill behind the church, the largest hoard of Roman coins found in Herefordshire was unearthed by workmen on the estate. An estimated 18,000 coins from the period AD 290-360 were found in two earthenware pots.

The church of All Saints was built in 1841 by John Partridge, the ironmaster. He also provided the furnishings. It was dedicated in 1845 and services are still held there every Sunday. Built of local stone, it is situated in the wood and several hairpin bends are negotiated to reach it. The church itself is not very ornate compared with others in the area, but its sheer simplicity gives it its unique beauty and peacefulness.

The school was built next door to the church in 1850, again founded by John Partridge. It is now a private house, appropriately renamed The Glebe House.

Kerne Bridge lies on the westerly edge of Bishopswood. The bridge itself was built in 1834 and is without doubt one of the loveliest bridges on the Wye. Stand on the bridge and look westward over the top of Flanesford Priory – you will get a magnificent view of Goodrich Castle nobly outlined against the skyline. The castle, which stands on a promontory overlooking the river, is about half a mile away as the crow flies. It would seem that until the building of the bridge this little part of Bishopswood was known simply as 'Kerne'.

The main Ross–Monmouth–Chepstow railway line which opened in August 1873 ran through Kerne Bridge until it closed to passenger service in January 1959. The station flower gardens were lovingly tended by the last stationmaster for many years until its closure and he was repeatedly awarded the trophy for the best kept station. Now it is used as an adventure centre for The National Association of Boys Clubs and has been renovated and extended.

Some 50 years ago most people were engaged in agricultural work or would have worked on the Bishopswood estate, which was sold off in 1949. Nowadays one source of employment is factories in Ross and the Forest of Dean while quite a lot of people commute further afield.

At present two public houses serve the community. There is an excellent village stores, post office and filling station at Bishopswood and the milkman delivers daily on the main road and every other day to the more remote places. A baker calls three times a week and a butcher twice a week. There is a limited bus service to Ross. Salmon fishing is world renowned on this stretch of the Wye but it is all privately owned.

BLAKEMERE

Blakemere is a small roadside village on the B4352 Hereford to Hay-on-Wye road. The focal point is the church, dedicated to St Leonard, the patron saint of prisoners, the sick and women in labour. It dates from between 1180 and 1200 but, owing to extensive damage by fire, was entirely rebuilt in 1877 in a very similar form. It was visited by the Rev Francis Kilvert and mentioned in his diaries. In the churchyard is a preaching cross dating back to the 14th century. The head is mid-Victorian but it is remarkable because the shaft is a single stone, which is very rare.

The village green boasts a rare gnarled Black Poplar tree of great age and a maple and a chestnut planted to commemorate the Queen's Silver Jubilee in 1977. The green is ideal for fund-raising events in the summer. Several ancient black and white cottages surround the churchyard and across the green there is a group of mellow Georgian red-brick farm buildings and a handsome house. Behind the churchyard the ground drops to a lake (probably the origin of the name of the village), then rises sharply to Blakemere Hill Wood on the outermost ridge of the Black Mountains.

There are about 35 houses and 70 residents in the village, all but two of the dwellings being detached. Many changes have taken place here in the last few years. An old coach house at Blakemere House has been razed to the ground, for instance, and a fine house of old red brick and stone and boasting a clock tower built in its place. One of the red-brick barns was converted into a house several years ago and another barn is now being converted into two houses, one of which also has a clock tower.

Travelling down through the village towards Hereford, the Raven Garage has disappeared and two houses have been built on the site. On the opposite side of the road is Well Cottage with its wonderful garden, open by appointment under the National Gardens scheme. At the furthermost tip of the village, Lower Blakemere Farm is now also the home of the Wiggly Wigglers Worm Farm, which has put Blakemere on the European map. Farming is still the main occupation in the village, with the addition of trees as a crop in many fields, and a nursery producing herbaceous plants.

BODENHAM

'A rich man's village' in Saxon times, and Bodenham's well favoured setting has maintained this description down the ages. There are some clues that Bodenham was intended to become grander than just a lovely village in the valley of the Lugg, as that river makes its meandering detour to skirt Dinmore (Din Mawr) Hill. On the village green stands a market cross – the market failed; the unique lantern of the church should have grown into a handsome spire – did the money run out?

The Arkwright dynasty, descended from the inventor of the spinning frame, paradoxically fixed the village in a pre-industrial golden age. From their seat at Hampton Court, they gradually bought up nearly every dwelling in the village, maintained them all with judicious improvements, made sure they all had ample gardens, built nothing new. The worst fate to be imagined by a cottager for over a hundred years is still reflected in a local saying – 'Either that, or leave Hampton!'

Modern Bodenham hides under the shadow of Queenswood through which passes the A49 trunk road. Follow the side road along the wood hanging over the lake, where deer steal down to drink in the dusk. Leave the old village over a graceful stone bridge and reach the newer settlement of the Moor, commanded by the England' s Gate inn on an ancient crossing.

A Middle Ages heatwave supported terraced vines on Bun Hill, and today at Broadfield Court, itself dating from the 14th century, excellent wines are again being produced as part of a modern farming enterprise. Also centred in Bodenham are two major potato handling operations, and the A417 which skirts the Moor has also helped the expansion of the grain drying syndicate. A thriving post office, garage and store, a joinery workshop and a famous bargain warehouse complement the commercial scene.

This widely flung settlement, the largest in north Herefordshire, is thus able to support an excellent primary school and a more than viable church congregation. It has a fine modern village hall, tennis courts and children's play area, and even an endowed group of sheltered homes, with resident warden, surrounding their own beautiful bowling green.

The valley sides are still heavily wooded, and cattle-grazing still predominates in the flood plain. The Hunt kennels are still at Ketch Gate, and the bells still ring out from that odd looking tower. But this is no heritage park – Bodenham balances old and new to display, on a good day, the very best of English country life.

BOLSTONE

Bolstone is a small parish seven miles south-east from Hereford, and a similar distance north-west from Ross-on-Wye. The whole parish is little more than 650 acres, mostly farmland with a good proportion of woodland. It was formerly part of the Holme Lacy estate, being joined ecclesiastically with the parish of Holme Lacy. Bolstone is now united with the adjoining parish of Ballingham.

It is unfortunate that the church is no longer used, although the burial ground is still available for interment. The church and the house nearby (now the farmhouse) were once owned by the brotherhood of Knights Hospitallers. The church was known as the chapel of ease of St John of Jerusalem in about 1050. It is a small compact building with seats for 60 people and there are two bells in a small open belfry.

A Norman doorway (now built up) is situated on the north side of the church, with gargoyles of two heads of fishes carved in stone and its dripstone ending in dragons. There are also five stained glass windows, one of the Nativity and another of the Resurrection. Among the windows is a very good group of three restored Norman examples in deep splays. The church was completely restored in 1877.

As one looks around from the tiny church tucked snugly away by an old timbered farmhouse, there is nothing to see, only hilltops and scattered dwellings peeping from the trees, amounting to 15 properties, the homes of Bolstone's 40 or so inhabitants.

What were tiny cottages, with the families employed on the land, are now mostly enlarged and modernized. One farm dwelling which was tenanted and farmed is now leased as a private house with the land also leased in various lots to neighbouring farmers. Bolstone is unique in that every house has water from a well or reservoir – no mains water being available.

BOSBURY

Bosbury is situated four miles from Ledbury and is a rural community with a population of about 800. It is one of the most important hop-growing centres in the county.

The Bishops of Hereford had a palace here, the gateway of which still survives as a tall archway with wooden gates and pedestrian entrance. Next to this was the gaol, a more refined building than most of the period. The walls are still standing.

The church is late 12th century of Norman design and stands on the site of an earlier church. It has a free-standing bell tower, one of seven in the county, and a ring of six bells. The large stone in the churchyard near the bell tower was found buried under the cross of St Cuthbert when the cross was moved to its present position. It is believed to have been used for worship in pagan times.

The grammar school for boys was founded by Sir Rowland Morton in 1546. It stands next to the gaol. The school is no longer used, having been replaced by a new building for mixed pupils in the 1960s.

There are many fine black and white houses in Bosbury. Temple Court, just outside the village, stands on the site of the preceptory of the Knights Templars, a military order established in 1118 and disbanded in 1312 on the orders of the Pope.

The Bell Inn was once two houses owned by the Bishops of Hereford, and dates from the 15th century. It was first mentioned as an inn in 1870. There were then five inns in Bosbury, one of which was The Dog, which is also 15th century and is situated in the main street. Another inn was The Crown, just beyond the bridge over the river Leadon. In Elizabethan times it was the house of the steward of the manor.

Bosbury House, an imposing Georgian mansion, lies half a mile from the village on the Bosbury-Cradley road. In the first half of the 20th century it was owned by the Buchanan family who after the First World War established several small-holdings called The Settlements, for officers returning from the war. Today these holdings are administered by the County Council.

Philip Clisset moved to the village in 1838 when he was 21 years old and set up as a chairmaker. His chairs became known all over the county. His ordinary wooden chairs sold in the markets for 2s 6d to 4s each, the armchairs at 8s 6d each. He became involved with the Arts and Crafts movement in the 1880s and died in 1913 aged 96. Many of his chairs can be seen in the collections at Churchill Gardens, Hereford.

Bosbury has its own carol which consists of 18 verses. The exact date and author are unknown but it had been sung for a hundred years in 1891 so it is over 200 years old.

On 27th May, known as Royal Oak Apple day, everyone used to wear oak leaves or oak apples to commemorate King Charles' escape from Cromwell's soldiers.

An annual fair used to be held with gypsies bringing horses to trade, and market stalls. People came from miles around to enjoy the fair. At hop-picking time families from the Black Country, South Wales, Bath and Cheltenham came to Bosbury every year and stayed on the same farms. This was their annual holiday. There are still six farms in the parish growing hops, with hop-pickers from as far afield as Poland and Australia, as well as South Wales.

Job's Well is to be found here, wonder-working for eye troubles and possibly for boils too!

In 1890 an ancient bronzed Celtic bell was found in one of the fields and is now in the Horniman Museum, Forest Hill, London.

BRAMPTON ABBOTTS

Two miles from the beautiful town of Ross-on-Wye, and close to the winding Wye itself, lies the village of Brampton Abbotts. It has been called 'The Peaceful Village', and was mentioned in the Domesday Book. Now, the old cottages and farms are surrounded by modern bungalows and houses, and the self-contained working community no longer exists.

At one time the four big farms, Netherton, Townsend, Overton and Gatsford dominated the life of the village. As well as the farm workers, who lived in small tied cottages, often with large families, there were the blacksmith, wheelwright, carpenter and basket-maker, all essential to an agricultural way of life. The waggons, the threshing machines and hand-shearing have long disappeared, as modern machinery and farming methods have taken over. The last cart-horse on Townsend Farm was sold in 1955, and around that time 25 village folk worked on the farms. Today, the villagers use their cars to take them to their businesses out of the village, and a new generation has come to stay.

The school, built in 1857, consisted of one large classroom where children from four to 14 years were taught by a headmistress. This room was also the centre where the whole village would gather for social occasions. Yet today the school lies empty and semi-derelict. There is a flourishing nursery school in the village, however, which

The village of Brampton Abbotts

welcomes local children and those from further afield.

The 12th century church of St Michael and All Angels is built on a hill, and from the churchyard lovely views extend over the Herefordshire countryside to the distant Welsh mountains. Along with many evidences of the church's Norman foundations, the architectural styles of succeeding centuries bear witness to its long history. The remains of fresco work on the walls, the wooden porch, two brass memorials to the Rudhall family (of much interest to visiting brass-rubbers) and the shingled bell-turret are among its many historical features.

The old manor house of Rudhall, for many years the seat of the prominent Rudhall family, was built in 1530 and much enlarged in the following century. It is believed to be in three parishes. In the 19th century the visit of Lord Nelson in 1802 stirred the imagination, and more recently the arrival of 40 Chelsea Pensioners during the Second World War must have added a touch of colour to the village.

The war years are memorable in the way of many country parishes. Young men and women left for the war, work on the land took on a new importance, and many families and evacuees came from the towns to escape the bombing. However, the village did not go unscathed, for nine high explosive bombs were dropped, one causing damage to old Netherton House, and about 300 incendiary bombs fell near the river.

Over a century ago the first post office was established in a part of one of the oldest houses in the village. Alongside it were the 'store' and the blacksmith's shop. Now after two moves it is a small sub-post office in a modern bungalow, and there is no village store.

BRAMPTON BRYAN

Travellers on the A4113 cannot fail to be enchanted by the peaceful village of Brampton Bryan. It lies in the northernmost corner of Herefordshire bordering Powys and Shropshire, where the river Teme, one of the fastest flowing rivers in England, runs along its northern side.

To the casual passer-by it would probably come as a surprise to learn that in 1643, during the Civil War, the tranquillity of the village was shattered by a fierce battle which was waged from the church roof. The Royalist forces bombarded Brampton Bryan Castle, which was bravely defended by Lady Brilliana Harley and her hundred-strong garrison. Earlier, she had taken the entire village into the castle for protection and, probably as a result of this, only one person, a cook, was killed.

The name Brampton Bryan originates from Brian de Brampton whose daughter married Robert Harley. The castle passed to the Harley family in 1309 and has remained in their keeping until the present day. The ruins, which cannot be seen from the road and are in the grounds of Brampton Bryan Hall, have received expert attention in recent years to forestall any further decay. There still remains part of the towered gatehouse containing a portcullis.

St Barnabas' church is one of the few churches in the country to have been built during the time of the Commonwealth in the year 1656. It can be seen to the right of the crossroads when travelling in the direction of Knighton. The building is plain without a tower or sanctuary, but inside it is beautiful with a magnificent east window depicting Easter scenes. The window was given to the church by Robert William Daker Harley and his wife, Patience, at Easter 1888. Materials from the castle were used to construct the church roof. Today, the church remains at the hub of much of village life, the parishioners raising funds by opening their beautifully-kept gardens on a weekend each summer.

The black and white cottages of the village, which are so much a feature of it, date from before the Civil War. Many were damaged and later renovated without losing their very special character. Some of the houses are built in an attractive orange and blue-tinged stone. This is Broomy Hill stone, an outcrop of preCambrian stone which was quarried in Brampton Bryan Park. These houses probably date from 1875 to 1900.

Numerous occupations are represented in the village. Although, nowadays, very few villagers are involved in agriculture, tenant farmers continue to make a living from the land. In recent years, the Harley Estate has changed the use of many of the old, obsolete agricultural buildings, bringing new businesses to the village.

Amongst these are a timber merchant, several carpenters, a coracle maker, an artist, a car mechanic and wrought-iron worker, garden ornament and pot maker, and farrier. The old forge is now a hairdressing salon. Amongst other occupations represented are a wheelwright, a gamekeeper and a landscape gardener. There is also a thriving village shop cum post office and cafe.

Another organisation which is at the centre of village life is the WI, which is the second oldest in the county. Since 1985 Brampton Bryan WI's enthusiastic members have become quite famous for their Christmas Pudding Mix-in. The pudding is mixed in the village hall on a Saturday morning in November. Members of the public collect the uncooked puddings in their greased pudding basins. The secret recipe is an authentic Victorian one. Over the years, the puddings have been taken as presents to many corners of the world.

Brampton Bryan Park is one of the oldest parks in Herefordshire and a place of great natural beauty, rising to nearly 1,100 feet. It has conifers at its peak, but below are many fine old trees, including some 300 year old Spanish chestnuts.

As recently as 1970, a horse fair was held in the village. This was known as the 'Bron Horse Fair' (Bron is the local name for Brampton Bryan), the charter for which was granted by Henry III in 1252. During its last years, it was not such a grand affair, but in earlier times it was quite an occasion with gypsies selling dolls and trading horses, and villagers selling 'Bron Fair Cakes' which apparently were similar to a Shrewsbury cake.

BREDENBURY

Bredenbury is on the A44, about three miles from the bustling town of Bromyard. As most of the older houses were built at the turn of the 20th century, the architecture receives either condemnation or adulation, depending on the current popularity of Victoriana!

The centre of the village lies deep amid the trees at Bredenbury Court, now a boarding/day school for over a hundred boisterous youngsters between the ages of four and 13 years old.

The Court was originally built by W. H. Barneby for his own

occupation. A wealthy man, owning most of the surrounding land and farms, he might well be considered the founder of today's Bredenbury. It was he who gave the land for the church and school, he who, as patron of the living, provided church bells, organ and clock; many of the trees that twist and fret in the tearing capricious winds were collected on his travels. He was later to sell the Court to the Greswolde-Williams and build Brockington Grange for his own family and, later still, his son built Brockington House.

The Greswolde-Williams divided their time equally between their estate in Africa and the Court. Here were kennelled the hounds of the North Herefordshire Hunt and here the family lived a fairytale existence. A matching team of ebony horses drew their black and yellow carriage while cart and shire (surely the most beloved of all transport) collected the fuel daily from the railway station at Rowden. Only open fires warmed the large house and the staff employed reads like a verse from a nursery rhyme – 14 maids, three footmen, housekeeper, butler, valets, nurses and grooms.

It seems absurd by modern standards that so many lives were spent in the service of so few but the Greswolde-Williams appear to have been a kindly family, taking seriously the responsibilities of their own good fortune. They built the Parish Room in an attempt to keep the men from the local pub though it is not recorded whether this was either successful or appreciated!

In the 1920s the Court was bought by R. Logan Kitson. The same luxurious standards of living were maintained but now cars replaced horses and much of the romance was lost.

When the local estate was sold in the 19th century the church, which was in its grounds, was demolished and an unexpectedly large one, with matching magnificent rectory, built by the road. The first rector walked Bredenbury accompanied by a St Bernard dog of substantial proportions, stately protectors of local morality. But times alter conditions. The rectory has been sold and the present incumbent lives in a convenient modern house. He is more likely to be seen on a bicycle gallantly struggling to meet the needs of the inhabitants of seven parishes.

One guide book caustically comments that the church is 'nothing special' but this is a church of a living faith – the kernel in the life of this small community.

There has been much change in Bredenbury during the past 50 years. The farms, once owned by the estate, are now all privately owned. The Barneby Arms, previously called the New Inn, used to house both post office and grocer's. But possibly the greatest change of all is the near doubling of the population by the erection of an uncluttered row of bungalows built to follow the contour of the horizon. Fortunate owners have a breath-catching view from the Malverns to Clee Hill.

BREDWARDINE

Bredwardine is an area of steep hills, narrow lanes, broad sunny fields and deep shady hollows. There are patches of natural woodland containing principally oak, ash, sycamore, birch and willow, with conifers and poplars on the hills. The Knapp, a hill of some 700 feet, dominates the village. A hundred years ago this was surmounted by a notable clump of beech trees, but these have since declined and, in 1984, a group of local people, 'friends of the Knapp', co-operated to plant a dozen young oak trees there, hopefully to preserve the ancient outline.

The church of St Andrew – partly Norman – is some distance from the main habitation, being close to the bridge on the river. Adjacent is the site of a medieval castle which doubtless protected the river crossing in days gone by. Very little now remains of it, not because it was razed in battle with the marauding Welsh, but because it was removed stone by stone in the 17th century and taken to Moccas after Frances, widow of Henry Vaughan of Bredwardine Castle, married Edward Cornewall in 1651.

In the churchyard lie several former inhabitants of Bredwardine worthy of note. Rev Francis Kilvert, who was vicar for about two years until his death in 1879, is well known for his diary which so well describes mid 19th century rural life and also the beauty of the local countryside. Another interesting grave is that of George Jarvis, who died in 1793. He was originally a tramp who visited the villages of Bredwardine, Brobury, Staunton and Letton. Later in life he emigrated to America where he amassed a large fortune. He left his money in trust for the benefit of the youth and poor of the villages which had befriended him. As the villagers of Bredwardine had been the most generous, they received the largest bequest. The villagers of Brobury had apparently chased him away from their doors, so they got nothing! Bredwardine's population increased to its peak of over 400 in the middle of the 19th century when squatters arrived to claim residential status in order to benefit from the Jarvis charity. Crafta Webb, where most of them settled, has disappeared, only a few scattered stones remaining, and the present population is less than 200.

A third grave of interest is that of Major-General Pitman, 11th Hussars, who lived at Brobury House until his death in 1941. His tomb is a ledger stone surmounted by a magnificent bronze replica of his dress uniform which was sculpted by Madame Sabatini, wife of the famous author Raphael Sabatini who once lived at Clock Mill on the road to Hay.

Notable buildings in Bredwardine mostly date from the 17th century or earlier. Several of the old farmhouses – Town House, Old Court, Woola and Benfield, where Augustus John stayed to paint, are especially noteworthy. Bredwardine Hall, now a guest house, was formerly known as The Cottage, and is later in origin. Kilvert was a frequent visitor there.

The building which can most nearly claim to be the centre of the village is the fascinating old Red Lion Inn dating from the 17th century. Externally this has changed little over the centuries and its forecourt was, and still is, the main meeting place for the villagers.

The village can claim two ghosts, one once occupying an upper room in the Red Lion, the other a very old part of a local cottage. Sadly, these apparitions are both now homeless. The room in the Red Lion has been converted into a bathroom, and the cottage has been extensively modernized and rebuilt. Perhaps the wind is not all that we hear howling up and down the hill on a dark winter's night?

BRIDSTOW

Approaching Bridstow from the nearby town of Ross-on-Wye, one crosses the river by a 16th century bridge, on which can be seen a curiously engraved sundial of the 18th century.

On the right bank are the ruins of Wilton Castle (13th century) and two of the nearby hotels have claims to fame as the old gaol and courtrooms. Some features, such as the barred windows, are still visible.

The original church of St Bridget at Bridstow is believed to be of the 12th century although the main portion was rebuilt in 1862, retaining many of the original features including the late 14th century tower.

BRILLEY & MICHAELCHURCH

There surely can't be many Women's Institutes where the members live, not in different counties, but in different countries, but this is the case with Brilley and Michaelchurch, for the former is in England, whilst Michaelchurch is in Wales. But the members couldn't be more friendly!

Each village has its own church, but that in Michaelchurch, although small and beautiful, is not easily seen unless one goes looking for it. St Mary's church in Brilley has a nave dating from the late 13th century, although the font dates from the 12th, indicating that there was a chapel there earlier. Both churches have baldacchinos over their altars to protect them.

In church records, it is interesting to read that parishioners complained, in 1397, that the current rector in Brilley was renting out the 'fruits of the church' without licence to do so, and not setting them aside for the church. One wonders what happened to him!

After various repairs throughout the next few centuries, the wooden tower and the west end of the nave of St Mary's caught fire in 1910 – the whole roof being saved by the efforts of one Thomas Price. The same roof remained until the 1990s.

Many of the houses, too, are centuries old. Llanhedry is said to be the oldest farm. The Cummau Farmhouse, perhaps the best known to outsiders, and its neighbour, Fernhall, are now National Trust properties, both lovely old houses, the former open for view on public holidays.

Another house, Pentre Jack, was built in the 16th century or even earlier. Records show that a William Powell lived there in 1642, but from 1776 it belonged to the Price family who were there for 200 years, and the oldest son was always named Thomas. They were coopers, but in 1878, when one Thomas Price died, his heir was said to be a machinist – the family had bought a threshing machine. When, in 1970, the Price family left Pentre Jack, there was still an earth floor in the house.

The New Inn, a house on the right as one drives uphill to Brilley, was first mentioned as being licensed in 1883 in the name of the son of John and Martha Pugh, innkeepers. There was a cider mill in the garden in which an old lady is said to have hanged herself! Attached to the inn is a small cottage, and a John Provert lived there until he became the innkeeper himself. However, in 1940 the last innkeeper did a 'moonlight flit' and left leaving many debts. It is said that people ransacked the place as it stood empty.

One amusing anecdote about the New Inn is about a neighbour from Little Merthyr, who used to frequent the inn. He was leaving it one night, rather inebriated, and met the vicar coming down the hill. The vicar greeted him with, 'Drunk again?', to which he replied, 'So be I,' and went merrily on his way.

In 1808, John Harris of The Cummau built a house near the church to be used as a school, and in 1819 when he died the sum of £5 was left, and a further sum of £5, charged on the Kintley estate, to be paid to a schoolmaster annually. A second benefactor left a further sum of £100 to enable a house to be built, adjoining the school, for the schoolmaster. He also left £50, charged upon Brilley Court estate (now owned by the Bulmers, famous for their cider manufacture), to be paid annually to the schoolmaster. Extracts of the school inspector's reports were published yearly, from 1876, showing the concern at poor attendance, and criticism of the standard of teaching. The inspector had hesitation in recommending the master for his teaching certificate. In fact he did not receive this until 1885.

When at last the building was deemed to be too primitive, and a new school was built in 1968, the old school was used as the village hall. It became the venue of the Brilley and Michaelchurch WI and many a good meeting was held there. In the winter the big stove was lit and gave out great heat during the meetings – in fact it was generally too warm to sit near it. And many were the concerts and festivals held there – packed to the doors. However, inevitably the repairs became too costly and the villagers set to and raised enough money to build a new village hall next to the present school. It is a most prestigious hall, and may also be used as a gymnasium for the children in school. It was opened at last in 1995, and the old hall was sold to be made into a private dwelling.

BRIMFIELD

Brimfield, which is some five miles from each of the market towns of Leominster (Herefordshire), Ludlow (Shropshire) and Tenbury Wells (Worcestershire), is a self-contained farming community with some associated businesses and much cottage industry.

The village shop and bakery dated back further than living memory and from 1908, when a quartern (4lb) loaf of bread cost 4d, was managed by the same baker's family into its third generation before its closure in 1995.

All the 18th century farms have continued to evolve with modern developments, but the cattle market on the corner meadow near the Salwey Arms has long gone. So has the canal, which used to bring coal to the foundry and sawmills, but which was never used to capacity and fell into disuse with the coming of the railway. The sawmills and the foundry flourish still although the foundry no longer provides for the traction engine and steam roller. Woofferton Junction station and the branch line to Kidderminster were closed in the 1960s, and now all that remains is the main line alongide the old canal route up to the crumbling tunnel skirting Brimfield Common.

Local commoners continued to practise their official grazing and turbary rights (lifting of turves from the common, especially peat for fires) on the rather damp and isolated common ground until the Second World War. The present inhabitants of the common's cottages have their own asociation and have taken the initiative in creating their own drainage scheme. They were also responsible for

St Michael's church at Brimfield

introducing Neighbourhood Watch which now operates throughout the village.

Between the common and the old village centre a much needed bypass was constructed in 1981, which informally defines the hitherto umarked boundary between Brimfield and Wyson, across which one would not venture 'in curlers and carpet slippers' – although such attire was acceptable on one's own side of the 'border'!

Before the bypass, the A49 road between Shrewsbury and Hereford used to wind its way through the village centre, but the village section of the old trunk road now carries only local traffic past the post office, the Roebuck and the 12th century St Michael's church with its 17th century black and white tower. Inside St Michael's hangs the parish quilt dedicated by the Bishop of Ludlow in 1988, which was designed and made by a number of local ladies at the Craft Centre at the top of the hill, an initiative which led to the formation of the Borderers' Quilting Group.

Stable boys and girls exercise racehorses from the local yard past a highly successful fudge-making firm, the founder of which, Maureen Foster, has now been succeeded by a second generation who have shifted the emphasis of the products and outlets, tailor-making quality confectionery to their clients' requirements, selling direct to the gift-trade.

An outhouse of the old manor house, Brimfield Hall, once occupied by the Salwey family, has been converted into a modern dwelling, as has the building housing the old inn and butcher's shop where the Brimfield Brass Band used to practise. It played at many local events between the wars, especially the renowned Brimfield Agricultural Show.

The only thatched garage and petrol station in Herefordshire was pulled down in 1987 to make way for a modern housing development completed on the 'Buck' orchard in 1989 where 'slang' (right of way and public footpath) which led from the former post office to the old village shop now winds its way through back gardens, up to the bypass and on to Wyson.

BRINSOP

The original village near to the church at Brinsop has long since vanished, but the platforms of former houses can still be seen in adjacent fields, and existing houses are now widely scattered.

Although the church itself is largely of the early 14th century, it contains a remarkable tympanum of about 1150 on the inside north wall, by the Herefordshire School of Norman sculptors, representing St George and the Dragon (St George being the patron saint of the church). There are also memorial windows to Wordsworth and his relatives who once lived at nearby 14th century Brinsop Court.

The Court is particularly noteworthy for its first-floor hall with cambered tie-beams and kingposts. Rev Kilvert, the Victorian diarist of Clyro, mentions several visits which he paid to the Court.

BROAD OAK

Broad Oak is a hamlet situated on the Ross-on-Wye to Abergavenny road, on the B4521, about two miles from the Welsh border. Half of it is in Garway parish and the other half in St Weonards.

It once consisted of twelve houses and a round house. The latter was on the side of the crossroads, with a pond opposite, and may have been a toll house. It was occupied until it was demolished in the late 1950s.

Ten more houses have been built in recent years; and the surrounding farms, which cover many acres, are all still intact. A garage was built in 1960, and recently a shop has been attached to it. Mains electricity came to the area in 1966.

There was a post office which was closed in 1961. In those days the mail was delivered on foot from there, and sometimes by bicycle. A Methodist chapel is still in use, as is a Catholic church built in the 1930s, but the small Anglican church is closed. All denominations were served, even in such a small area. Beside the Catholic church is a pound; although much overgrown now, it was presumably used to house stray animals. Perhaps it may be uncovered again one day.

There were once two public houses, only a few yards from one another. The Southwell Arms served only cider and beer, in china pint pots, and closed about 1928 – it is now a private house, with the adjoining ground sold for building. The other, the famous Broad Oak Inn, was a thriving pub until it was sold in the late 1980s and is now a private residence. The oak tree still stands outside. It was the 'last pub in England', and when there was no Sunday opening in Wales, the coaches used to arrive in droves on a Sunday evening from the valleys. This continued until Sunday opening was allowed in Wales. The Broad Oak football team was very successful.

The fox hounds used to meet outside the pub once a year, which was a very colourful scene. Sales were held every spring and autumn in the field behind the inn, where there were permanent pens. The farmers walked their stock to be sold until the 1950s. There was little traffic on the roads then – this would certainly not be possible now! It is a very busy road these days.

The local policemen used to arrive on bicycles – one from St Weonards and one from Llangarron. Then the sergeant arrived in his little car, and they would have discussions by the pool at the crossroads. Sadly, all that has gone – including the pool.

BROMYARD

The Domesday Book of 1086 records Bromyard as a large manor belonging to the Bishop of Hereford. In 1652 Silas Taylor wrote: 'Bromyard is a market town, situate very pleasantly betwixt hills, the inhabitants whereof boast themselves to be the inhabitants of one of the most ancient market towns on this side of England.'

Although Bromyard no longer has a market, the High Street and Hop Market Square make a pleasant, busy shopping area with interesting timber-framed architecture. The 16th century Bridge House has herringbone timber framing and a jettied front overhanging the road. Tower Hill House is a superb example of timber building, and Georgian facades disguise 16th and 17th century timber buildings, themselves built on medieval foundations. St Peter's church with its unusual exterior stair-turret is mainly 14th century.

Bromyard has its own community hospital and an excellent leisure and sports centre. The Heritage Centre recounts the story of Bromyard and the influence of hop-growing on the life of the area. The Conquest Theatre is the centre of cultural and social entertainment and all kinds of groups flourish here, catering for cultural and recreational interests. In late June or early July Bromyard hosts the Great Gala and Steam Rally and in September you can join in Bromyard's Folk Festival. Both these events attract visitors from other counties and countries.

Above Bromyard are the Downs, reaching to over 800 feet and offering superb views of the Midland Plain, the Malvern Hills and the mountains of Wales.

BROXWOOD

Three miles west of Pembridge is the hamlet of Broxwood, which has a very interesting history. The Manor has been in the hands of the Snead and Cox families for over 300 years. It once belonged to the nuns of Limebrook Priory and after the dissolution it passed to the Lingen family. Dame Alice Lingen sold it to Richard Snead of Eaton Bishop in 1664. Later the Sneads married into the Cox family – hence the name Snead-Cox.

In 1851 Richard Snead-Cox inherited Broxwood and decided to make it his home. Having chosen a site he engaged a well-known architect, Charles Hansen, to design the house and a well-known landscape gardener, Nesfield, to design and lay out the grounds. Having settled in with his wife Maria Teresa and their eleven children, Richard embarked on a large building programme – a Roman Catholic school, new cottages to house estate workers, and a fine Roman Catholic church. Richard Snead-Cox left diaries written daily from 1840 to 1899, describing vividly the life of a country gentleman of the day.

The school had competition from the Church of England school erected shortly after, and closed down in 1920. During the Second World War the mansion was used by Mrs J. B. Priestley as a home for bombed-out mothers and babies, and later for an evacuated school. It was demolished in 1955 and a much smaller house erected in its place.

Broxwood was once a busy little community, having a church, school, a post office and shop, a pub, a chapel, a carpenter and undertaker, and a stonemason. Alas, they have all gone, and today it is just a pleasant, quiet hamlet.

BULLINGHOPE

A settlement existed in Bullinghope well before the Norman invasion. Until the Middle Ages, Bullinghope and Lower Bullingham were one entity. In 1341 they became Bullinghope Superior (Bullinghope) and

Bullinghope Inferior (Lower Bullingham). By 1831 the Ordnance Survey map showed them as Bullingham and Upper Bullingham, and in 1872 they were shown as Bullinghope and Lower Bullingham, which is how they stand today.

The ancient church of St Peter was built around 1150, with chancel, nave and turret containing one bell. Although repaired in 1817, the church is now in ruins. The stone for the new church was laid in 1878, and work was completed in 1886 costing around £2,000. Its design is Early English and the architect was F. R. Kempson, a local man.

Bullinghope's principal landowners were the Ecclesiastical Commissioners. The Parsonage, built in 1868, is now a private house. The National school (now also a private house) was built in 1886 by the Misses de Winton, and enlarged in 1889/90 for 60 children. The school was once the centre of all village activities, including a men's club, whist drives, dances etc. There was also an excellent church choir.

Before the Ross Road was developed, in the mid 1930s, farmers used to drive their livestock along the road. Some were quartered overnight on the meadows alongside, for which farmers were charged twopence a head for sheep and sixpence a head for cattle.

Today, Bullinghope is little changed, being still essentially a farming community.

BURGHILL & TILLINGTON

Burghill parish is situated just north-west of the City of Hereford. Besides the main village, which contains the parish church, there are also the hamlets of Tillington and Tillington Common on the road to Weobley and of Portway on the A4110. A large number of houses will be built soon on the site of the former County Asylum which was itself built in 1871, enlarged in 1900, and in more recent times became St Mary's Hospital. The two Italianate towers are a local landmark and it is hoped that they will remain to remind us of earlier times.

The large parish church of St Mary plays an important part in the life of the parish and it is lovingly cared for. There are visible Norman remains in the chancel, a window and a doorway, but mostly it is of the 13th and later centuries and it was much restored in 1880. Edward Elgar, who lived in Hereford for over seven years, once cycled to the church and wrote about it to one of his musical friends. He sketched the Norman font with its figures of the apostles and of our Lord and noticed a brass in the chancel to the left of the altar. This brass is dated 1619 and is dedicated to Robert Masters who sailed around the world and visited Virginia in 1585. There is an unusual separate brass showing a terrestrial globe. In the churchyard is a large, hollow yew tree which is traditionally associated with a visit by the poets Wordsworth, Coleridge and Southey. Wordsworth often visited nearby Brinsop Court where lived the brother of his wife, Thomas Hutchinson. At the northern end of the parish is the Methodist chapel built in 1857 which is still in use.

The area surrounding the church is one of the rather few Conservation Areas in Herefordshire and this includes the early-Georgian Grange with its dovecote dated 1717 and the Manor House. Nearby is Burghill Court of 1775, probably by the architect Anthony Keck (who also built Moccas Court). The Court had been bought in 1874 by John George Woodhouse whose family were notable benefactors of the church. It was the scene of the tragic death of his two unmarried daughters in l926 when they were shot by the butler, who had just learned that he was to leave the Court due to his drinking habits.

Nowadays the only hostelry in the parish is the popular Bell Inn at Tillington but formerly there were at least four others. There are the remains of hop kilns at most of the large farms of the parish but hops are no longer grown. Much fruit is still grown for pick-your-own purposes, for cider-making and for sale to the retail trade. A popular 18-hole golf course has been developed in recent years on land formerly used for fruit growing.

There was a school in the parish in the 18th century but the building of the present thriving school (and former school house for the master) towards Tillington was begun in about 1851. A former resident of Burghill Grange, Albert Simpson, financed the building of 'reading and recreation rooms' in 1909, designed by local architect

Mr Bettington, which were later extended and are now the Simpson Hall.

An earlier house near to the present Tillington Court had distant connections with the Mynors family, now living at Treago, and their name is reflected in several old field names. By the will of Thomas Carpenter, who lived in this earlier house in about 1700, there were to be distributed 'six fourpenny loaves every week to the poor of Tillington'! Tillington also had connections with the renowned horticulturalist Thomas Andrew Knight (1759–1838) who was born at nearby Wormsley Grange and whose tomb is in the graveyard of Wormsley church. He owned orchards at Tillington and produced many new varieties of apple and pear including an apple named Tillington Court.

It was at Tillington that the Romans coming down their road from Chester would turn sharply right towards the town then at Kenchester (Magnis), along a road which is still in use from nearby the Bell.

Nowadays the majority of working villagers find employment which is not connected with the land; but even though lacking a shop and a post office we are still a village with traditions. A village where you can watch the local cricket team; some can take up their rights on the eleven acres of common; and most can hear the bellringers practise on Monday nights!

CALLOW

The small rural village of Callow, surrounded by farmland, has changed little over the years.

High on Callow Hill stands St Mary's church, overlooking the southern approaches to the city of Hereford. On a clear day, when the sun lights up the cathedral tower and sparkles on the river Wye flowing past the Bishop's Palace, the view is breathtaking. The church was rebuilt in 1830, although the font dates back to an earlier building on this site, possibly of the 13th century. The church was closed in 1994. In the 19th century, the Pearle Charity was established, whose object was the annual distribution on St Thomas'

Day of the income derived from the rents of 21 acres in Much Dewchurch parish for the relief of the poor and elderly. The land has now been sold and the proceeds invested to provide income for charitable purposes.

The Forge has played a very important part in the history of Callow for 400 years, and the Howells family have lived there almost as long. It ceased to be a blacksmith's shop in 1944, and Mr Frank Howells opened a grocer's shop there in 1949, combined with the post office which was opened in 1964. However, its doors were finally closed in 1985 with the retirement of the postmistress. This was a great loss to the village and the surrounding district, and at the Harvest Supper that year a presentation was made to the three sisters who ran the shop.

The school which closed in 1953 is remembered by pupils who are living in Callow today, but in 1906 children began their first lessons with a small tray of sand and a wooden skewer and were taught to make letters and figures before progressing to a slate. After closure the building was used as the parish hall and as such helps to maintain the life of the village.

Callow is not without its ghost stories although the ghost of Callow Hill is not a person but a house! In the early 19th century Callow Farm, which stands behind the church on Callow Hill, used to be a coaching inn where travellers broke their journey for the night. The old coaching road, which is still in existence in part, runs past the inn and on down the hill and there in the darkness figures have been seen carrying something ungainly between them as they cross two fields to a house. Then they return carrying nothing – and it is said that one morning the coach continued with one less passenger! Within living memory people have claimed to have seen the house on Callow Hill although now only a mound in the grass remains.

Callow Farm itself has its own ghost story, a rather charming one in contrast. Many years ago people living in the house would see a little girl entering a certain bedroom, and although dressed as if for a ball she was always weeping and seemed distressed – and one of her slippers was missing. In the 1920s alterations were made to the building and when one wall of that bedroom was demolished, behind it was revealed a small powder closet and inside it a little blue slipper.

CANON FROME

Canon Frome, in a beautiful valley of some 1,050 acres of rich farmland, is superbly situated west of the Malvern Hills.

The first traceable occupation of the site was in the early days of the Roman Conquest, when a fort stood near the river Frome, the remnants of which remain to this day. The Canons of Llanthony established themselves here in 1280.

The Hoptons came to prominence through the marriage of Michael Hopton of Shropshire, to a widow named Martha Hareford of Canon Frome estate. Thus, in 1591 began a 300 year period when the Hoptons resided at Canon Frome Court.

During the Civil War the 'Strong House' at Canon Frome was ransacked and some 70 men of the Royal army garrisoned there were killed by Cromwell's men. Another 80 were taken prisoner and many of the dead were buried where they fell. Cromwellian times are still in evidence; a house more than 300 years old bears the title 'Cromwell's Walls' – Cromwell is purported to have tethered his horse there to rest before the battle of Ledbury, and a field is aptly named Bloody Acre.

The driveway to the Court is flanked by imposing red brick pillars dated 1905 and surmounted by unusual sandstone carvings, one the figure of a griffin's head, in its mouth a bloody hand, the other a talbot hound, chained and wearing a floral collar, resting its paw on a saltire – St Andrew's cross; these figures are depicted in the Hopton family crest. They are the most striking landmark of the area and the topic of many a conversation.

St James' church is the third sacred building to occupy the site close by Canon Frome Court, built in 1860 by John Hopton jnr at a cost of £3,000 in memory of his wife. The tower and bells date back to 1680.

The Swiss Cottage, an interesting building, is a replica of Queen Victoria's house on the Isle of Wight; it was built, and the waterfall made, near Mill Cottages, the site of the old Canon's Mill. The waterfall was utilised for an electricity plant supplying electricity to Canon Frome Court in 1900.

Herefordshire County Council purchased Canon Frome Court and

35 acres of land in 1952 and converted it into a school for 13–15 year olds. Sadly in 1978 it was held to be no longer economically viable, so the children moved to school in Ledbury. The Court was purchased by the Windflower Association, who have converted it into 15 flats; many new young families have come into the area to live there and travel to work in the towns and cities.

Wargent Engineering is the oldest established business of the parish. Mr Tony Wargent, the present proprietor, is the third generation, his great-grandfather, William Jauncey Wargent, having arrived on his bicycle in 1868 as the local blacksmith. They have continued on the same site ever since.

The cricket club is very active and celebrated its Golden Jubilee in 1989; the club house and pitch are situated in the parish of Ashperton. Likewise, through the same anomaly, the post office and village shop, run by the Matthews family, where the locals could meet and set the world aright, was also in Ashperton; sadly it has now closed.

CANON PYON

Canon Pyon lies on the A4110 roughly halfway between Hereford and Leominster. Dominating the skyline is Pyon Hill, a thickly wooded pyramid of cornstone, a type of red and green mottled limestone. In days gone by this limestone was quarried in the surrounding hills.

Cromwell's men came to Canon Pyon in June 1649 and surveyed the parish. A Jury of Tenants was called which valued and listed all the properties in the parish. Of the twelve jury members, descendants of John Yeomans and Thomas Jay still survive.

In the 18th century another member of the Yeomans family joined the Canon Pyon branch from Cowarne and brought the *Foxwhelp* apple which, with the *Kingstone Black*, became the most sought after cider apple. Cider made from these apples won top prizes at many shows well into the 20th century.

Yeomans Bros Cider Makers was formed and produced cider in Canon Pyon on a site alongside the main road. There were hop kilns, a granary and two wooden buildings housing the mill presses, bottling plant and coopers' shop. The plant employed a large number of men during the season.

The cider mill was originally driven by steam power which also supplied hot water for the bottle washing. The steam engine was replaced by an oil engine which in turn gave way to electricity. This change to electric power gave electricity to Canon Pyon before most Herefordshire villages.

The whole area around the buildings would be covered with apples to a depth of three feet at cider-making time and it was hard work keeping the mill running. The apples were loaded into wooden wheelbarrows with a wooden shovel as no steel was allowed to come into contact with the fruit. The barrow was then pushed up a long wooden walkway and the apples tipped into the chute above the mill where their own weight fed them through.

The resulting pulp dropped into below-ground-level brick-built tanks. These tanks were open topped, always wet and slippery and people would frequently fall (or be pushed) in. Luckily they were only three feet deep as no helping hand was extended to the victims, who were in an awful mess when they got out. It was all considered to be great fun.

Cider was delivered to public houses and fine hotels over a wide area, reaching as far as Aberystwyth.

The cider which was produced for the farms was made from several different varieties, all mixed up, such as *Tom Putts, Lady's Finger, Russetts, Old Norman, Cowarn Reds,* and *Cats Heads*. They made a very good harvesting cider, not too strong in case the men were overcome with sleepiness!

Later in the 20th century the site became a bus garage, still in the ownership of Yeomans. More recently, after being empty for some time after the garage closed down, the site was let to a new firm making powered parachutes.

The church of St Lawrence, the oldest part of which is 13th century, is well worth a visit. It lies in peaceful surroundings half a mile west of the A4110, on the road to Weobley. On the south side of the churchyard – which is kept tidy by a band of volunteers from the village – runs a brook. Beyond that is a meadow, home to wild daffodils.

The only common land now left in the parish is that on top of Westhope Hill. There were two common fields, one at Derndale, the other on the Kinford to Westhope road. A bare-knuckle fight took place on the latter field at one time. After the fight the skins of two freshly killed sheep were wrapped around the fighters to draw out their bruises.

Today, the village is a community of scattered dwellings; some black and white timbered and stone cottages remain – the oldest of which is believed to date from the 1600s – but many of the old buildings have been lost. There has been some new housing built since the Second World War, the most recent being two detached dwellings adjacent to the old Yeomans' site, one of which is used as the vicarage.

There are three pubs, The Bush, The Plough and The Nag's Head. The latter once brewed its own beer but now the brewhouse has been transformed into bedrooms and bathrooms for the holiday trade.

Unlike many villages Canon Pyon still has a village shop with post office and its school. There is also a garage and service station with shop at Bush Bank.

CAREY

Carey is a tiny hamlet of approximately 20 inhabitants, between the villages of Ballingham and Hoarwithy.

Its main feature is the local pub, much photographed by visitors. It was formerly a couple of workmen's cottages and was originally called the Miners Arms after the Miner family who resided there. An owner and licensee since the Second World War had the great foresight to change the pub's name to 'The Cottage of Content' and fame had arrived; Carey was on the map.

CASTLE FROME

Castle Frome is situated twelve miles north-east of Hereford. It occupies about 1,500 acres and it is named after a wooden castle which stood on the hill overlooking the church. All that remains is the castle mound.

Below the mound is the Norman church of St Michael and All Angels. Here can be seen a fine Norman font of old red sandstone, said to be one of the masterpieces of Romanesque sculpture in England. It is the work of the Hereford School of Carvers and is dated about 1170.

In 1840 an American Mormon missionary, Wilford Woodruff, baptised the first Mormons in the West of England in a pond at the Hill Farm, Castle Frome. Meetings continued to be held at the Hill with Wilford Woodruff preaching. The local vicar was concerned and sent the parish clerk and churchwarden to find out what was happening, but Woodruff converted and baptised both – he also baptised the village policeman, who had really gone to arrest Woodruff! In all 600 people were baptised into the Mormon faith in the space of one month. Six months later 50 converts from the village and surrounding area set sail for America, to be followed over a period of ten years by some 1,200 others. The Mormons have dedicated the pond and erected a tablet at its edge and every year hundreds of Mormons from all over the world visit the Hill and occasionally baptisms take place there.

Another point of interest in the history of the village was the Fromes Hill Climb. On 17th June 1905 a Hill Climb was organised by the Hereford Automobile Society on Locks Hill. A silver cup was offered to the car to climb the hill in the fastest time. Ten cars entered, but not all reached the top. It was won by Mr R. J. Hopkins of Canon Frome in Colonel Hopton's 20 hp Wolsley. From a standing start the race took three minutes five seconds.

Today Locks Hill is notorious for a different sort of hill climb – that caused by icy roads and impatient drivers in the winter months, but the improved conditions on the hill have afforded the motorist a magnificent view from the top, where there are pull-ins to allow a moment to 'stop and stare'. Looking westward one enjoys a wide panorama from the Severn Vale, across Gloucestershire, the Wye valley, Hay Bluff, the Black Mountains and Brecon Beacons and on into North Wales and Shropshire. A survey map and binoculars are a must on this occasion.

There have been many changes in the village, especially in the agricultural industry. In the 1930s hop farming was all done manually, many villagers worked permanently on the hop growing and in the picking season train loads of pickers came into the area. Working in the hop fields provided a paid holiday for city dwellers and there are many stories of births, deaths and marriages amongst these colourful visitors to the village.

Many country crafts are still practised in the village and once a year in October a Ploughing Match is held at a local farm. Whilst great store is put on the art of ploughing (both ancient and modern) and the quality of cereals, root crops, hops, hay and livestock, there is also an exhibition of local talents in cookery, preserves, flower arranging, embroidery, dressmaking and many other crafts, when cups and prizes are earnestly competed for.

Like most villages, the school has long been closed and there is no village shop. The post office is housed in a cottage with vines and roses around the door and provides an informal community centre! Half the cottages and houses which were once homes for agricultural workers are now occupied by folk who travel to town to earn their living or newcomers who have come for retirement.

Although the times are changing rapidly, the countryside in Castle Frome seems to mark time and the discerning visitor can seek out many lesser known wild flowers, watch kestrel, jays and even buzzards, wheeling above the woods. Foxes and badgers set out on their evening sorties as the sun sets over the distant hills in a myriad of beautiful colours.

CLEHONGER

Clehonger is situated some four miles from the cathedral city of Hereford and has a population of approximately 2,500, a startling contrast with the census of 1901 when the population was just 430. The village is unfortunately split in two with the new village sited some three quarters of a mile from the church and the old village.

The church dates back to the 12th century and contains the tomb of Sir Richard de Pembrugge (Pembridge), one of the first knights of the Order of the Garter, founded by Edward III. Also within the church are the Barre brasses dated probably around 1490. The male figure represents Sir John Barre and the female represents his second wife, Joan. It has been discovered that these brasses are almost unique and they have been removed temporarily for professional restoration.

One of the windows in the church was designed by A. W. N. Pugin, an eminent Victorian architect who also designed the neighbouring Belmont Abbey. Within the churchyard is the grave of Private Benjamin Preece of the 1st Dragoon Guards, who fought at Waterloo. He died in 1870 at the age of 87.

The major part of the village contains a post office, two shops, a garage, primary school and village hall. There is also one public house, The Seven Stars. Most residents now work in the city of Hereford but originally work on the land was the major occupation plus limited employment at the local cider works which closed in 1950. During the Second World War the cider works also provided transport for the area Home Guard detachment.

The village at present has no local policeman but records show that in 1755 a local constable was employed with the princely salary of seven shillings per annum and it is believed that for this sum the constable was expected to maintain the local lock-up originally sited at the Bowling Green. Further records show that he was paid 'bounty money' to arrest and detain a local vagrant. His fee amounted to one shilling and upon transfer of the prisoner to Hereford the parish had to pay the 'Bridewell' keeper the sum of five shillings.

Whereas nowadays the local bus service is quite frequent, in the 1930s there was no public transport whatsoever and the only way to visit Hereford was by walking or by local carrier's cart which provided transport on Wednesdays and Saturdays.

Clehonger possessed its own flour mill but this is now used as a private residence. Sited on the bank just above the mill is a tiny Methodist chapel, now disused, but this possibly reflects the influence of the nearby Welsh valleys and the strong evangelical movement at the turn of the century.

The descendants of many of the old villagers still live locally. Most of the property in the village is now quite modern but there are numerous old cottages and farm buildings still to be seen, some well over 200 years old.

CLIFFORD

Clifford is a very scattered community and the village itself has lost many of its focal points. The lord of the manor, many years ago, would not allow pubs within his estate boundaries and the cider house (The Old Castle Inn) was closed when the irate wives of the estate workers complained that their menfolk were spending most of their wages on their way home. There are two pubs now but they are not in the village – the Castlefield Inn is on the Bredwardine side of the parish and the Royal Oak is on the Golden Valley side.

In more recent years the village has lost its own vicar, policeman, nurse, post office and village shop but Clifford is one of the few civil parishes to have two churches. Clifford church is very old, dating back to about 1200, and is situated in a picturesque position – although an uphill walk from the village. One of its treasures is an old coffin lid, carved from oak – an effigy of a monk. The old 12th century priory is near the church.

Hardwicke church is a beautiful little church on the Golden Valley side of the parish and it was built in 1860 by the lady of the manor for her new son-in-law, who had been ordained but did not have a living.

The Golden Valley railway used to come through Clifford but only the level route remains, a grassy lane surrounded by trees and much frequented by wild life. The ruins of Clifford Castle still stand sentinel over the village and the river Wye, proudly overlooking the common – now a nature reserve. The castle goes back to Roman times, rebuilt by the Normans in the 11th century. During some excavations there in the 1960s, a sandal buckle and a toga clip were found. Henry II is reputed to have visited the castle in the 1100s, where he met his Fair Rosamond. The castle ceased to be of importance after 1485 but has many interesting areas for those inclined to delve into the past. The local schoolchildren make periodic visits to the castle and re-enact appropriate activities, like storming the gates.

A notable piece of history, often passed by, is a very old post-box in the wall near the chapel. It is one of the very few Victorian letter-boxes still in regular use.

A favourite tale about a local character is of an old man who was very partial to his cider – sadly he died a few years ago. He rode a bicycle and used to collect his weekly shopping in Hay-on-Wye, three miles up the road. He frequently set off home with his shopping, having enjoyed his usual cider and it was remarkable how he meandered his way along the country road, until he eventually arrived home and soon went to sleep in his armchair. His groceries used to arrive later – at intervals, picked up off the road by caring neighbours or children, who quietly put them on his doorstep.

CLODOCK

Nestling at the foot of the Black Mountains lies the sleepy hamlet of Clodock. The ancient parish church of St Clydawg was named after Prince Clydawg who was a son of Clodwyn, king or ruler of Ewias in the 5th century AD. Clydawg and his brother Dedyw did much missionary work in the area but as he was hunting one day he was killed by someone who was jealous of his friendship with a certain lady. Legend has it that on the day of his burial, the two oxen pulling the cart containing the coffin refused to cross the river at the ford and the yoke broke. He was therefore buried near the river bank and, because of his godly life, such an act of murder made him a martyr. The people he ruled gathered at his tomb to worship, and pilgrimages were made there, especially on his day, 3rd November.

As time passed, a simple wooden church was built and later a stone building was erected. The church as we know it today dates mainly from Norman times. The church furnishings are mainly of wood, with box pews, a three decker pulpit, a minstrel's gallery and solid oak chests – one of which dates from around the 12th century.

Clodock church was chartered as a 'place of refuge' for those escaping from their enemies. The Welsh Border runs alongside the mountain and there was much rivalry between the Border people, hence the strong solid door dating from around the 15th century. The church is full of history, with wall paintings, murals, coats of arms and a Decalogue. It has a memorial stone which is thought to date from around AD 750-850, 'To the dear wife of Guinndo, a resident of this place'.

Clodock Mill is a listed building now standing idle, although the mill machinery inside is still preserved. The impressively large wheel was made at Leominster in 1868 and the thick walls and large oak beams tell the age of the building. There are two pairs of grinding stones, one for flour and one for animal feed. On the left bank of the Monnow is the Holy Well.

The Cornewall Arms, looking towards the Black Mountains, has changed very little with its flagged floors and oak settles. It is a place where fishermen enjoy a cool drink after a peaceful hour or two wading down the river, trout fishing.

COLWALL

The most spectacular approach to the ancient parish and village of Colwall is by way of the Wyche cutting through the Malvern Hills, originally a track for pack animals carrying salt from Droitwich. After leaving the grandeur of the scene across the Severn plain, another magnificent view spreads itself before the unsuspecting visitor, right across to the Welsh mountains.

Other travellers, approaching from Ledbury and the west, follow a winding country road with stone walls and fences protecting fields of sheep and cattle. There are enough hedges and trees to give a welcoming, bosky feel, with the outline of the Malverns a constant backdrop. Colwall Green is the first settlement reached, a pleasant triangle of common land with handsome trees edged by houses, bungalows and sports fields. Some distance from the main road lies the parish church of St James the Great, with a half-timbered farmhouse adjacent, said originally to have been the hunting lodge of the Bishop of Hereford when exercising his feudal rights over the deer of Malvern Chase.

Colwall possesses more facilities than many villages, both body and soul being well catered for. There are four places of worship in addition to the parish church. Residents can buy meat, vegetables, groceries, and newspapers from a number of well stocked shops; they can visit the doctor and get the prescription filled by the chemist. They also have a post office, hairdresser, and an estate agent.

Colwall is well served by public transport. There is a bus service to Ledbury and Malvern, and it is the only village in the county with a rail service, including 125 mph Expresses to Hereford, Worcester, Oxford and London. The station has been transformed by Colwall WI from near dereliction into an attractive garden area with lawns, flowering shrubs, and a seat given by a grateful resident.

The coming of the railway caused the heart of the village to move to where it is today, around the Colwall Stone, a block of limestone about which legends abound. It is said that the old giant of the hills, looking down and seeing his wife being friendly with someone else, heaved a great boulder at them, but it is probably nearer the truth to surmise that it was a mounting block for huntsmen!

The visionary entrepreneur who excavated the original railway tunnel through the Malverns was Stephen Ballard, who was truly a man of many parts. Colwall was where he settled and where many of his descendants still live. He led the fight to preserve the hills and surrounding commons which the unique body of Malvern Hills Conservators continue today. His sons were as inventive as their father, and such enterprises as brickmaking, a gas company which lasted until nationalisation and a vinegar factory all flourished in their time. Two others are still active, Old Court Nursery, well known for Michaelmas daisies, and the spring water bottling plant, famous for Royal patronage. Few realise that the Malvern water bottled today actually comes from Colwall in Herefordshire.

A nature reserve has been created on an area of land near to the station, given to the village by the late Charles Ballard, a descendant of Stephen Ballard. In the past Colwall had a golf course, and even a racecourse! The handsome Colwall Park Hotel still standing near the station was built to accommodate visitors, while the Horse and Jockey hostelry housed the grooms.

Retired people now form a large part of the population. Apart from farming, local shops and schools, employment is provided by the bottling plant, and an industrial estate on the site of the old station buildings.

There is a pleasant mix of buildings, from ancient thatched or black and white, to solid Victorian villas and modern bungalows. Many are in sight of the Iron Age hill fort known as the Herefordshire Beacon, or British Camp, reputed to be the site of Caractacus' last stand against the Roman invaders.

Few of the multitude of motorists who take the spectacular Jubilee Drive linking the Wyche cutting and British Camp, created for the Malvern carriage trade after 1887, realise that all of it lies within Colwall parish. Longer stay visitors are mostly hill walkers, but once a year women's cricket teams from all over England, with visitors from Holland and Ireland, meet in the oldest festival in the women's game. The first matches were arranged in 1926 by Mrs Molly Scott-Bowden of the Colwall Park Hotel and led to the formation of the National Women's Cricket Association.

CRADLEY

Just within the Herefordshire boundary from Worcestershire, the village is protected by the beautiful Malvern Hills and the fortunate inhabitants enjoy extensive views along the range, especially from the Upper Westfield side. These hills have been a source of inspiration to artists, authors and musicians from early times until the present day, one of the most famous being Sir Edward Elgar.

Now the village falls naturally into two parts, separated by the burbling stream known locally as Cradley Brook. The lower and original half includes the church, old post office, two rectories, old and new, and some fine old black and white and half-timbered cottages still retaining their old world charm. The local people were very proud of the 'Old Rectory' which was considered to be one of the finest in the county, boasting 20 bedrooms with a coach-house and stables at the back. The modern, smaller and much more convenient rectory was built some years later on glebe land.

The church of St James the Great nearby contains many interesting features and is well worth a visit. The church register dates from 1560 and the porch was built some 300 years later. There is a fine belfry with interesting tablets round the walls and a board setting out the ancient rules and penalties for disobedient bell-ringers. There is a wonderful view from the top of the tower for those who care to climb the steep ladder inside. There is a pleasant well-kept churchyard surrounding the church, a lychgate and a sundial erected to commemorate Queen Victoria's Golden Jubilee. The tower, with its 15th century upper section and Norman base, dominates the very attractive black and white houses nearby.

Farther along Church Lane there is a marvellous example of the type of building of 500 years ago. This is black and white, half-timbered and was presented to the parish as a boys school in 1674. It is now the village hall and is widely used for present-day activities.

Years ago, agriculture was the main activity of Cradley and this still carries on today, albeit to a somewhat lesser extent. Hops were the main crop and hop-picking was perhaps the most important annual event. People from all over the parish joined in, women and children especially and the school holidays were extended to cover the entire hop-picking period. Labour was also forthcoming from Birmingham and the Midlands and many gipsy families took part. It must have been a colourful sight when a long trail of caravans filled the main roads en route for the hopfields. Most of the families returned year after year, generation after generation, the women telling fortunes and selling pegs when time permitted. The village was like a second home to them with a mutual exchange of customs and ideas.

In the early 1900s most of the women stayed at home in the village, occupied with the family, probably larger than families of today. They made jams and pickles and wine from the local fruit; some made gloves for the famous Worcester glove firms. These were stitched at home, being delivered and returned by the local carrier.

Cradley folk, today, are as proud of their gardens as they were in the past. Every summer, in July, a number of gardens are thrown open to the public on a Sunday afternoon.

CRASWALL

The parish of Craswall nestles under the eastern flank of Crib y Garth, the most northerly ridge of the Black Mountains. The river Monnow rises at the top of the parish, high on the mountain in the Red Dingle, and flows down the valley followed by the road from Hay-on-Wye to Longtown. Along its banks, the imposing mountain with its heather and whinberries, hill farms and cottages meets the gentler, kinder south-facing slopes of the Cefn Hill with its more substantial houses and richer pastures. With Welsh names scattered amongst the English, Craswall feels almost as Welsh as it is English.

Following the Welsh pattern, there is no village nucleus but rather a scattering of farmsteads and cottages, a welcoming pub and the tiny church of St Mary's standing towards the head of the valley. It stands alone without even graves for company because of soil too thin for digging, but it does have a musicians' West gallery, a cock pit, and a Fives court against the north wall, evidence that Craswall has long had a rich social tradition. It is said that the East window of the church came from the much more imposing Grandmontine Abbey, whose ruins lie further up the valley. This was one of only three houses of this austere French order in Britain and is the only one with substantial visible remains.

Below the church lies the pub, the Bulls Head, which until recently had been in the ownership of the Gane family for 125 years. Beatie Lewis, the last member of that family to live there, played Craswall's church organ for every service for over 50 years.

Despite its apparent isolation, Craswall is well known for its strong sense of community, fostered by the unaffiliated Craswall St Mary's Women's Guild. This organisation was started in 1950 for the purpose of supporting the church 'and having a bit of fun along the way', in the words of the vicar of that time, Rev Tom Cann. Today, in addition to its monthly meetings held in members' homes, the Women's Guild organises an annual Harvest Supper, a Parish Christmas Party and a Whitsun Barbecue as well as a series of increasingly popular classical concerts featuring rising young soloists.

The Victorian village school which was closed in 1957 was bought by the parishioners in 1975 with the proceeds of a lamb sale. This is now the village hall and provides a venue for parish events and a meeting place for the Thursday Club for older residents from the surrounding area, and Craswall Young Farmers Club. This club, founded over 50 years ago, is famous for its hedgelaying skills and remarkable for its prominence in competitions – success which, alongside Craswall's other longstanding organisations, says something about the strength of this little parish with just over 100 on its electoral roll.

CREDENHILL

Credenhill village has had military connections since about 80 BC, when Celts constructed an earthwork defence system which still remains. After trial and tribulation the Roman town of Magnis evolved, at what is now Kenchester, abandoned by the Romans when Picts and Scots made their raids and the Roman legions were withdrawn. In AD 428 Magnis was destroyed by fire, and it was about AD 480 before the old fort was taken over by the Saxons. The Saxon chief Creda occupied it in about AD 540, and Creda's Hill gave its name to Credenhill.

During the First World War, land in Credenhill was occupied by an Army unit to store ammunition. In 1939, this land was requisitioned for defence and became RAF Hereford. A 112-bed hospital was prepared and much used later. The flag, or ensign, of RAF Hereford is now laid-up in the church since the Camp closed in 1994, and work is in progress for the Army to take over that site.

Credenhill was then a long winding road from the Camp to the railway station. Poplar trees lined a lot of the route, edging fields on either side of it. There were few houses and several farms or smallholdings. The old railway station is now home to the Credenhill Social Club and Credenhill Community Hall, alongside a playing field at the lower end of the village.

There is a good and frequent bus service to Hereford although the local shops supply most everyday needs. Village housing has increased considerably since the Second World War and the 1997 house building in the main street has softened the visual aspect and made it more pleasing.

At the top end of the village are the schools, both old and new, and a cluster of black and white timbered houses around the old chestnut tree that stands in a green island where the road divides. A listed dovecote is behind the school, near a small expanse of water where swans come in their season.

The church with its 14th century tower lies under the hill, opposite to the Old Rectory, still the home of the Bulmer family whose ancestor, the Rev Charles Bulmer, made the first now world-renowned cider. The new rectory in front of the church has a fine view over Credenhill, the distant hills and the Beacons. Inside the church is a 14th century glass window depicting Thomas of Hereford and Thomas of Canterbury with hands raised in blessing.

One notable incumbent other than the Rev Bulmer, was the Rev Thomas Traherne, mystic poet of the 17th century, whose works are remembered yearly on Trinity Sunday in St Mary's church. There is also a Traherne Association which explores and promotes his recently discovered poems and writings 'in the pursuance of Felicity'.

DEWSALL

Dewsall lies about five miles south of Hereford, to the west of the A49 and below Callow Hill. It looks out towards Wales and the Black Mountains. The Welsh influence is marked in its name 'Dewi's Well', Dewi being St David. More a scattered hamlet than a village, Dewsall has two distinctive buildings – its church and the large house of Dewsall Court adjacent to the church.

The little church, dedicated to St Michael and All Angels, dates from about the 14th century and has a font of the same date. It has a shingled bell tower and the remains of an old preaching cross. There is a monthly evensong service and one morning communion service.

Immediately facing the church is Dewsall Court, built in the 17th century for the Pearle family who were large local landowners. Here was born in 1674 James Brydges (a descendant of Sir John Brydges

The Ark, Dewsall

and Mary Pearle) who later became Paymaster General to Queen Anne and did very well out of it, becoming Duke of Chandos and fabulously rich. It was for him that Handel wrote the Chandos anthems. However, the Duke was also spectacularly extravagant and in 1731 the Herefordshire estates were sold to Guy's Hospital, who remained landlords of the Dewsall area until the 1950s when the estate was bought by Sir Charles Clore. The estate – not the house – is now owned by the Prudential Assurance Company.

The rectory, which was also built in the 17th century and enlarged in the 1830s, was sold in 1937 and is now a private house called Farmore. On the road between Farmore and the church is The Ark, a cottage that at one time was an alehouse.

Most of the land around Dewsall is farmed by the Prudential. Dewsall Court, after 30 years of emptiness and decay is now privately owned, restored and occupied. Monkhall Court, like Dewsall once a large tenanted farm, is occupied but not by a farming family, and the land that used to go with the house is farmed by the Prudential. Most of the other dwellings are occupied by retired people, or people working in Hereford, but the aptly named Cold Nose Farm is still being worked by a traditional farming family.

Dewsall and Callow are adjoining, and share the same village hall; village fetes and activities are supported by both communities, and now that Callow church is closed, Dewsall church serves both. However, the few people who live there still think of Dewsall as distinct, and although so close to Hereford the village has a character of its own.

DILWYN

Dilwyn is a 20th century village. One hundred years ago about 35 houses plus the 13th century church made up the heart of the parish. Most have survived, to be joined by 60 new homes, mainly in cul-de-sacs, and 20 conversions of farm buildings. It is this latter group, clustered around another innovation, the village green, that gives today's Dilwyn its character and 'old world charm', the appeal of the year 2000.

Of course we remain a farming community. Five of Dilwyn's farms in the Domesday Book survive today with their names unchanged. There are fewer but larger farms employing fewer people and more machinery. The very big farmhouses have become private homes. The Great House in the centre of Dilwyn is an excellent example. Pevsner said 'the house is unattractive, but it has tall gatepiers with a fine wrought-iron gate. Early Georgian.' Since he passed by, the owners removed a hideous false second-storey facade, and the decorative centre piece over the gates was sold to an American couple, who fortunately have preserved it as a bed headboard. The house has a substantial Tudor section.

St Mary's church, on its slight rise, keeps an eye on the village. The tower was built onto an earlier nave around 1200. Later in the century the living passed into the hands of the Prior of Wormsley who in the 1290s 'gave' Dilwyn its fine chancel. The village was left with the task of pulling down most of the existing nave, and building anew. Only the tower remained, acquiring an extraordinary door, half in the south aisle and half in the nave. Two acolytes swing censers high over their heads in a window in the chancel, the only surviving medieval glass. An anonymous donor provided a large elaborate south porch at the beginning of the 16th century. The church registers date from 1558, the first entry is a marriage. Since then galleries have been added, and taken away. Restoration in 1867 removed them and much else, but added a magnificent Nicholson organ. Now an active ingredient of the Leominster Team Ministry, St Mary's continues to fulfil its mission in the community.

Possibly because the centre of Dilwyn is compact, village life thrives. There is, of course, a very active WI! But there are also regular meetings of the Mothers' Union, the Over 60s, the Trefoil Guild and, for youngsters, the Tuesday Club and the Rough and Readies. If you fancy hard work, then there are the Parish Council, the PTA, the Neighbourhood Watch, the Hall, Dilwyn Show Flower Show, etc Committees! Dilwyn is a community.

DINEDOR

The village of Dinedor lies sheltered at the foot of Dinedor Hill, a local landmark rising to 600 feet above the river meadows just two miles south-east of Hereford. It consists of a pleasant mixture of old and new houses, of well-tended gardens and country hedgerows, with outlying farms and cottages spread round it, in a patchwork of fields and woodland. The little church of St Andrew has held its central position since medieval days, and still keeps the ancient name of Dyndor, but only the walls of the former 14th century tower remain. The church was rebuilt about 1867, and consists of a tower with a pyramid roof, a nave and chancel. An interesting feature is a brass tablet commemorating Bertie Davies, who died saving two men from the river Wye.

Nearby is the old village school. It was built in 1839, extended in 1896, and in its heyday housed nearly 50 children, finally closing, as did so many village schools, in the 1950s. The building was used for some time as a public meeting place, but has now been superseded by a new village hall.

One annual event is firmly fixed in the local calendar. This is Dinedor Sports Day, traditionally held on the last Saturday in July, come rain or shine (and it seldom rains). It began in 1935, organised by a local Ladies Club, and took place in the rectory garden, later being transferred to a nearby field, where it is still held.

No doubt Dinedor had its share of old country customs and superstitions, but only two can be found recorded. The first concerned the Holy Well. These were believed to have curative powers, and were quite widespread in medieval times. The well in Dinedor is clearly marked on old maps, and the name survives in the existing Holywell Farm. On New Year's Day there was great competition to draw the first pailful of water, called 'the cream of the well', which was said to promote health and happiness through the year. If a maid could procure it for her mistress she was rewarded with a shilling.

The other old custom was that of wassailing on Twelfth Night. All over the countryside fires would be lit in the fields, twelve in a ring, with a big one in the middle, with merrymaking and drinking of health to the next year's crops. Large Twelfth Night cakes were baked in a ring shape.

Dinedor Hill was the scene of some very early history, for it is the site of an Iron Age hill fort, the ramparts being still clearly visible. Excavations have produced evidence of extensive occupation from the late Iron Age to Roman times. Some pottery, coins and other finds are in the Hereford Museum. Troubled times came to it again in the Civil War when, in 1645, Cromwell's Scottish army, with 8,000 foot and 4,000 horse, besieged the city of Hereford. For six weeks that summer they camped on Dinedor Hill, within striking distance of the city, but it was said that the men were badly paid and badly fed, roaming the countryside eating green corn and unripe apples. Eventually, on hearing that King Charles was approaching with a large force, they retreated from the area.

One important part of Dinedor's past has vanished almost without trace. In the river meadows bordering the Wye, in the north of the parish, stood Rotherwas House, a large mansion set in beautiful parkland. This was the seat of the Bodenham family, principal landowners for hundreds of years.

The estate was sold in 1912, the mansion demolished in 1924, and the land was used by the government for a munitions factory and ammunition stores in both World Wars. The derelict wartime buildings have been gradually removed, and a large industrial estate is taking their place. One tiny piece of the past remains: Rotherwas Chapel stands in a little green oasis by the river. It was the private chapel of the Bodenham family, part of it dating back to the 16th century. It is listed as an Ancient Monument and can be visited at weekends in the summer. Otherwise little trace of the former magnificence remains, except for some garden walls. The remaining stately park trees, and a pool, look oddly forlorn among the warehouses, wartime concrete and wire netting.

Dinedor Hill has long been a local beauty spot, the views from the summit stretching from the Black Mountains in the west, past the Shropshire Hills, to the Malverns in the east. There was such public concern when it was put up for sale in 1912 that Hereford City Council bought some of the land, including the cottage whose tea rooms had been open since the turn of the century. The cottage has now been converted into a hostel for youth groups, and the tea rooms replaced by picnic tables under the magnificent beech trees. Its future as a public park has been assured.

DORSTONE

Linking the Stone Age with the present, the village of Dorstone nestles at the head of the Golden Valley, sheltered by the Black Mountains to the west and Merbach Hill to the east. Here is Arthur's Stone, a Neolithic burial vault from between 2000 and 3000 BC – a great slab, set on upright stones, and the only cromlech in the county. Whoever was buried here still has the power to draw archaeologists on pilgrimage to their grave. From Merbach Point eleven counties can be seen on a clear day.

In the village below the river Dore rises from the Golden Well where, legend has it, St Peter's fish was caught – a carp with a chain round its neck, a sculpted model of which can be seen in St Peter's church, Peterchurch. Was the name Dorstone derived from Dwr – the Welsh for water, or a corruption of d'Or – the French for gold? Certainly the valley is truly golden in spring, with daffodils.

For generations Dorstone has retained its olde worlde charm with a traditional village green encompassed by the post office, the Pandy Inn, and until 1965 the village school.

The school was built in 1603 for 60 boys and girls, an endowed Free School helped by charities arising in part from the sale of land between 1623 and 1737 and amounting to £90 annually. Today the charities are administered by trustees towards educational activities, help in sudden bereavement or misfortune and 'at the marriage of poor deserving virgins, bona-fide of the parish'! After its closure in 1965 the school was used as a meeting place until 1988 when it was completely renovated as a village hall.

The Pandy Inn – thought to have been built in 1185 by Richard de Brito to house his workers while building Dorstone church – is said to have been visited by Oliver Cromwell during the 17th century. On the village green opposite stands the old village cross, turned into a sundial in 1812. An older sun clock is to be seen on a stone ball in the churchyard.

The present church of St Faith was largely rebuilt in 1889. One of the four knights who murdered Thomas a Becket, Richard de Brito, took sanctuary in Dorstone and after serving 15 years' penance in the Holy Land founded a chapel here to expiate his share in the murder. One of its treasures is a tiny pewter chalice from the 13th century, kept behind glass in a recess in the chancel. Three of the bells are of the 17th century but one, a hundred years older, boasts in Latin 'it will ring for ever'.

Legend has it that on the eve of All Souls a man called Jack of France was walking home past Dorstone church. Hearing something going on inside, he peeped through the keyhole and saw the Devil in the pulpit reading out the names of the people who were to die during the coming year and heard his own. Having been rather a bad character he tried reforming his ways but it was too late. He died as he had heard he would.

In 1881 the Golden Valley railway brought the opportunity to local farmers of a wider market for their produce. Parishioners too were able to get to Hereford, Abergavenny, Hay-on-Wye and Brecon – many for the first time. However, after 60 years, bus competition siphoned off the passengers and the railway was only used for agricultural supplies and products, and the station at Dorstone was finally closed in 1950. Although many of the hill farmers continue today with their sheep and cattle, the larger valley farms are chiefly arable and one of the country's largest potato growers employs many local people.

The organisations in Dorstone thrive and work together and hold many local events. Best Kept Village Competitions were won three times between 1973 and 1980. In 1978 the village decided to rent a piece of glebe land to provide a playing field. Here cricket and football are played in ideal surroundings, watched by spectators from a spacious pavilion. There is also a thriving Bowls Club using a Crown Green designed and laid out by the members themselves. At the other end of the village the Golden Valley Cricket Club, whose members come from miles around, have their own ground and pavilion.

EARDISLAND

Eardisland, which is situated on the river Arrow between Leominster and Kington, is an essential part of the 'Black and White Trail' which is followed by many tourists who find themselves drawn to the rural charms of Herefordshire.

In days gone by the village was noted for serious flooding, and tractors were used to rescue schoolchildren and take them up Broom Lane, and to take supplies to the village centre past the Cross Inn. However, in recent years only the eastern edge of the village has been affected, a traffic hazard rather than flooded living-rooms and cellars – until October 1998, when the worst flooding for 50 years occurred! Milk and newspapers were delivered by boat and canoe, and over a dozen houses (as well as the village hall) were seriously damaged by the water. The WI had to meet in a member's house (on high ground!) the following month, while the floor of their usual meeting room was replaced. The village was cut off for some time, the water having risen to well over five feet on the main road at the west end of the village, where flooding is normally quite rare. The east end, which is the area that has permanent road signs warning of flooding, was passable for part of the time.

St Mary's church has always played an important part in the lives of the villagers. The peal of six bells is so highly regarded that bellringers come here from many parts of the country. The church itself is 13th century, though it was rebuilt in 1864.

As visitors wander near the bridge, they pause to admire the half-timbered cottages and also the historical grammar school (now Bridge Cottage) which became reading rooms in 1936, where one can still see the iron rings of an ancient whipping post. A ruined 18th century dovecote can also be seen near the bridge, in the grounds of the 17th century manor house. One of Eardisland's millennium projects is the restoration of the dovecote, which now belongs to the village; its ground floor – which used to be a dame school – will be open to the public, and will contain a permanent interpretation board and other items of interest.

The manor house itself had a Queen Anne front built on and has

Bridge over the river Arrow at Eardisland

been extensively restored and rebuilt. At least two previous owners have described feeling 'a presence' there – and the impressive 14th century yeoman's house known as the Staick House on the east side of the bridge is also reputed to have a ghost. A large building next to the manor house was a furniture store for some years, but has now been transformed into a row of attractive houses by the local firm Border Oak (which built a 'Tudor village' in Japan, and helped to rebuild The Globe theatre in London). Border Oak also built, circa 1988, a row of nine houses on the main road, with a communal garden and a 'Tudor dovecote' in front – one with a utilitarian purpose! Eardisland is not yet on mains drainage, nor does it boast street lights.

There is a thatcher's needle on a cottage wall, a reminder of the great need for this craft in days gone by; two thatched cottages still remain, towards the west end of the village. The smithy is now a private dwelling, having been used as a shop and a meeting place for the Home Guard, the WI and other local organisations.

Near the river stands the Mill House, where even today one can see the millstream passing underneath part of the modern house, just as it did in former times.

There are two ancient mounds, one beside the church with a moat around it, probably the site of a pre-Conquest wooden castle. The second, a much lower mound on the other side of the river, is known as Monks Court, and is thought to have been the place where monks met their tenants to discuss problems.

The village has always been a thriving community – although at the present time there is no shop, no school, and the future of the White Swan Inn is uncertain. The old school has become an excellent village hall and is well used by the community for a variety of events and activities. The Bowling Club has its own premises just beyond the village hall, and the Cricket Club has recently been re-established, and now puts on an annual Cricket Event. Behind the village hall is the recreation ground. A mini-fete beside the bridge is now held each August, providing entertainment for the villagers with a raft race, duck races and stalls.

Other social events are held at Burton Court (mentioned in the Domesday Book), where visitors – before succumbing to cream teas –

may enjoy the tour of a distinctive costume exhibition and the 14th century Great Hall where Henry V once stayed. Other people enjoy picking soft fruits in the tranquil grounds overlooked by a most elegant mansion, which makes the picking an unusual experience!

In the absence of a village school, a bus transports younger children to Kingsland, and the bus stop provides a sociable meeting point for children and parents alike. Nearby, a part-time post office provides a much appreciated service for the residents.

A large, beautifully kept caravan park is situated on the north bank of the river, opposite to a new lay-by on the narrow Broom Lane, with picnic chairs and tables; a bridge was built here in the 1970s, replacing the old ford crossing. A small parking area is also sited beside the bridge in the village itself, where the swans and ducks come to meet residents and visitors in the hope of being fed.

Well known for its orchards and rare old English apples, Eardisland, which used to lie on the A44 Aberystwyth road, was by-passed a few years ago and no longer has to suffer the constant stream of heavy goods vehicles – a welcome relief to most of the residents.

EARDISLEY

At first glance Eardisley appears to be simply a long straight street running purposefully from the Hereford direction to Kington. Drivers are usually only aware of close-packed cottages, black and white and picturesque, before they find themselves again in open countryside. If they chose to stop and take a look around they would probably be surprised and certainly delighted.

Starting at the lychgate to the churchyard at the Hereford end of the village, there is an instant reward at the sight of timbered tithe barns – a ciderpress beside them converted into dwellings and retaining much beauty. Behind the church a pleasant Georgian farmhouse sits peacefully in front of the ancient castle mound, once home to the famous Baskerville family, Lords of the Manor of Eardisley for over 500 years. Today this 'tump' is the only relic reminding the visitor that the village had a turbulent past, situated

Sonia Taylor

Upper House Farm, Eardisley

on the fractious borders of three cultures – Celtic, Saxon and Norman – for many of its early years.

The church of St Mary Magdalene has been there since the early 12th century and remains an integral part of the life of the village. Its Norman font is acknowledged to be one of the finest examples of Romanesque carving in England. In high relief, within a Celtic endless chain of plaiting (once thought to have magic properties), angry knights wielding weapons, startled saints and fabulous beasts struggle to tell their story for story. This priceless treasure, sensitively restored, attracts visitors from many countries.

Out in the long street the exasperation of present-day traffic can be forgotten in enjoyment of the timber-framed houses, many centuries old, companionably shouldering each other. At the far end stands Upper House, an ancient monastic lodging, with its massive beams, overhang and central medieval hall. Behind some of the cottages, and predating them by many hundreds of years, the strip-like gardens reveal the ancient Saxon layout of the first village.

The village hall stands back through an archway off the main street. It is a Victorian period piece, new at the beginning of the 20th century and now admirably brought up to date. It was originally provided by the rector of the village, Canon Palmer, and was built on the old tennis court of the Eardisley Church Institute. In addition there were two other rooms at the archway entrance, both still in use and recently modernised. They are the remaining parts of the Curzon-Herrick Institute, founded in 1877 as a challenge to the public houses, where working men could obtain recreation and education without recourse to drink. The Curzon-Herrick family were the last of the village lords of the manor, their great estate being broken up in 1918.

The two inns face each other at the top of the main street, across the old market square. On the evening of 12th May 1959 Eardisley's worst-ever flood swept mud and destruction through the village. The square was four feet deep in water, but the challenge was made for someone to swim across between the two inns to win a tankard of ale. It was taken up by one of Eardisley's legendary figures who swam both ways to make sure of his future fame.

The New Strand (previously the New Inn) bears the date 1902 on its main roof beam, commemorating the rebuilding of the original half-timbered New Inn following its destruction by fire one snowy day in December 1901. There was no efficient and speedy Eardisley Fire Brigade then as there is today so by the time the firemen arrived from Hay-on-Wye they only had cinders to hose down.

On the opposite side of Tram Square sits the Tram Inn's black and white building, part of which is the original 14th century hostelry. Its unusual name recalls a marvel of invention in the early 19th century – a horse-drawn tramway on cast-iron rails which brought Welsh coal from Brecon to Eardisley first in 1818. Its success led to its extension to Kington and its use lasted until the steam railway arrived in 1864. Both the Tramway Wharf and the Midland Railway station were at the opposite end of the village, the former now providing sites for small industries and the latter almost completely disappeared except for the road bridge at the entrance to the village.

Eardisley is fortunate in being a working community still, retaining young people in employment.

The church school, provided by William Perry-Herrick in 1857, is a flourishing hive of young life, learning and discipline with over 100 pupils from the village and surrounding neighbourhood.

The main street is by no means all there is of Eardisley. To the right of Tram Square a road leads past attractive houses to Almeley, and to the left there are more old houses, including the 600 year old Cruck House standing alongside the village pump-house which supplied water until the 1960s. Some little distance further along this road stands Eardisley's oldest living inhabitant – the 800 year old Great Oak. Despite its hollow interior it still flourishes, providing much wonder for young children. It is probably the sole survivor of the forest that surrounded Eardisley at the time of Domesday.

Back again to the Tram, where the near-mythical Eardisley Fox Pie first appeared in the Second World War, served up as a practical joke for a visitor. It achieved fame by causing the Nazi radio propagandist 'Lord Haw-Haw' to announce that the starving English had been reduced to eating foxes!

Eardisley, never dormant, was the first village to offer Village Holiday Breaks, an enterprise which is now known world-wide for its contribution to the concept of Sustainable Tourism, and which annually attracts visitors from Japan, North America and Australia. Visitors stay with families in their homes and gain an insight into village life and the surrounding countryside.

In this quietly vibrant village it is not only the houses which support each other, but the generous community. There are the true Eardisley born-and-bred, but also over the years 'incomers' who have become absorbed as part of the village. Everyone takes part in such annual events as the Flower Show and Sports at August Bank Holiday, and the Festival. To herald the first of these Festivals on 11th August 1974 a record peal of 15,000 Doubles lasting 7 hours 22 minutes was rung on the church bells; in campanology this record still stands. Their peals will ring in the millennium – the third in which this fortunate village has flourished.

EASTNOR

Eastnor is situated on the Tewkesbury road, two miles from the market town of Ledbury. This delightful village, with many half-timbered cottages in beautiful surroundings, is on the fringe of Herefordshire's south-east border and commands splendid views of Midsummer Hill and the Holly Bush, part of the Malvern Hills.

The main interest in the village is Eastnor Castle which contains many art treasures. It was built by the first Earl Somers in 1812 and the architect was Sir Robert Smirke, who planned the British Museum. Within the grounds a large lake provides a home for wild duck, and in the 500 acre park there is a variety of trees, many of foreign species, and a herd of red deer. There is also a proud obelisk which commemorates the deeds of the Somers family.

The parish church of St John the Baptist was rebuilt in 1852 but a Norman arch and pier can still be seen at the east end. The old font which was discovered during the rebuilding is possibly one of the oldest in the country as it was made to enable babies to be totally immersed, and it could only be used by the priest as it had a locked cover.

EATON BISHOP & RUCKHALL

Eaton Bishop, with its neighbour Ruckhall, lies close to the south bank of the river Wye some five miles west of Hereford. Its rich undulating pastureland, lush river meadows, and tranquil views towards the Black Mountains in the west and the Malverns in the east, are typical of Herefordshire countryside at its best. Centuries ago, the Romans forded the river near Lower Eaton to reach Magnis (Kenchester) to the north, and indeed a stretch of the old Roman road from Abergavenny forms the western boundary of the parish.

A hundred or so years ago, Eaton Bishop was a fairly self-contained community, little having changed since medieval times. Two or three major landowners, several farms and at least two working mills provided most of the employment. The village had its own school, post office, grocer's shop, a butcher and a baker, a blacksmith and a wheelwright, a tailor and a boot and shoe maker. All these have now disappeared, and only the fine old parish church, with its early 14th century stained glass window, remains as a focal point for the community. In the late 1920s, however, it was felt that a village hall was needed for social activities, and by vigorous fund-raising efforts, and small loans from the villagers themselves, the present hall was eventually built.

Several good farms continue to flourish in the area, and sheep still graze Honeymoor common in summer - though not the donkeys which were once a vital part of village life. These long-suffering animals, which lived on the roughest food and in the most primitive of shelters, were used for ploughing, hauling carts, transporting people and goods to town, and taking poultry, pigs and sheep to market. A donkey and cart could be hired for the day for one shilling. Often the animals were named after their master's trade – Mr Jones the blacksmith called his donkey 'Pig Iron', Thomas Mason the postman's was called 'Letter Bag', and the Camp Inn donkey rejoiced in the name of 'Beer Barrel'! Affluent folk, of course, travelled in style with a horse and carriage.

The recollections of older villagers make fascinating reading: farm workers' wages in the early part of the 20th century were 12s 6d to 14s a week, and hours were very long. Workers had three days holiday a year. Every home in the village had a good garden, and the occupiers grew their own vegetables, kept a pig and some chickens, and made jam and cider from their own fruit. After gleanings from the cornfields had been ground into flour at the mill, bread would be baked 'the likes of which you cannot get today'. Coal was brought by barge up the river from Hereford to Ruckhall, and the villagers collected it themselves.

Eaton Bishop possesses an interesting Norman church, parts of which are believed to be Saxon. Apart from the beautiful stained glass windows and many interesting features, the church contains a memorial tablet to Richard and Margaret Snead, who died within a few months of each other in 1678, which deserves to be mentioned for its charming inscription. It reads:

> One bed we shared; one tomb now holds us,
> And our bones, mingled with dust now lie together.
> One death was ours; one year took us away,
> One day saved us and gave us back to God.

One of the major landowners of Eaton Bishop in Victorian times, in effect the squire, was Sir Joseph Pulley, a member of the London Stock Exchange. He and his wife spent only part of the year at their property by the river at Lower Eaton, but he appears to have been regarded with great affection by the villagers. He died in 1901, and his nephew Charles inherited the estate. Charles, however, died childless, and the estate was split up and sold in 1947.

The proximity of the river adds to the attraction of the villages, and in pre-war times an outing was popular with Hereford folk, who came by punt or rowing boat up the river, or on foot or bicycle by road. Their destination was Ruckhall, where delicious ham and egg teas could be enjoyed at the Laurel tea rooms, or the Camp Inn high up overlooking the river. The river meadow below was an ideal spot for a picnic. Today the tea rooms are no longer there, but the Camp Inn has been renamed the Ancient Camp Inn (there was an Iron Age fort nearby).

EDVIN LOACH

This small parish situated three miles north of Bromyard was once in the county of Worcestershire and completely enclosed by Herefordshire. The parish was transferred to Herefordshire in 1893 and was part of the Saltmarshe Castle Estate owned by the Barneby family until 1953 when the estate was sold.

When Edvin Loach was part of Worcestershire, fugitives escaping from the law would flee to a point on the boundary locally known as Catchem's End. Once in Edvin Loach they were out of the jurisdiction of the Bromyard police, thus avoiding capture.

The Gothic-style church of St Mary the Virgin was built about 1860 near to an old 11th century Saxon church. The old church, now a ruin, was originally, with Lower Sapey (Worcestershire), the daughter church of Clifton upon Teme, and a gift of three shillings had to be paid annually to the Mother Church as late as 1536. The herringbone masonry in the north and south walls, the arched entrance and the tower have been preserved. It was still the custom in the early 1840s, every Palm Sunday, to decorate the church with yew boughs, the same being tied to the seat ends, a relic of pre-Reformation Palm Sunday ceremonies.

There are fine views from the churchyard to the Malvern Hills in the south-east and the Clee Hills to the north. The rectory was sold in 1945 and is now a private house. The church joins with Tedstone Delamere, Upper Sapey, Wolferlow and Whitbourne to form the Greater Whitbourne Group of parishes. Each church celebrates its Patronal Festival and services are held only in the respective church on that Sunday.

The two oldest houses include The Hope, built in the 16th century. It has a two-storeyed porch with oak posts; the sides have turned balusters and on the projecting upper storey are two panels carved with fleur-de-lis and other ornamentation. The other house,

The Hope at Edvin Loach

The Steeples, is a c1600 timber-framed house through which the parish boundary runs. There are nine other dwellings. Of these, four have been built since 1963, two have been converted from old buildings, and another old house is now being restored.

Edvin Loach is mainly a mixed farming community. At the Wild Perry there is an old perry pear orchard and perry is made every year. It is an excellent drink, especially when the pear juice is fermented in fresh empty rum or whisky barrels!

EDVIN RALPH

The village lies about three miles north of Bromyard and is situated in pleasantly wooded countryside, looking towards Bromyard Downs and the Malvern Hills. It is a community of about 150 people. There is a church, a sub-post office and a village hall. The first village hall was at one time part of an American Military Hospital and re-erected by the inhabitants after the Second World War, having been removed from Mansell Lacy. The village hall, recently rebuilt with the help of grants, now houses the sub-post office.

The centre of the village in ancient times was set in the vicinity of the church, where there was also a religious community. Visitors can still see the moat and traces of a fortified mound on ground where the village stood prior to the disaster of 1348, when the Black Death decimated the population. There is also a hollow in this field which is believed to be the pond where the monks did their fishing. After 1348 a small number of houses sprang up on the road to Tenbury about a quarter of a mile away from the church, and it is in this vicinity that the village hall now stands and limited developments have taken place.

Fascinating stories abound in this North Herefordshire village of how Baron Ralph and Lord Edvin, once friends, fell out over the love of a fair lady. The duel was fought to the death 'with rage, hatred and revenge' close to the old bridge leading to Buckenhill, and this tragic event gave the names of these knights to the village for all time. According to the legend the lady over whom the duel was fought threw herself between the combatants and was mortally wounded.

There is an element of truth in the story, because these warring knights did exist and their effigies can be seen lying with their families, under the tower inside the church of St Michael. You will see seven monuments in a fine state of preservation in one of the most interesting collections to be found in any parish church in Herefordshire. All these monuments were unfortunately removed from their niches in the chancel where they had lain since the 14th century, to their present resting place under the bell tower in 1885, to make way for choir stalls.

The heart of the village is, and has always been, around the Norman church and the adjacent farms. The church, which was built in the 12th century, is approached by a path under a bower of yew trees. The modern porch shelters a Norman doorway with a 13th century arch and a stoup in the wall. There is also a Norman arch, rebuilt in the 13th century, which is now the doorway to the vestry. Visitors will find much to admire in this well loved yet simple church, particularly the lancet window in the west wall which glows a beautiful red when seen at sunset. The tower is distinctive, unbuttressed with a broad arch towards the nave, and later a truncated pyramid roof and spire were added.

This part of the county is renowned for high yields of best quality wheat, barley, oats and potatoes, and is fortunate to have many hopyards and cider orchards in the area. Much of the land in Edvin Ralph produces milk, but many fat cattle and sheep are raised here on the excellent grassland in summer, and on the hay and silage made in that season for winter fodder.

EWYAS HAROLD

This is a fairly large village, population approximately 900, just off the Pontrilas by-pass on the A465, the main Hereford to Abergavenny road, and about 12 miles from each of these two towns and 1½ miles on the English side of the Welsh border.

The most popular meaning of Ewyas is 'Vale of the Yew Trees' and the Harold who gave his name to the village was the son of Earl Ralph, a nephew of Edward the Confessor, who occupied the Castle of

Ewias. Little now remains of this castle except a mound known as the 'Castle Tump' which is on private ground overlooking the village.

The village today caters extremely well for the physical and spiritual needs of its residents. It has a grocery and wine and spirits store which also houses the post office; a general store, a butcher, full time doctors' surgery, dental surgery and a veterinary practice. In the centre of the village are the two pubs – The Temple Bar and The Dog Inn.

The modern village school accommodates the five teachers and 120 pupils now on register. Unlike many villages, Ewyas Harold still has a resident policeman.

Modern homes are springing up in the village and small factories and an engineering works are thriving and yet the village has retained its rural charm and tranquillity.

Entertainment, through the many societies, is centred on a large hall built as a memorial to the young men of the area who gave their lives in the Second World War. There is also a beautiful recreation ground situated near the parish church which caters for the village's sporting needs. The annual Carnival and fun day is held every July on this field, as is the annual parish Bonfire Night Party.

On the spiritual side, the parish church is dedicated to St Michael and All Angels. The tower and chancel date back to the 13th century.

There is also a delightful small modern Roman Catholic church served from Belmont Abbey and resident ministers at the long established Methodist and Baptist churches, all in the centre of the village.

EYTON

Eyton, some two miles north-west of Leominster, boasts some of the oldest buildings in the county, the church of All Saints dating back to the 12th century and Marsh House to the 14th.

Marsh House has been extensively renovated and is now a high class hotel, with the old hop kiln transformed into a 'baronial hall' and used as a dining room for guests. A far cry from the men's club of long ago, which used it as their venue for air gun shooting! Marsh

House was once the social centre of the village.

Opposite is Eyton Court, a black and white house of architectural interest. Not far away is Pondside Cottage, another black and white building which has seen great changes of recent years. The grounds are surrounded by a high wire fence, which runs through a wet pool adjoining Eyton Common. The common provides a safe haven for several species of water birds and pondlife.

The parish also has some very old families, still represented by members living within its boundaries. The Coates family at Eyton House, opposite the church, goes back for ten generations, and gets a lengthy mention in Alec Haines' book *The Standard of Mercia*.

There are still several members of the Dale family living in the parish, although sadly Frank Dale of F. H. Dale Ltd is no longer alive. The Dales not only provided work for the people of Leominster town, but a number of Eyton's parishioners worked at Dale's Nursery at Eyton Hall, and lived in houses provided by the company, still known locally as 'Dale's Houses' and named after the family racehorses.

Agriculture is still the main form of employment in the village, with a large fruit farm on the Kingsland road out of the village, operating on a pick-your-own basis during the summer months. At Hill Farm, the third generation of the Morgan family occupy the farmhouse.

Although several properties have been renovated with love and care, several have disappeared too. This is most noticeable at the Riddle, where only two of the original cottages remain. However, a new house has been completed nearby, and a riding school has also been established in this small section of the community.

Eyton lost its school in the late 1960s when the new school was built in the neighbouring village of Luston. Miss Groves, the last headmistress at Eyton, lived in the schoolhouse, but now this has been converted, together with the school building, into a large private house. The school gate used to be the meeting place for the village boys, who congregated there to chat on long summer evenings. Opposite the school is an old gate in a wall, which is the entrance to a passage leading to the cellar of Eyton House. Known locally as 'the dungeon', this passage was used as storage for, and movement of, cider barrels to and from the cellar, which housed a cider press. The 1953 Coronation celebrations, a sports day, followed by a village supper, were held in the gardens of Eyton House.

FORD

Ford is a pretty little hamlet of around 303 acres with the river Lugg running through. It lies in the Lugg valley, protected by the Welsh mountains on one side and the hills of Worcester and Malvern on the other.

It once had a station and signal box, but the Shrewsbury to Hereford and South Wales line now runs through without stopping. Ford does have a nine hole golf course with driving range, which is very popular – by eight o'clock on Saturdays and Sundays the car park is full. Fishing is also available.

There are several orchards and one or two old oast houses. Deer are to be found in the nearby woods. Wild daffodils and primroses are abundant in the spring. It's amazing how much mistletoe grows on the trees!

Ford Farm is a rambling old stone building with barns and outhouses, and still a working farm with plenty of sheep set alongside the river with ducks and swans. There was a medieval village on the banks opposite and beside the farm is a little chapel dedicated to St John of Jerusalem, which dates back to the 12th century. It was rebuilt in 1851 by John Arkwright of Hampton Court and seats about 50 people. Many original features are still there and there are some interesting paintings in the dome over the altar.

There are good walks along the lanes to Stoke Prior, the nearest post office and village. In the other direction is Hope-Under-Dinmore, with lovely Queenswood high on the hill with a special viewpoint. Several old Iron Age forts can be seen, as well as many pretty black and white houses. Other than the new road it has hardly changed over the years. One can still find peace and quiet – apart from the sounds of so many birds!

FOWNHOPE

Fownhope is a picturesque village surrounded by lush meadows, bordered by a fine river with a background of wooded hills. During the spring the wild cherry blossom covers the hill leading to the Iron Age hill fort of Cherry Hill.

Outside St Mary's church you can still see the old village stocks and in the corner of the churchyard there is a strangely accurate milestone giving an exact distance to Ross-on-Wye. Inside the church can be seen a fine Norman tympanum on the west wall.

The Green Man inn is steeped in history. During the Civil War Colonel Birch, the Roundhead leader, halted here overnight after his siege of Goodrich Castle before proceeding to besiege Hereford. Tom Spring, Fownhope's famous prize fighter, is featured in a mural in the Naked Boy Restaurant, painted by Trevor Makinson. The mural also reminds us that petty sessional courts used to be held at the inn.

There are many old cottages in the village, but perhaps one of the most interesting is the timber-framed Bark Cottage, formerly called Bark House. Its name was derived from the bark-stripping industry carried on years ago when the ricks of bark stood in what is now Fownhope Motors, awaiting their transfer by barge on the Wye to the tanneries.

One much more morbid reminder of days long ago is the garage at Bark Cottage for it was once known as the Dead House, recalling the fact that when drowning tragedies occurred occasionally in the swift flowing Wye, the bodies were laid there. As the petty sessional courts used to be held at the Green Man inn, it is possible that the inquests were held there too.

Another house with bark industry connections stands close to Holme Lacy bridge. This too has been named Bark Cottage, but in the older days it was called the Warehouse. This was in the days of considerable navigation on the Wye, when the then tenant kept three barges on the river, and a wharf was attached to the building. Bark was the main commodity then carried, and an old iron mooring ring and some remains of the wharf can still be seen.

In the 17th and 18th centuries, Fownhope had a thriving lime

Fownhope

industry, and as the lime burners found working on the kilns was very thirsty work it was natural that there were several small inns in the village which supplied ale and cider to slake their thirsts. There was also a flourishing brewery in the last century at what is now the Rock House.

At the beginning of the century both the Nupend Mill and the Pentaloe Mill were working. The Nupend Mill only worked about two days a week, when local cottagers could be seen carrying sacks of gleaned wheat upon their heads, returning later with their sacks of flour. The Pentaloe Mill catered for the farmers who arrived with carts filled with sacks of corn.

There were several places where ferries could be hired, though they usually were run for private profit only, and not as a full time job. Boats were kept at Lechmere's Ley (a difficult corner and barges often needed help), Mill Farm, Ferry Lane, Leabrink, Mancell's Ferry, opposite Ballingham, and Alford's Ferry under Capler Wood.

The Fownhope Heart of Oak Friendly Society meet on (or as near as possible to) Oak Apple Day, and when parading to church for the service at 11 am carry their 'club sticks' on which are wooden oak apples. The ceremony is certainly colourful and there is much friendly rivalry over the decoration of the sticks with fresh flowers. Preceding them is a member carrying an oak bough with red, white and blue ribbons attached and four others carrying the historic banner.

There have been several earth tremors within living memory and just over 100 years ago there was the great Herefordshire earthquake of 17th December 1896 when much damage was done in Fownhope. The walls of some houses were cracked, slates shaken off the roofs and many chimneys fell. It is thought it was caused by a slip along a fault running parallel to the Woolhope Dome.

FOY

Foy, lying in one of the most beautiful areas of the Wye valley, has been accurately described as 2,366 acres of 'land and water'. Welsh Foy or West Foy is a peninsula almost two miles long in a great hairpin bend of the river. English or East Foy, much of it wooded and rising 400 to 600 feet above the river, curves round it from north-east to south-west, rather like the rim of a shell. The Wye 'acres', part of the boundary of the old kingdom of Archenfield, make the whole an Area of Outstanding Natural Beauty, but they also make it a sharply divided community. In previous times there were ferries and a ford and, it is said, a tunnel under the river. Now there is the suspension bridge, erected for £800 in 1876 and rebuilt for over £2,000 after it was washed away in 1919, but only pedestrians, horses and bikes can get across. Cars must go the eight miles round by Wilton bridge.

The church, from the 11th century, stands on a terrace on the peninsula. It was quite a wealthy church with significant additions over the next two centuries but never as important as the nearby Sellack church. In 1280 John de Tregoz came to Foy and built his castle at or near the site of Court Farm in East Foy. From then the area was known as Eton Tregoes and it was not until somewhere between 1805 and 1835 that the name 'Hole-in-the-wall' appears on maps.

During the 19th century, when the river was used for navigation, the old Gatehouse, the only building on the river side of the road, was used as a warehouse. There are canals where the boats were drawn out of the current above the staunch and the remains of the paving where the horses were stabled. The school house was built in the middle of the 19th century to replace the schoolroom which was previously over the cider press attached to the Gatehouse. The school closed again in 1959 and the few children went to Brampton Abbotts. Both the Gatehouse and the new school were built high above the flood levels, but children could not get to school from the other side when the river was in flood.

The Abrahalls of Eton and later of Ingstone were first heard of in the 15th century as knights of the shire. They became patrons of the benefice and the family provided a succession of vicars from 1642 till 1937 with only three exceptions in all that time. The names changed as the line passed through the daughters to Evans, Jones and Wilton – quite a remarkable record.

Foy was never a nucleated village. What are now scattered farms – Hill of Eaton, Ingstone, Underhill – were described as townships. Equally scattered were the labourers' cottages, except at Hole-in-the-Wall where they were doubtless built from the stones of the castle when the Abrahalls moved across the river to Ingstone. The cottages at Brickend and Hillcrest only date from the 19th and 20th centuries and all have had electricity and running water since the 1950s.

The Bennett family lived at Ingstone for 99 years from 1816. James Bennett, born in the huge old Jacobean mansion in 1821, grew up on this most compact of farms. It filled the broad top of the peninsula and was so fertile that it was spoken of as the 'Fatlands'. In the late 1830s the decayed mansion, ravaged by fire in 1785, was replaced with a Georgian farmhouse, though many of the old buildings and the hop-kilns remained, including what was reputedly the largest barn in the county of Herefordshire.

James Bennett founded not only a flourishing family of eleven children, but also the Royal Hotel, the Waterworks and the Alton Brewery in Ross. The tenancy of Ingstone was passed to Philip Charles in 1893. James died at Coughton in 1903, and his wife Mary in 1919. Both are buried at Foy. Mrs Hone, who succeeded as mistress of Ingstone, is remembered for having raised fabulous crops of peaches, bringing in over £1,000 a year.

In the 1930s, under the Roberts family, the great revolution in farming practice took place. The 23 horses used for work dwindled in number, each new machine displacing about six. The last two or three became too fat to work through lack of employment and finally disappeared. Much use was made of the railway at Backney for corn and sugar beet. With the arrival of the first harvester combine, harvesting no longer took four to five weeks. The great 'ginny-ring' which used six or seven horses tied to poles for threshing or four or five for pulping roots lies now in the Gaff next door. Hard work was the rule; but the fishing season and hare shoots were great occasions, and there was dancing at the Christmas feasts.

In 1965 the Court Farm at Hole-in-the-Wall was bought by Peter Lawrence and the PGL canoe centre developed. Hillcrest, in West Foy, was bought a few years later. Gradually the inhabitants of Hole-in-the-Wall have died or moved away and several houses are now empty and derelict. Most of those still living in Foy no longer work on the land but still appreciate the lovely area.

GARWAY

Garway is in a beautiful setting on a south-facing slope of the Monnow valley. The banks of the river Monnow, which separate England from Wales, were settled by early man, and the Romans built a fort at the narrowest part of the valley between Garway Hill and the Graig Hill. The whole area was laid waste by the Welsh, according to the Domesday Book, and from the 12th to the 16th centuries the manor of Garway was owned by the Knights Templars and the Knights Hospitallers, who built the church in 1180, and the beautifully preserved dovecote in 1326. A return to the Bishop of Hereford in 1394 tells us that the people of Garway spoke only Welsh and that the curate spoke only English!

About the year 1690 there was a vicar of Garway called Jeremiah Jackson who seemed to be greatly at odds with his churchwardens; so much so that they sent complaints about each other to the bishop.

The churchwardens complained that the vicar did not wear his surplice on Sundays and set his neighbours against one another, and the vicar complained that the churchwardens brought their children up as Papists and that they invited their cronies into the church, got them drunk, and rang the church bells all day!

The parish is a scattered community with no main centre but with several small hamlets. At the Turning is the church, and the Baptist chapel; a hundred years or so ago there were also shops, a post office and a forge. The Garway Moon Inn, in another part of the parish, looks out over 23 acres of common land, part of which, by the efforts of the villagers, has been made into a fine cricket and sports field. There are houses and cottages around the common, and nearby a row of houses built by the council in the 1950s which are now mainly privately owned. Several new houses have been built in recent years, bringing more young families to the village.

High on the slopes of Garway Hill is the hamlet of White Rocks, which is reached down a single narrow lane. It is probable that this was a much larger community in the Middle Ages. Now there are scattered cottages and small farms which have grazing rights on Garway Hill common, which rises to 1,200 feet. Right at the other end of the village, almost seven miles from White Rocks, is a hamlet on the crossroads called Broad Oak. 'The Broad Oak' is a very old tree which stands in front of the former inn, now a private house. Here was once a toll gate and toll house on the Ross to Abergavenny Toll Road, which was part of the main route from London to Milford Haven. The farm called Southwell Court was once a coaching inn on this road, and takes its name from Viscount Southwell who was Lord of the Manor of Garway in the early 19th century.

Almost all the land in Garway is farmed and there are some very old farmhouses. The population is now small at a little over 200 people, but a hundred years ago there were more than 500 people in a thriving self-sufficient community. It was the 1930s before water was piped to the village, and the 1950s before electricity was installed.

The last shop in the village was owned by Miss Lawrence who was postmistress for over 50 years. She kept a shop and post office at the common until she died in 1978 in her eighties. The shop had never been modernised and the locals well remember the row of biscuit tins on the counter in which the sweets and chocolates were kept. Buying a bar of chocolate involved opening tins until the right one was reached! There is still a sub-post office in the village, and the garage at Broad Oak now has a shop.

Garway is fortunate in still having its school. The first school was built in 1878, but before that a school had been held in the church vestry and in a specially built schoolroom over the Baptist chapel. The present school was built in the 1960s.

HAMPTON BISHOP

The village of Hampton Bishop is situated on the B4224 road between Hereford and Mordiford approximately three miles south-east of Hereford. It is bounded by two rivers, the Wye and the Lugg. The lord of the manor was the Bishop of Hereford, which explains the addition of 'Bishop' to the name of the parish.

In the past basket making was an important occupation in Hampton Bishop. There was also a forge and a wheelwright and a toll had to be paid at Lower House for cattle crossing from Ox Ford to Hampton Bishop. However, although the village remains largely agricultural, these old crafts are no longer practised and many of the homes, both new and old, house families that are no longer connected with agriculture.

Nevertheless, the character of this 'black and white' village stays the same because Hampton Bishop is a conservation area with many listed buildings. Consequently, although new residences have been built the old black and white houses, some of which date back to the 16th and 17th century, cannot be demolished and over the past few years they have been beautifully restored by their owners.

The principal building in the village is the church, which has been lovingly maintained by the villagers over the centuries. It was first built in the early 12th century but was found to be too small and enlargements and additions were made in the late 12th and 14th century. The stained glass in the windows is of the 19th century and the roof structure is described as a simple braced collar roof. The six bells, five of which were cast in the 17th century, are still rung regularly by dedicated campanologists.

The story of Hampton Bishop through the ages has been a story of the battle against flooding. Flooding occurs when the two rivers, the Wye and the Lugg, are carrying abnormal quantities of water and the Lugg, unable to flow into the Wye at Mordiford Bridge, backs up onto the fields at Hampton Bishop. Some of the older residents of the village can remember boating or skating over the fields when they were children.

In December 1960 there was a particularly memorable flood. The twelve foot embankment, known as the Stank, gave way under the pressure and millions of gallons of water swept over the village, inundating lanes, fields and the ground floors of many houses. Troops of the 22nd SAS Regiment helped to evacuate marooned residents by boat and helicopter. It was a strange sight to see the boat gliding along the lanes with people standing in it clutching a treasured possession or household pet. The roar of the river could be clearly heard half a mile away. After the flood the Stank was repaired and raised 15 inches above the 1960 flood level in order to protect the village.

However, on a happier note the floods provide lush meadow grass for the cattle to graze and the beautiful rivers provide endless pleasure for walkers, canoeists and anglers. The river Wye is one of the best salmon rivers in England and the stretch running through Hampton Bishop purports to be the finest stretch for fishing on the Wye.

Hampton Bishop has many footpaths and forms part of the Wye River Walk. The village public house, The Bunch of Carrots with its large car park, is conveniently situated beside the river Wye and provides an occasional venue for village functions.

There are twelve properties in Hampton Bishop that have 'commons rights' of grazing and mowing over three areas of the parish known as Hampton Meadow, Big and Little Million and Swan Bed. Their activities are recorded in a minute book which dates back to the year 1896 and at this time several of the commoners still exercise their rights.

HATFIELD

Hatfield is a rural parish situated on a by-road which runs parallel to the north of the A44 Leominster to Bromyard road, and is on the border of Worcestershire. It is in a green belt area, so it has retained its natural charm and beauty.

It consists of private houses, farms, the church, post office and the mansion of Hatfield Court, once the home of the local squire. It is approached along a country road, bordered by farmland and woods with the occasional farmhouse.

The railway which ran through the parish from Leominster to Bromyard was closed in 1952. A short time afterwards, the rails were taken up and the land sold to neighbouring farms. The station office and waiting room at Fencote station were sold, and houses built there.

The church of St Leonard dates back to the 11th century, and boasts a fine Norman doorway in the north wall, now filled in but still visible, and good examples of herringbone masonry. The walls are of local sandstone and tufa. The timber supports of the bell turret are said to be medieval. There are two 13th century bells, but they are not inscribed.

Hatfield school and the school house were built in 1852 with money provided by a local gentleman, Thomas Ashton Esq. After the school closed, it was used for the social life of the parish and as a meeting place, but it was sold in 1981 and is now a private house.

In 1957, when the owner of Hatfield Court – Miss Chambers – died, the estate was sold to sitting tenants. This ended the era of the local squire and that way of life for Hatfield parish.

Until a few years ago, most of the inhabitants were employed on farms in the parish or in the neighbouring ones. They would walk to work with their food in a pack over their shoulder. Quite a number of the girls were employed as maids in the big houses in the area before the Second World War.

The farms are now privately owned, employing very little labour, only the family. The larger farms have bought up nearly all the smallholdings, where the smallholder would keep a pig and a few animals, and he would work away for a few days of the week, to keep his family. Now, most of the young people work away from the parish.

Opposite the church is the Court Farm, built behind the remains of the once magnificent Elizabethan house known as Hatfield Court. The last remaining wall of this splendid house was pulled down in the 1970s. In the churchyard are monuments to the Colles family who lived in the Elizabethan house from the 16th century until the end of the 17th century. When the present Hatfield Court was built, the oak staircase was taken from the old house to the present one, along with other parts of the old house. Foundations which are believed to be of the medieval village can clearly be seen in the orchard of Court Farm.

The Old Hall, said to be the oldest house in the parish, dating back to the 16th century, is a typical example of a yeoman farmer's house, and it still retains an olde worlde charm.

There is an art gallery at Rough Cast Farm, 'The Coltsfoot Gallery', where paintings are displayed and sold.

HOARWITHY

Hoarwithy is a pretty riverside village consisting of cottages, houses, farms and barns built along a steep bank overlooking the beautiful river Wye. Its attractive name means 'at the willow tree on the boundary' and its earliest mention appears in 1005. The linear village includes settlements at Altbough, Tresseck, Llanfrother, Red Rail and Shepponhill, all situated within the Herefordshire parish of Hentland. At the census in 1981 the population of the parish was 399, which shows a considerable decrease since 1861 when 647 heads were counted.

The present day inhabitants are mainly retired or employed in farming, tourism, crafts or professional occupations. Hoarwithy has an inn, post office, two guest houses, church, redundant chapel and a reading room where meetings are held. Since the stores closed some years ago, bread, meat and groceries can be delivered. Books can be chosen from the monthly mobile library. An irregular bus service still operates between Ross-on-Wye and Hereford.

During the 19th century the picture was quite different with the rural population employed as agricultural labourers, fishermen, shopkeepers and tradesmen. Five inns were listed, together with three watermills, two schools, a church and chapel. The village was self-sufficient and the nearest public transport was available from Fawley railway station. Cricket was a popular pastime and social gatherings were held at the school and in the reading room.

St Catherine's church is an unusual Italian-style building constructed in the 1880s around an existing chapel of ease erected during the mid 19th century. Built of red sandstone, the building has not weathered well, so restoration work commenced in 1971 with further work undertaken in 1980 and 1988. Weekly services are attended by a small enthusiastic congregation.

The toll house and bridge stand on the site of an ancient ford and ferry crossing, connecting the adjoining parish of Kings Caple with routes into Hereford and Ross. The tall toll house has stood beside the Wye since the building of the first timber toll bridge in 1856. After 20 years of use it was replaced by an iron structure which measured 260 feet long and 15 feet wide. A novel feature in the construction of this bridge was the way it was built on top of the old one and lowered by hydraulic pumps. In 1935 the Hoarwithy Bridge Company sold the bridge to the Herefordshire County Council who immediately freed it of tolls. It deteriorated and became unsuitable for today's heavy traffic so a new bridge was built in 1990.

Tresseck lies in a delightful valley formed by a tributary of the river Wye. The attractive house consists of two storeys with attics partly built of timber and local sandstone. It is possibly of medieval origin with 16th and 17th century work remaining, together with later additions of the 18th century. Documents relating to Tresseck date back to 1200, and the name is derived from 'village built on drained land'.

Another interesting site is in an isolated position overlooking the Wye valley. Llanfrother is traditionally associated with the legendary St Dubricius who founded a monastic college here in the 6th century. In 1633 its remains were recorded and today mounds are still visible. The L-shaped house is of two storeys with attics and cellars dating from the 16th century with the upper part rebuilt in the 17th century. It has been much altered since this date. Llanfrother is well documented from 1500 when it appeared as Henfrowther, 'Church of the Friars'.

The greatest attraction at Hoarwithy is the lovely river Wye which flows from mid-Wales through scenic countryside to meet the Severn at Chepstow. Hoarwithy lies almost midway where an important and convenient river crossing was established. In earlier times barges loaded and unloaded goods, and bark from nearby woods was conveyed by river to local tanyards. At Hoarwithy the Wye provides an ideal recreational area for fishing, canoeing and raft racing while the banks are popular with walkers, bird watchers and painters.

Hoarwithy cannot be mentioned without reference to the Rev William Poole, a well connected Victorian cleric. By 1854 he had become vicar of Hentland and Hoarwithy where he stayed until 1901, a year before his death. Throughout these years the parish benefited from his generosity and supervision with the building of the school, vicarage and reading room, the restoration of cottages and the rebuilding of Hoarwithy church in the Italian style. During his 82 years as a bachelor he led a full life dedicated to his clerical duties, diocesan affairs and the growth of education. His photograph and brass memorial can be seen in Hoarwithy Reading Room.

HOLME LACY

Holme Lacy lies some five miles south-east of Hereford, set in pleasant wooded countryside, with water meadows stretching down to the south bank of the river Wye. The village takes its name from a famous Norman, Walter de Laci, who was rewarded by William the Conqueror with large tracts of land in the Hereford area, including the manor of 'Hamme'. For 400 years it was virtually one large private estate, with Holme Lacy House, the principal seat of the Scudamore family, as its focal point.

Holme Lacy House was built at the end of the 17th century. It is an imposing mansion of sandstone which originally had a very lavish interior, with moulded plaster ceilings in the Italian style, much oak panelling and a profusion of wood carvings, many of them by the famous Grinling Gibbons. The gardens were designed like those of

Hampton Court, with vast avenues of yew hedges, a maze and many examples of topiary. Some of the yew hedges still survive, with wide lawns sweeping down to a lake. After changing hands many times this century, the mansion was used as a hospital for some 50 years. It is now a well-known country house hotel. The house has been extended and restored to much of its former glory.

The Scudamore family produced many illustrious men, of whom two were particularly renowned. Sir James Scudamore, a distinguished soldier and horseman in the age of Elizabeth I, was knighted for his bravery at the siege of Cadiz, and immortalized by Spenser in *The Faerie Queene* as 'the gentle Scudamore'.

It was Sir James's son, John Scudamore, later 1st Viscount, who brought the most fame to his family and country. For four years he was Ambassador to France, and when he returned to his estates he brought new French varieties of cider apple, including the famous *Redstreak*, which improved his own orchards and those of his neighbouring landowners, thus laying the foundations for Herefordshire's still flourishing cider industry. An ardent Royalist, he was imprisoned for four years in the Civil War, and when released devoted the remainder of his life to good works, restoring devastated churches and giving away vast sums of money in charitable causes. The Lord Scudamore School in Hereford still bears this name. He died at the age of 70, and is buried in Holme Lacy church, without memorial.

The church of St Cuthbert is tucked away in a beautiful isolated spot by the river Wye, about a mile from the present village centre. It is a fine church, surprisingly large, mainly 14th century, but with many later additions, including some spectacular monuments. The church was declared redundant in 1994, and is vested in the Churches Conservation Trust. Since then it has been extensively repaired and is now open to visitors. The visitors' book shows that people from all over the world manage to find it! Nearby is the former 17th century vicarage, now privately owned. There is a remarkable story about a pear tree there, which the vicar of the time thought worthy of an entry in the parish register! A large branch of this tree had been broken by the wind, and the drooping head tip-rooted to form a growing arch. The vicar layered other branches in the same way, and formed a complete arched orchard from this one tree. In 1776 it yielded 14 hogsheads of perry.

Holme Lacy is still mainly an agricultural area, with 1,000 of its 1,300 hectares given over to farming. It is particularly well known today as the home of the Herefordshire College of Agriculture, now known as Holme Lacy College, which is set in attractive grounds near the southern entrance to the village.

Because fewer people are employed in agriculture in this age of mechanisation, most of the working population commute to Hereford or further afield, or are self-employed. But the village retains its own identity, with a school, a post office and a thriving village shop. The attractive Tudor-style village hall was given to the village in 1920 by Lady Lucas-Tooth, then owner of the manor house, as a memorial to her two sons, killed in the First World War. It is well used by local people, and is at present undergoing renovation and modernization. The large playing field behind the hall has a football pitch and a children's play area with modern equipment.

HOLMER

Holmer, Without and Within, sits astride the A49 two miles north of Hereford and includes Twin Tree Tump, the reputed geographical centre of the county. It is the fast developing northern suburb of Hereford, following part of Holmer and Shelwick being designated Holmer Within by Local Government order in 1884. In 1902, the ecclesiastical parish of Holmer was reduced to form the city parish of Holy Trinity.

Today, everything one can imagine in a modern community seems to be in Holmer. In addition to the old church and three daughter churches, the school and original buildings, there are now an ever-increasing number of houses, a travel hotel, the leisure centre, some heavy industry, and an increasing number of small trading estates, some new and some converted from factory premises into car showrooms, offices and industrial concerns. A large area has been developed as a retail park for out of town shopping. There is still agricultural use and original playing fields, but the racecourse incorporates the county cricket ground, a municipal golf course, football pitches and an athletics track.

St Bartholomew's church is stone built in Norman and Early English styles with a chancel, nave and porch. A string course runs round the church showing the sloping floor level when congregations stood for services. The church's detached tower and bells are of particular interest. The tower is 13th century grey stone for two storeys with a black and white belfry containing six bells, which are some of the oldest in Herefordshire. The fourth bell was believed cast between 1400–1420 and installed in 1552; it is long and narrow, unlike the usual bell shape. A new vestry has been built to blend in with the church, a Grade I listed building. The vestry was dedicated in 1997 by the Bishop of Hereford and is a memorial to Prebendary John Dale, Vicar of Holmer for 28 years.

An incident occurred shortly after Holmer school's foundation in 1857, when at the end of the second summer term, the Headmaster was dismissed. No reason was recorded for this decision – although he had just asked for a loan to buy coal! The second school built in 1874 still exists and has amalgamated with the adjacent infants school built in 1906. The school has been considerably extended during the past few years giving new classrooms, work and playing areas for the 380 pupils.

Shelwick Court was a crumbling ruin saved from demolition and beautifully restored by a Trust Company. Its medieval chamber has a six-bay open timber-framed roof whose massive timbers are cusped and chamfered in the Herefordshire manner. The former owner told tales of witch burning in the grounds, but there is no evidence and details died with him. The building is now let for holiday use.

In the l9th century, Turvey Hall became the home of the Oliver family. About 1884, Mrs Oliver disappeared and rumours abounded that she had been murdered by her husband and buried in the garden. All family burials are recorded except Mrs Oliver's!

Burcott Farm epitomises the development of Holmer. It is an arable and beef farm and the farmhouse was built about 1720 and was originally black and white. This century it was pebbledashed, but retains its character. All the farm buildings are modern following a disastrous fire. In the 18th century, the Hereford-Gloucester canal was cut through the land and a canal bridge constructed which is still a focus for canal enthusiasts today. In the 19th century, before the canal was finished, the railway line was cut. In the 1960s the North Sea gas pipeline was installed and fields have been lost to development. It is possible the proposed Hereford bypass, should it materialise, will cut through the farmland, and will affect the whole community. Holmer is a very busy and bustling place.

HOPE-UNDER-DINMORE

The village of Hope-Under-Dinmore is situated on the north side of the densely wooded Dinmore Hill, a short distance from the Hereford to Leominster main road.

In the 1930s it was just a hamlet with farms and cottages, the church being quite a distance from the village. The main form of transport was pony and trap, with no buses and only one car, although trains could be caught at Dinmore station, and unlike today the roads were gated.

The majority of work was farming but Cadbury's factory was built during this time which created more employment. At the outbreak of the Second World War searchlights were erected to guard the railway tunnel, and army huts built to house soldiers.

In the 1940s the 'scrambles' were started and are still going today with keen interest from the children. The first four council houses were built in 1947 on the same site as the army huts, and in 1965 a council housing estate was built at the other end of the village. This very much changed the style of Hope.

The old village hall, built by John Arkwright, was originally used as a reading room and a rest room for the workmen on Dinmore tunnel. In 1970 a much needed new hall was built.

There are several listed buildings including Hampton Court, which has the legend of the Hounds. A picture of hounds hanging in Hampton Court must not be removed – if so death will prevail! The Court was used as a hospital for soldiers during the war. Dinmore Manor is a magnificent building situated in beautiful gardens with its own chapel, which is still used.

Sonia Taylor

Entrance to the Music Room at Dinmore Manor, near Hope-Under-Dinmore

St Mary's church, although small, is lovely and stands proud on Dinmore Hill. The north transept was built as a memorial to John Arkwright. The old vicarage, which is a distance from the church, has now been turned into a children's care centre, namely Solutions. Next to the church is the Church of England primary school. This dates back to the 1800s. In October 1985 it was in danger of closure due to falling numbers but an action group of parents, governors, staff and villagers succeeded in keeping it open and numbers are steadily rising.

Queenswood is undergoing major changes. From rambling woods it is now becoming commercialized and laid out, but still attracts many visitors from far afield.

The village has expanded over the years, including the building of the Little Chef in 1986, creating employment for the younger generation, and the building of twelve new houses. Despite all the change there are still very few amenities, although there is an hourly bus service between Leominster and Hereford.

HUNTINGTON (NEAR HEREFORD)

Only two miles north-west of Hereford Cathedral lies the little village of Huntington, which despite its proximity to the city might as well be in the depths of Herefordshire.

Anyone who turns left off the Hereford to Canon Pyon road (A4110) into Huntington Lane will find the little church of St Mary Magdalen worth a visit. There are wall tablets in the church to members of the Tulley family, famous for their association with Hereford cattle. In 1799, Mr G. Tulley took first prize at the Smithfield show for his 1,925 lb Hereford which carried 288 lbs of fat!

Huntington Court stands near the Yazor Brook. This is a late Georgian house. The Bishops of Hereford used to hunt from here. Huntington House, a black and white house near the Yazor Brook, was formerly known as Pool House. In days gone by the Yazor used to flood into a lake in winter and skaters enjoyed good sport until 1906.

Now from the little stone bridge you will be more likely to see a few ducks or maybe a swan or two.

HUNTINGTON (NEAR KINGTON)

You could easily pass through Huntington without noticing it, for it is a very small scattered village. The school, now closed, is a mile from the church and the church is approached through a farmyard, fortunately a very clean and tidy one!

The manor of Huntington was mentioned in the Domesday Book as belonging to Earl Harold who was killed at the Battle of Hastings. The extent of the manor then was three miles from east to west and nine miles from north to south-west. Today the parish extends to no more than one and a half miles in either direction.

There are about 70 persons on the electoral roll. The most historic building is the castle which was built around 1200, probably on the site of an earlier motte and bailey. As well as a look-out and fortress, it was used as a sanctuary for the people and their animals whose homes had been destroyed by the pillaging Welsh!

There is another mound known as the Turret Tump a mile west of the castle which it was thought had been a look-out, but there is now a theory that this dates from prehistoric times.

The church was built in the early part of the 13th century, probably on the site of an earlier building. The circular churchyard indicates a very early date. There is a story that the church was built by Richard de Brito, one of the four murderers of Thomas à Becket who then, having seen the error of his ways, dedicated it to St Thomas.

St Thomas à Becket was also commemorated by Huntington Fair which was held twice yearly until 1956. The first recorded fair was in 1403. Originally for all kinds of livestock, for the past many years it had become a horse fair and was mainly famous for the mountain ponies, known locally as 'Munts'. These ponies were gathered by their owners from the surrounding hills and driven to Huntington. Traditionally the pony which realised the highest price of the day was ridden through the inn – sometimes causing considerable havoc!

There is no record of when this custom started, but villagers remember seeing it done.

The school was founded in 1791 by Edward Goff, the son of a local labourer. He went to London in 1763 when he was 25 and became a wealthy coal merchant. Feeling the disadvantage of his own lack of education he founded the school at Huntington. Under the terms of the endowment the schoolmaster was required to conduct a religious service in the school room each Sunday.

One of the earliest masters was Rev Thomas Rees, a distinguished scholar and a great preacher. When he arrived in 1802 he found 'the moral and spiritual state of the neighbourhood truly deplorable'. His preaching was not well received at first and once when speaking at Gladestry a wild bull was set loose among his listeners. Preaching at Eardisley in 1804 he was shot at from a pistol! Today three of Thomas Rees' direct descendants live in Huntington.

While the Trust continued to support the school the Congregational church, which later became the United Reformed church, was formed and had its own minister. Both school and church used the same building until 1953 when the school was closed. Church and Sunday school remain.

Huntington is not notable only for its past. It is still an interesting and friendly place to live. It is a very rural community, and only six houses have been built in the last 50 years. Agriculture is still the only industry. In this upland area it is mostly livestock farming. There is one modern dairy retailing farm in the parish where several people are employed but apart from that fewer people are working on the land than in years gone by. Dr Philip Cleland and his wife run a rare breeds farm.

KENCHESTER

The village of Kenchester lies five miles from Hereford towards Hay, and consists of three farms – Magna Castra, Kenchester Court and The Old Weir. The New Weir is now a nursing home. Cottages and bungalows number about 20, although only four now house agricultural workers. Most other occupants commute to Hereford, and the ex-village school belongs to a vet. Lady Southampton's chapel and St Michael's church still hold services, but the parson is shared with five other parishes. The nearest pub and garage are at Bridge Sollars.

Since the footpaths have been opened the village sees many more strangers. The 22 acre site of the Roman town of Magnis attracts students and archaeologists, although there is nothing to see above ground. However, older villagers talk about the ghosts of Roman soldiers marching on certain nights of the year. One old lady (now deceased) insisted that they marched right through her house every full moon, and another that they camped in her garden!

KILPECK

Open any book on the history of church architecture and almost invariably you will find an illustration of the very remarkable south doorway of Kilpeck's St Mary and St David's church – the most famous church in Herefordshire.

Apart from a corner of the nave which is Saxon, some medieval windows and a 19th century restored bell-cote, it all dates from the third quarter of the 12th century. Its red sandstone has stood up uncommonly well to 800 years of weathering.

The south doorway has a wealth of grotesque carvings. There is a continuous corbel table round the building with the corbels carved with all manner of beasts – the gaps, it is said, being caused by the Victorians who removed those which they considered unsuitable!

The castle lies west of the church although very little of it remains. As a stronghold it was part of the fortified village set up in the time of King Offa as an outpost in the defence of Hereford. The medieval village which lay outside the castle area covered some six acres.

Kilpeck lies eight miles south-west of Hereford off the road to Abergavenny. Its name is derived from the British 'kil' or cell and Pedic – the cell of St Pedic.

KIMBOLTON

The centre of this large parish straddles the road from Leominster to Tenbury Wells, the A4112, the land continually rising to 750 feet. The name of Kimbolton does not appear in the Domesday Book, although the hamlets of Hamenes (Hamnish) and Stocktune (Stockton) do feature. The civil parish of Kimbolton is reputed to be one of the largest in area in the whole of Herefordshire.

It is well watered with three brooks, Cogwell north to south, and Whitty and Yolk east to west. The Ryde Wood is an outstanding landmark on the ridge parallel to the A49 and into the next parish. On this road, one mile out of Leominster on the parish boundary is the wharf where coal was brought from Stourport on the old canal and stored on the banks. Evidence of this can be see at The Moors further along the A49.

Historical evidence of ancient settlements can also be found within the parish boundaries. The Iron Age camp at Upper Bache and the medieval village of Stockton are in a field owned by Stockton Bury at the rear of a building called Spice House.

The present house of Stockton Bury was built in 1970 on part of the foundations of the previous Georgian building, The latter was the home of 'Squire' Herbert Smith-Williams, who had purchased it from Lord Rodney of Berrington Hall in 1887, when parts of the Berrington estate were sold off to settle gambling debts. An ancient round dovecote, a tithe barn and the outlines of a large fish pond can be seen south-west of the house. The gardens at Stockton Bury are now open to the public. Pigeon pie must have been frequently on the menu. There is space for hundreds of birds!

Thomas Carwardine, a renowned breeder of Hereford cattle, farmed The Bury between 1868 and 1884. One of his bulls, Anxiety IV, was exported to America in 1880. It is claimed that 95% of all present day American Hereford cattle can trace their ancestry back to this bull.

The parish boasts another dovecote – this one being square and situated at Upper Bache where reputedly prisoners of war were housed during the Napoleonic Wars.

Stockton Bury Dovecote and Tithe Barn at Kimbolton

The Lea, 'up the Lever hill', is over 300 years old. It was farmed at the end of the 16th century by the originators of Lloyds Bank, known as the Quaker Lloyds. The chimneys here are of interest – three diagonal shafts – while the front door is of solid oak, brass studded. Here is situated a Berrington barn recognised by the arched window-like features with open brickwork. Two others are sited at Endale and at Rowley Field.

Rowley Field, Sweet Appletree Field and Grantsfield offer, to the discerning, traces of the three-field system, as their names imply. Grantsfield, once a cottage yet extended several times during the 17th and 18th centuries, was owned by the Hutchinson families. The Rev Thomas Hutchinson was for 62 years vicar of this parish. He was the nephew of Mary Wordsworth née Hutchinson, the wife of William Wordsworth, and members of the family are buried in the south-west corner of the churchyard.

The 12th century church of St James commands this rural scene some 410 feet above sea level and possesses outstanding views as well as being prominent itself from many vantage points.

The Church school was opened in 1856 with two rooms. The infants were in a classroom while the seniors and juniors were in one big room divided by a green curtain. This Victorian state more or less existed until 1972 when it was modernised and extended. The new village hall was opened in 1997 and is the venue for an increasing number of activities.

Stockton forms an ancient township within the parish of Kimbolton. Lower Stockton or 'Bottom of Stockton' was known as the Old Workhouse, consisting of four cottages, two from the 15th century with a 17th century north wing and an 18th century south wing. The premises were used in the 19th century as the parish workhouse after which division was made into the four cottages.

Stockton Cross Inn greets the traveller passing through the village and to the left of it is a development of bungalows for the elderly, with a further development of houses on part ownership with a Housing Association. These dwellings are known as Stockton Rock, that being the name of the field on which they are built, where in the 17th and 18th centuries an annual fair was held.

Pateshall, which can be seen from the church and approached along the lane at the side of Stockton Cross, is a stone-built farmhouse of the 16th century with five gables on the front, each with a blocked window.

Hamnish was a township with the lord of the manor at Hamnish Court. The church of St Dubricius dates back to 1910. This replaced a corrugated iron hut of 1897 which now serves as a church hall.

KINGS CAPLE

Situated in a large horseshoe bend in the Wye valley, the dominant feature of the parish is the church standing on high ground adjacent to The Tump and divided by the Roman road once known as Caple Street. This ancient track crosses the Wye into Hentland at Red Rail, words derived from the Welsh words rhyd-yr-heol, 'ford on the street'. The parish name is derived from the Norman-French word 'Capele' meaning chapel.

The 13th century church of St John the Baptist was a chapel of ease annexed to Sellack. Restoration work was carried out in 1884 at a cost of £600. The huge cedar tree crashed in the 1947 gale fragmenting the head of the 14th century standing cross. Much parish history was lost in 1968 with the destruction of many gravestones. The spire was partly rebuilt in 1982 and the fifth and tenor bells were rehung in 1993.

The Tump, an ancient monument standing in a salient position, is the site of a Norman motte and bailey castle. Commanding wide views, it was ideally placed to strike terror into the local peasantry. It possibly had its origins as a meeting place in ancient times. Up until about 1930 it was the setting for the traditional 'Caple Feast' held on Whit Tuesday when parishioners gathered for dancing, nine-pin bowling and much fun and games. In recent years it has hosted PTA barbecues, a church fete and of course the annual WI bonfire.

The river provides a strong visual impact forming three quarters of the parish boundary. The Hoarwithy ferry operated by William Fido ceased with the construction of a timber toll bridge on stone piers in 1856. This was replaced by an iron bridge in 1876, which in turn was replaced by a stronger span capable of coping with the heavier and bigger vehicles on today's roads. Sadly, this much abused bridge with its seven ton limit is soon to be replaced. The Sellack ferry operated by George Harris ended with the erection of the suspension footbridge in 1895. In 1995 the centenary was celebrated by both Sellack and Kings Caple with a weekend of special events, culminating with a riverside service, which has now become a regular event.

The Free Fishermen of the Archenfield Hundred were finally banished in 1909 following legal actions epitomizing a misuse of wealth and power. The riparian owners led by Lord Chesterfield and Mrs Foster took legal action against George Harris and Frank Bailey which finally went to the House of Lords. The ancient charter was written off and might triumphed over right. The quarry pool at Aramstone produced some huge salmon caught by Jack Wyndham Smith and his daughter Barbara. In 1914 the Squire landed a record sized 51 pounder.

The largest single impact on the parish must surely have been the arrival of the railway with its Fawley station and goods yard in 1855. In addition to cheap coal it brought an escape route for those in rural poverty. In 1947 a great disaster occurred when, following a great flood and gale, the Strangford bridge collapsed. The railway closed in 1964 but plans now exist for the reinstatement of the line.

Elementary education came in 1840 with the building by public subscription of a National school. This was a Sunday and day school for 55 pupils and financed by the children's pence. After surviving for nearly 60 years, a new school for 65 pupils was built in 1899. In 1995 this was enlarged and redesigned at a cost of £250,000. The old school is now a parish room. This too has been extended and renovated to provide a very pleasant meeting place.

Many social changes have taken place since the Second World War. Aramstone, Pennoxstone and Poulstone, seats of the local gentry, are no longer large employers and the present owners are in farming. In their heyday, each provided a magistrate to dispense justice and keep the peasants in order. A great loss to the village took place in 1959 when Aramstone was demolished. Built in 1730, this beautiful mansion was considered to be the most important house of its period in the country. While a preservation order was being considered, demolition men moved in to bring about the end of an era.

The arrival of electricity in 1952 followed by mains water and the proliferation of motor cars opened the door to city folk. The indigenous population has largely disappeared together with its characters. None of the thatched cottages survived and Davies the thatcher died in 1952. The butcher, grocer, basket maker, dairyman and post office have all closed their doors; but the British Lion pub, true to its name, refuses to die, and in the hands of new local owners is going from strength to strength. The smithy closed in 1951 when the last heavy horses went to the knacker's yard, and the gipsies turned to motor cars. The Women's Institute and Monday Club are well established. The Parish Council meets several times a year. A mini bus provides a service to Ross on Thursdays and Hereford on Wednesdays and Saturdays.

KINGSLAND

Kingsland, a village almost a mile long, lies alongside the old Roman road from Hereford Lane to Street, with the added hamlets of Shirlheath, Cobnash and Aston. Owned by the Crown, it had a Norman moated castle, the remains of which, known as the Mound, lies west of the church.

The church had its first rector in 1285 under the patronage of the Mortimer family, and its unusual Volka Chapel was probably the burial place of a Mortimer. Parish records date back to 1538, and are now held in the County archives.

On the Great West Field was fought the Battle of Mortimer's Cross in February 1461. This was a crucial battle in the Wars of the Roses and resulted in the Yorkist Edward IV being crowned King. A monument to commemorate the event was erected nearby in 1799.

Many black and white houses were built in the village; many more than are apparent today, because John Gethin, who owned a local brickworks, added brick fronts to several, the 15th century Angel House being a notable example.

John Gethin was born in 1757 and became a master stonemason, living at Brick House and then Stoneleigh. He and his brother rebuilt Aymestrey bridge after its destruction by flood in 1795. He then rebuilt many others and became surveyor and inspector of all Herefordshire bridges till his death in 1831.

Farming has always been the most important industry. Arrow Mill, Lugg Mill and Waterloo ground corn, while cider was made at Must Mill, and at Bone Mill bones were ground for fertilizer. The work of the wheelwright, saddler and blacksmith were also linked to farming.

An ancient fair, dating from 1305, was held on 11th October on a field to the east of the church, and the same date was kept for a later foal show on Boarfields.

An old custom which only ceased at the outbreak of the Second World War was the tolling of the church bell to announce a death. The bell rang four times for a man, five for a woman, and then the age of the deceased.

The Church school, of local stone, was opened in 1846, replacing one over the rector's vestry in church. It catered for children up to 14 years old but in 1963 it became a primary school.

The railway station opened in 1856 with the line from Leominster to New Radnor, and a branch to Presteigne. Crossing gates were operated by the occupants of the cottages at the Brook, Station, and Waterloo. At this last cottage, Freddie Fox, the notable flat race jockey, was born. A unique aerial railway three and a half miles long carried timber for pit props to the local sawmills.

Kingsland has been proud of its fire service since its inception in 1893, when a horse-drawn engine was given by Mrs Price of Stanley Villa. More modern engines replaced it over the years, till today's up to date equipment, housed in Harbour Lane, can cater for all types of fires and accidents. When the old engine was housed at the Croase, much excitement occurred as the old fire bell was rung to summon the men. Many villagers, and especially the children, would turn out to see the engine set off.

The post office dealt with letters, telegrams and telephones. Many remember Mr and Mrs S. D. Williams who manned the telephone 24 hours a day. For a local call it was often only necessary to ask for a name rather than a number. Sometimes the reply would be, 'No good ringing her, she's just gone down the village.'

Electricity came in 1935, but the installing of mains water and drainage signalled a bigger change. Many new houses were built, and the development still continues. The opening of the Coronation Hall meant that organisations now had suitable premises for their meetings. KATS puts on two theatrical performances annually to appreciative full houses and the annual Flower Show has been revived.

KINGSTONE

Kingstone is a village situated seven miles from Hereford. It boasts two public houses, a village hall and an attractive church. The church is not architecturally important although the flowing tracery of the west window is unusual for Herefordshire. The simple breccia font of the 13th century and the long 'dug-out' chest of about the same time are both interesting. The church now boasts a ring of eight bells, previously six. These were acquired with the help of a legacy from a redundant Welsh church at Llanbradach.

The village has two shops, one incorporating the post office. The children are fortunate in having excellent schools within walking distance. During the Second World War, Kingstone became home for a large contingent of RAF personnel, associated with the Madley airfield. The temporary accommodation left behind after their departure, served to provide housing for families and also to provide the start of what is now a school complex for infant, junior and senior pupils.

The school has recently celebrated its 50th anniversary. All the wartime huts in which the school started have been demolished and a very large well-equipped building houses the latest educational facilities for its pupils. The catchment area stretches from South Hereford city to Ewyas Harold, eleven miles away.

The village is well served by three resident doctors and also has an adequate bus service. Houses in and around the village vary from black and white timber-framed to modern centrally heated, with various other periods in between. Many new houses have been built on what was open farmland, thus changing the balance of the village. Some small industry has moved into the village and has provided employment for several local people.

The village has a thriving Sports Association which organises many activities on its grounds. The Association has plans for a Millennium project which will provide a sports complex with permanent facilities for all sport, so much fund-raising will have to take place.

KINGSWOOD

Kingswood lies roughly one and a half miles south of Kington in north-west Herefordshire. The population is about 150.

With Kington its origins go back at least to AD 50. In 1252, when the neighbouring manor of Eardisley was conveyed by Humphrey de

Bohun to Walter de Baskerville, the great wood extended from Eardisley nearly to Kington, but that part known as the 'King's Wood' which pertained to Kington, was excluded from the Baskerville lands. Until 1868, when the Kingswood estate was sold and broken up, the area was managed as an ancient 'Standard and Coppice' woodland adjacent to Kingswood Common, which was itself owned by the manor of Huntington.

The stone cottages, many doubtless gained by 'squatters' rights', were scattered amongst the woodland tracks. There were, and are, very old farms; Apostles, Lilwall, The Birches, The Pound, The Mere, The Rodd, Moseley, Bredward and Chickward. A brickworks was established long ago to take advantage of good clay deposits and local employment was found in connection with brickmaking, on the neighbouring farms and in woodland management. There was no 'great house' or church; Kingswood then, as now, belonged to the ecclesiastical parish of Kington. One or two cider houses existed for the refreshment of travellers and residents.

The Royal Commission on Historical Monuments (Herefordshire North-West, Vol 3) mentions Apostles Farm, which is stone built and partly timber-framed, the oldest section of medieval origin, as was the dovecote and stable block which has been re-erected elsewhere in the county. Leading to the farm is Apostles Lane with its Apostles Stone where, legend has it, St John once preached. Where Apostles Lane crosses over the main road from Kington to Hereford, at the cross, it is said that a gallows once stood.

After the sale of the Kingswood estate the 'Great Wood' was cleared and several new farms were established, these houses built of local stone and brick. A few cottages came into being as well. The common too was absorbed into enclosed agriculture. It was on the common that, on 1st May 1863, the newly-built, stone Wesleyan chapel was opened amidst celebrations, and several generations of local families attended its services and Sunday school. They remember with pleasure the school outings, sometimes to Aberystwyth, sometimes to a local farm. The chapel has now been converted to a house.

Modern Kingswood is still a small, scattered community but it is active and aware of its separate identity from Kington. The village hall was built by local subscription and was opened in 1960. Since then the hall has become a strong focus of local life, holding parties, meetings, whist drives, religious services and, as always, plays a large part in the successful annual August Fete and Horse Show. The grandson of the original benefactor lends his adjacent field as the show ground.

With such a history, naturally most local inhabitants are still engaged in agriculture or ancillary employment. The brickyard was demolished in about 1970, victim of mass production, but there are other options, including caring for the elderly and sick in Kingswood Hall.

KINGTON

Kington is a small friendly place, 19 miles north-west of Hereford and two miles from the Welsh border, which still has regular livestock markets.

In the Domesday Book of 1086 it was spelt Chingtune meaning 'royal manor or town', possibly referring to King Offa who built a dyke two miles to the east of Kington. The original Kington was built around the Castle Hill and the church, but as early as the 13th century, the present one came into existence, built on a grid pattern typical of medieval times. Little is left of 'old' Kington but many of the houses in present day Kington date back at least 300 years.

The parish church, dedicated to St Mary, is believed to be on the site of a Saxon church. This was replaced by a Norman church from which the font bowl and bell tower remain today. Other parts of the church date from 1220 through to modern times and include a fine range of lancet windows in the Early English chancel and the 15th century tomb of Thomas Vaughan and his wife.

Hergest Court, built for the Vaughan family in 1430, (where the ghost of the Black Dog walks) is a little to the west along Hergest Road. Opposite is the ancient mount of Castle Twts. Under the will of Dame Margaret Hawkins (a member of the Vaughan family), the grammar school was opened in 1632. It is now Lady Hawkins' Secondary School and with the Leisure Centre is sited down the slope from the old school. It is fed by local primary schools including Kington's in Mill Street, which was built in 1896.

A little earlier, in 1888, on the other side of Kington, the Cottage Hospital was opened and continues to serve residents in and around the area today.

Hergest Croft in Ridgebourne Road has famous gardens which are open to the public. They contain a great variety of trees, shrubs and flowers (some very rare) and a glorious display of rhododendrons.

For long distance walkers, Offa's Dyke path runs through Kington and the Mortimer Trail goes from Kington to Ludlow. Hergest Ridge with its old racecourse, Bradnor Hill with the much used highest golf course in England, Rushock Hill and the old tramway provide good local walks. In fact, to walk out of Kington in any direction provides spreading views into the Welsh hills or over the adjoining English counties.

Today, Kington offers good shopping, good pubs and eating places, plenty of accommodation and a caravan and camping site by the river next to the recreation field. There are many societies and clubs providing a wide range of interests and sports. Kington is lucky to have retained its St John Ambulance and also Guides and Scouts. Annual events include a two-week festival in June, a vintage car rally in August and, on the second Saturday in September, the Kington Horse and Agricultural Show which originated from the Horse Show started in 1881.

KINSHAM

Kinsham is a hamlet of some 18 households with five outlying farms, situated mostly in the Lugg valley four miles east of Presteigne. The nearby hamlets of Byton and Combe form a rough triangle around the eastern edge of what was once a glacial lake, the last vestige of which still remains as Byton bog, now designated a Site of Special Scientific Interest. Towards the end of the Ice Age, melting ice forced its way out, forming a gorge below Kinsham Court through which the river Lugg now runs. Of other historical interest is the hill fort at Wapley which some experts believe may have overlooked the valley for 3,000 years, and on the valley floor are three well documented Bronze Age burial mounds.

The 'big house' is Kinsham Court, said to have been built on the site of a priory and inhabited in the 15th century by the Blaney family. Subsequently the house formed part of the vast estates of the Earls of Oxford and was used by members of the family, a fine memorial to Thomas Harley being in the church which is situated in the grounds. Lord Byron rented the house from Lady Oxford in 1812/13, and some say he wrote *Childe Harold* there. Another tenant for a time was a Mr Nightingale, whose daughter Florence spent part of her childhood at Kinsham.

The church is of simple design, dating from Norman times with a small single belfry and no chancel arch. Until 1982 Kinsham and Byton formed one parish, their churches being of very similar construction and both situated to command striking views over the valley to the west. Kinsham now forms part of the group parish known as Presteigne and Discoyd, Kinsham and Lingen and is used regularly for worship.

The Arkwright family – of 'Spinning Jenny' fame – came to Kinsham in 1910 and owned the estate which then included most of the cottages and farms. The years between the wars saw Kinsham a thriving community with a village hall, cricket pitch and tennis court. Sir John and Lady Stephanie Arkwright had two sons, the elder of whom sadly went down with his submarine in 1942; a window in the church is dedicated to his memory. The younger son, Mr David Arkwright, died a bachelor in 1984, one of his last acts being to give the village hall in trust to the village. The house is now owned and lived in by his cousin, Mrs Susan Wood, and her family.

Several houses in the area are of stone and timber-framed construction, the most interesting and ancient in Kinsham being Lower Court which lies close to the river and was formerly moated. Now three dwellings, Lower Court has parts dating from the 14th century, as do parts of Combe farmhouse and the Court House at Byton.

To the north is Cole's Hill, shown on old maps as Cows Hill, rising to just over 1,000 ft and giving spectacular panoramic views. Footpaths traverse the valley from Byton to Kinsham and are crossed by yet another which follows the river from Kinsham Bridge to Rosser's Bridge on the Presteigne road.

Earlier mention was made of the gorge which lies under the church and Kinsham Court. Tales are told of soldiers escaping the Battle of Mortimer's Cross in 1461 who were captured and slaughtered there. A nearby sharp rise in the road at Lye is known as Slaughterhouse Pitch and similar stories arise here. Also a track leading down to the river from the Lingen road is known as Dead Woman's Lane. However grisly its past, the gorge today is a place of peace and beauty.

THE LEA

The Lea is a small village with a population of approximately 600, and is situated on the A40 between Ross-on-Wye, four miles away, and Gloucester twelve miles away. It is right on the border with Gloucestershire in the south-east.

It is always referred to by the inhabitants as 'The Lea', not just Lea, and newcomers are quickly put right about this. Early transcriptions of old documents of the 17th century call the village 'The Lake', or 'La Lea'. The Old English word Laecc or Lec denoted a stream, and as the Rudhall stream runs through the village at its lower end, there is the probability that at one time this broadened out into a lake. There is certainly swampy ground at one point. Another theory put forward is that the name is derived from Lacu, the name of an ancient family, the principal landowners in the 11th and 12th centuries.

The Lea owes its existence to the fact that it has always bordered a thoroughfare. Even from Roman times it was on the route between Gloucester (Glevum) and Weston-under-Penyard (Ariconium) and also the Forest of Dean, where the Romans obtained the iron ore which they smelted at Ariconium.

Some of the oldest village houses have at some time or another been inns. One reference in old documents tells us that a hostel or hospital existed on the crossroads at The Lea. This house still stands. It now has a fine Queen Anne facade, but medieval building is still discernible at the back, and probably it has been built on an even older foundation.

The Crown Inn also dates from medieval times. It is said that on dark, still nights, the clatter of hooves, the creaking of springs and the crack of a whip may be heard, as a phantom coach and horses rounds the corner near the Crown onto the old coach road. There is a lane about a mile away called Cut-throat Lane which certainly puts one in mind of highwaymen or footpads.

Any visitors to The Lea must visit the lovely little church of St John the Baptist. It is built of the local red sandstone, now mellowed to warm pink. It began life as a chapel of ease in the 12th century. The tower was begun in the 13th century and the slender spire was added in the 14th century. It was not consecrated for burials and baptisms until 1418.

Inside the visitor will be delighted to find a most unusual font, one made of Italian marble and estimated to be about 900 years old. How it came over to this country is not known, but it was given to The Lea church in 1907, by the daughter of Sarah Decima Bradney, in commemoration of her mother.

After the Second World War there was some new housing development which increased the population somewhat but in recent years there has been a spate of new building. An estate of 14 executive-type houses has been built on the site of Mitcheldean Road Station, through which the Hereford-Gloucester railway ran until 1965; while alongside the road to Aston Ingham there is a new estate of 40 houses. In 1990 the new village hall was built together with six houses alongside. In the village there is another small estate.

All this has had a beneficial effect on the village, bringing new life into it. There is a thriving village stores, a post office which also sells groceries, and one garage. The village school has 80 pupils and when sufficient money has been raised there are to be new buildings.

There doesn't seem to be the local characters about these days, like the old man with his donkey and cart and little dog, who came every year and camped in a nearby lane. He never came to beg but seemed to get by on the coppers he charged the local children (about 3d) for donkey rides. Another sideline was his flea circus for which he charged 1d a show and his little dog doing tricks was thrown in free of charge. After a week he would move on to the next village.

Part of the original Royal Forest of Dean borders the village on the south-east side. This wood is called 'Howly Grove' or 'The Wild Wood'. It is a beautiful sight in early spring and autumn. The lords of Lea claimed rights in the Forest and control over certain territory or bailiwick. Even today part of this district is known as Lea Bailey, and lies within the parish of The Lea.

LEDBURY

Ledbury is now a small, busy market town, with the heart of a village, nestling in the foothills of the Malverns. The Bishops of Hereford had a palace here and the place grew around its minster church, built in Norman times on the site of a Saxon church. A market was held on the village green (the first charter dates from 1138). The road from Hereford to Worcester (and the old salt track to Droitwich) crossed the road from Bromyard to Gloucester at the Lower Cross. Burgage plots were developed on either side of the Homend and the High Street, and many frontages of the present-day shops still show the width of these plots, with fascinating alleys in between.

There are many timbered buildings. Ledbury Park, at the Upper Cross, is a fine example of a Tudor manor house, now used as offices. Opposite is a house on stilts, which overhangs the footpath and is constantly being threatened by passing lorries. St Katherine's Hospital, built in 1532, has been restored and is now used as a meeting hall for many societies and activities, including a thriving WI market. The original chapel, screened off, is still used every Friday morning.

The black and white Market House, on its 16 massive oak pillars, is very splendid. In the nearby – and very much photographed – cobbled Church Lane, is the 16th century building which now houses the Council offices. Also in Church Lane are the old grammar school, restored as a heritage centre and museum, and the Butcher Row House, one of a row moved from near the Market House. Now on its third site, and carefully rebuilt by the Ledbury and District

Society, it is used as a folk museum. Burgage Hall, also restored by the Society from the derelict Congregational church, is now a fine meeting place for all to use.

The parish church of St Michael and All Angels stands at the top of Church Lane. It was described by Sir Nikolaus Pevsner as the premier parish church of Herefordshire. It is very impressive in size, and contains fine monuments and stonework. For many years the Chapter House was used as the Baptistry, but it has now been converted into a room for meetings, divided from the north aisle by a glass screen engraved by Kenneth Knowles.

The font has been resited in the north aisle. During the alterations the remains of an earlier font were found buried in the floor below the font now in use; this is presumably the font referred to in the 17th and 18th century church records and which now stands in the south aisle. At the side of the church is a large detached tower and spire, with a peal of eight bells and a carillon which plays hymn tunes at certain times of the day.

Ledbury had many crafts in the past, the main ones being cloth-making and tanning, and the making of gloves and shoes. Blacksmiths and other trades flourished to support the local farming and hop-growing communities.

Today there are still busy cattle markets, held off Bye Street every Wednesday and third Saturday. On Tuesdays and Saturdays, stalls are set up under the Market House, selling plants, cheeses, fish and other items, adding extra colour and interest to the High Street.

Modern-day industry includes stationery and office equipment, plastic packaging, preserves and fruit juices, a huge cold store for fruit, and a cheese factory which employs many people. Although many people are employed locally, others commute to the cities nearby.

The annual carnival has been revived, and is held on August Bank Holiday Monday. The much older Mop Fair fills the streets in the second week of October.

Many years ago, there were about 40 public houses in Ledbury. There are now about twelve inns or hotels, which is quite a good number for its size. The Feathers Hotel, an old coaching inn, is host to the Ledbury Hunt on the morning of Boxing Day, watched by crowds who are then entertained by the Silurian Morris Men beside the Market House.

LEINTHALL STARKES

Leinthall Starkes, often referred to as Long Leinthall, is a village of farms. It has lost its school, chapel, public house and like most other villages its smithy and wheelwright's shop. Fox House, a three-storey stone building in the centre of the village, was The Fox public house. The Norman church of St Mary Magdalene is a little away from the village.

The school was founded under the will of Thomas Allen dated 25th April 1704. He laid down that Limebrook Farm where his brother John lived should provide £14 a year forever to pay a teacher to teach the children of the parishioners, both boys and girls, to read English and instruct them in grammar and writing. This endowed school had its ups and downs and finally closed in 1946 when the building became a house. The £14 a year is still used for educational purposes.

Little so far is known of the early story of the chapel except that in 1884 a rent of 30s per year for the 'Chapel Room' was being paid to Harriett Preece. Was this for a room in the timber-framed house known as Chapel Cottage today? In 1920 Evan Dyke and Cecil Griffiths, owners of the reading room with land adjoining, sold part of it for £15 to the Primitive Methodist Circuit of Leintwardine on which to re-erect the iron building from Adley Moor which had been closed some twelve months. In 1946 Mrs Ann Elizabeth Griffiths according to her late husband's wishes gave the reading room to the trustees of the chapel. This chapel closed about 1983 and has been removed.

In 1801 there were 136 inhabitants which increased to 147 in 1841; since then there has been a decline to 70 in 1971. Some development has taken place within the village environs.

LEINTWARDINE

Leintwardine is a picturesque and historic village located close to the borders of Powys and Shropshire, at the meeting of the rivers Clun and Teme. The village is built on the site of the old Roman fort of Bravonium. A number of archaeological digs have been done and many Roman remains can still be found. A Roman bath house was situated near the bridge where Griffiths' Garage and the Lion Hotel now stand.

Beautifully situated in the centre of the village is the church of St Mary Magdalene, built on the site of an old Saxon church. Its large square tower can be seen on all approaches to the village. The oldest part of the present church is a blocked up 12th century doorway in the west wall of the nave, but even more ancient, beneath the chancel, is the Roman vallum (a rampart or stockade).

On the banks of the river lies the village green where the locals can often be seen fishing from the bridge. There is an abundance of wild life including otters and kingfishers. Between Watling Street and High Street are many old and interesting houses and near the north end of the village is a 400 year old black and white thatched farmhouse known as The Plough, which was once a coaching inn.

The old school, built in 1845, has now been converted into a community centre, which at present houses the library, the resources centre, the Age Concern office, the Youth Club and the thrift shop. This together with the village hall caters for the many activities and organizations of the village.

The village and surrounding areas are well served by a new primary school, many old established shops, a post office and a bank. With all these amenities available it is not surprising that there has been new development, but this has not changed the character and friendly charm of Leintwardine.

LEOMINSTER

Leominster lies midway between Hereford and Ludlow on the main

A49, and is only twelve miles from the Welsh border. It has a population of 10,000.

The first recorded name is 'Llanlieli', the Church or Town in the Marches. It was renamed by the Saxons, possibly after Leofric, the husband of Godiva, in the 9th century. In the 13th century Leominster became prosperous through its woollen trade from the local Ryland sheep, and this became known as 'Leominster Ore'.

The Charter of Incorporation was granted to Leominster in 1554 by Queen Mary Tudor. The streets follow the medieval grid plan except for the Georgian modernisation of Broad Street and Etnam Street. Church Street also contains elegant brick-built Georgian town houses. The timber-framed Market House which stood at the junction of Broad Street, Church Street and High Street was built by John Abel, the King's carpenter, in 1633. In 1855 this building was sold to a Mr Arkwright, of the Spinning Jenny family, for £95; he moved the building to its present site in the Grange, and lived in it. In 1939 when a buyer from America was interested, the council bought it and it is now Council offices. Leominster's motto is inscribed along the frieze above the pillars and reads, 'Where Justice rules there Virtue flows'.

The impressive priory church has three naves, the north nave being strongly Norman. Inside the church is England's last-used ducking stool, used in 1809 when Jenny Pipes was ducked in the river near the Kenwater Bridge. The ducking stool is described as 'an engine of universal punishment, for common scolds and for butchers, bakers, brewers, apothecaries, and all who gave short measure, or vended adulterated articles of food'.

Nearby is what was once part of the Old Priory, which over the years has served as the Leominster workhouse and latterly as a geriatric hospital. Leominster's museum is housed in what was the Mission Chapel in Etnam Street. The Lion House, formerly the Red Lion Hotel in Broad Street, an important coaching inn, has recently had its magnificent Regency ballroom restored.

Hester Clark's Almshouses in the Bargates were built in 1736 and rebuilt in 1874 and recently modernised further; they housed four widows. A figure on the wall has lines under saying, 'He that gives away all before he is dead, let'm take this hatchet and knock him on the head'.

Leominster has a wide range of amenities today. There are three state schools; nursery and infants in Hereford Road, the junior school in George Street and the Minster College in South Street. The Fine Art Saleroom attracts buyers from home and abroad, as do the many antiques shops. The two main hotels in Leominster are the Royal Oak and The Talbot, with numerous B & Bs offering first class accommodation.

There is a community hospital in South Street, the fire station is in Bridge Street, the railway station in Worcester Road and the bus station in Dishley Street. There are three superstores and free car parking in all central car parks. Friday is market day with stalls in the Corn Square, and the WI Market in Grafton House.

During June a very popular Music and Drama Festival is held for two weeks in the town. May Fair Day is 2nd May with amusements in the town centre streets. There is a children's playing area in The Grange, given by Stanley Holland, freeman of the Borough, and the Sydonia is home to the 1938 council-built swimming pool. In Coningsby Road is a Sports and Leisure Centre with a fine fitness suite. The brand new £3.2m Bridge Street Sports Park offers a wide variety of sporting facilities, while Scouts, Cubs, Girl Guides and Brownies meet in their respective halls each week. Leominster has always been a hospitable and friendly little place.

LINGEN

A traveller approaching Lingen from Wigmore will cross Deerfold and look down on the village set snugly in the hills at the south end of a wide valley running north to Leintwardine.

Lingen was included in the Shropshire section of the Domesday Book (1086) and it is of interest that the community does not appear to have varied greatly in numbers since that time. As the raising of sheep and cattle are still the principal local occupations, the essential nature of the village has not changed much either. There is now a large alpine nursery as a modern innovation and centre of interest.

Little is known of Lingen Castle, the motte only being plainly visible behind the Court House Farm. Originally retainers of the

Mortimers of Wigmore, the Lingen family owned the village from 1256 to 1583 when the estate was confiscated by the crown, to be restored under James I and finally sold in 1685, cutting the family connection with the village.

Ralph of Lingen founded the nunnery at Limebrook (approximately one mile from the village) in 1190, but today only one wall, overgrown with ivy, remains in this lovely secluded spot. Nearby, Limebrook Cottage (16th century) was no doubt built from materials from the priory, including moulded beams and a handsomely carved string to the staircase. Now the home of a herbalist, it is a happy thought that the healing mission of the nuns survives.

The nuns had originally lived on Deerfold, at the site of the present Chapel Farm (15th century or earlier) and moved to Limebrook when the land was granted to them. Chapel Farm is also believed to have given sanctuary to Sir John Oldcastle for four years when he was wanted by the authorities for his support of the Lollards in the 1400s.

The church was burnt down and rebuilt in 1891. The old pews

St Michael's church, Lingen

are early 16th century and scorch marks can be seen on some of them. In 1877, horse chestnuts were planted around the churchyard and 100 years later the WI planted a red maple to commemorate the Queen's Silver Jubilee.

The Methodist chapel was opened in 1877 with a splendid ceremony, culminating in a tea for nearly 400 people, some travelling from as far away as Ludlow, a considerable distance in the days of foot and horse travel.

The majority of houses in the village are old and give a good idea of how self-contained life was here until recent times. The Gisborne family were local benefactors who lived at Lingen Hall for several generations from the reign of Victoria to the 1940s when the estate was broken up. By the stream is the wheelwright's house, where it is still remembered wagons were left in the water to swell up the wood. Next to the church to the west was the forge and next door the old school, which became the village shop when the Victorian school opened, but is now a private house.

The Tan House, Wigmore Road, was where the cobbler plied his trade and Brook House was the home of the Mellings family for 200 years – the village carters and carpenters, transporting all necessary supplies, coal, bricks, and furniture wherever required, by horse and cart. At Archer's Ford upstream, the stone knappers lived, breaking stones for both buildings and roads. Above their house, six lynchets (ridges from prehistoric ploughing) are clearly visible on the hillside and further up the brook was a mill, keeping the area supplied with flour and meal, but of this echo of the past, no trace is left.

Today The Royal George is the only inn, but in the days of no Sunday opening over the nearby Welsh Border, the Rose and Crown across the road joined in the resulting flourishing trade.

Possibly the oldest house of all is the Turn Farm (15th century), reputed to be a pound house, with the pound field over the road. It is said that the road passed in front of the farm at one time, emerging at the far end of the village.

In the hills above the village are the ruins of Willey Old Court, occupied by the Legge family at the time of the Civil War. Whilst Mr Legge was with his men gathering the harvest, Cromwell's soldiers, looking for the King, sacked the house and violated the womenfolk.

Returning to find the reason for no lunchtime victuals for the harvesters, the master was outraged at what had happened, gathered his hands and gave chase. On overtaking the culprits, he killed their leader with a pitchfork. It is not known what happened next, but the pitchfork was a Legge family heirloom for several centuries.

At Willey Hall there is an ancient oak with a circumference of 26 ft, said to be at least 500 years old, possibly even 800. The Goat House Farm is the highest inhabited farmhouse in Herefordshire.

LINTON

Linton is pleasantly situated on rising ground close to the south-eastern boundary of the county, five miles from Ross-on-Wye. The parish includes most of Gorsley, a virtually separate and expanding village to the east. Although the M50 passes under a bridge near the village, only twisting minor roads lead there and visitors often lose their way. A weight-limit excludes the heaviest vehicles so that apart from the drone of tractors and the occasional irruption of low-flying fighter planes the village is peaceful and unspoilt.

This has always been an area of small farms combining corn-growing with cattle. The extensive orchards of earlier centuries have dwindled; Revells Farm no longer carries on its once-flourishing fruit-juice business. More land is devoted to root-crops and there is a thriving Forest Nursery.

Around AD 300 the Romans had a large iron-working settlement at Ariconium on what became the parish boundary near the hamlet of Bromsash. In the 17th and 18th centuries there were iron and steel furnaces around the village. On the western edge of the parish was Eccleswall Castle. Only the odd fragment of it remains at Eccleswall Court, but it was once the chief residence of the Talbot family, lords of the manor from the 12th century to the 17th.

St Mary's church in the centre of the village was held at the time of the Domesday Book by the Norman abbey of Cormeilles. Built in the local red sandstone characteristic of the village it has a 14th century spire and an interior which contains a mixture of styles from

Norman to Victorian. The hollow yew tree in the churchyard is among the oldest in the country. A tablet in the chancel commemorates the Rev Arthur Matthews who died in 1840 after 28 years as vicar. 'His premature decease', according to Duncumb's *History....of the County of Hereford*, 'was occasioned by the injuries he received from jumping imprudently from a stagecoach, the horses drawing which had become restless.' Some of his successors, such as Edward Palin, vicar from 1865 to 1903, were colourful and dominant characters. Today the church is run by the Ross team ministry.

Next to the church the Victorian school, closed despite strong protests in 1958, is now the village hall. It has recently been improved and extended and is the centre for most of the community activities. One of the latest, the Toddlers Group, shows a welcome influx in recent years of younger families. Here too the Parish Council alternates its meetings with those in Gorsley. Some of its meetings, partly open to the public, provoke lively debate in a village with a strong social sense.

Sadly, there is no longer a shop: the former post-office/store has become a two-day-a-week 'community post office'. Some older residents remember Mr Langley who ran the post office and also acted as undertaker. He used the sidecar of his motor-bike for transporting coffins and sometimes parked it (with laden coffin) outside the Alma when he went in for a pint.

Because the County Planning Office restricts building in the village, the cluster of houses faced in local stone which stand opposite the post office form the only new development apart from some infilling. By contrast the oldest cottage (Priest's Chambers) with its original cruck construction still detectable through the rendering is a few yards away down the lane by the churchyard. The only big house, Burton Court, stands in the valley between Linton and Bromsash. It is mainly 18th century, a handsome brick-faced building with a large garden which is sometimes lent for fund-raising activities. Close by is the 17th century Burton Mill on the Rudhall Brook. It was still in use in the 1940s, but now the mill-wheel lies smothered in undergrowth and the lake that used to feed the mill-race has been drained and turned into pasture.

Beyond the church the village straggles up to the top of Linton Hill, a ridge with immense panoramic views. Most of the cottages are late 18th century or early 19th. Many were built from small local quarries by their future occupiers, mostly agricultural labourers living always on the edge of poverty, sometimes with six or seven surviving children. These houses are now renovated, some unrecognisably, and all extremely comfortable. In several of them there once lived various members of the Webb family, who rose from being humble artisans in Queen Anne's day to become prosperous 'monumental masons'. W.J. Webb became in the first quarter of the 20th century a great village figure, buying houses, lending money and managing the affairs of the community.

There are no longer the blacksmiths, butchers, dressmaker and cordwainer who existed here in the 1840s. The old way of life changed with the coming of mains water and electricity in the early 1960s. Now the population includes a furniture restorer, an upholsterer, a music teacher, two craft workers in metal and a 'restorer of classic cars'.

LITTLE BIRCH

Little Birch is situated on the east of the A49, six miles south of Hereford. The name derives from the large number of birch trees which grew in the area several centuries ago. Little Birch is a scattered settlement of 81 houses with the church a mile away from the village hall and the pub in between. The first church dated from 1306 but was replaced in 1839. In 1868 it was decided that the new building no longer met the requirements of the population and the then rector, Rev Stephen Thackwell, paid £3,500 for the third and present church to be built on the site.

Near the church is Higgins Well, an important and unfailing supply of water for the village. There is a legend connected with the well which was told by a local man, Mr. H.W. Southey, to the *Hereford Times* in 1900 as follows:

'The original outlet for the waters of the well was in a meadow at the top of the steep bank which rises above the present well. The owner of this meadow became so annoyed at the trespasses of the villagers across his land to the well that he had it filled up. However, shortly afterwards, while smoking his pipe in the great chimney corner of his house, he was startled by a sudden eruption of water under his feet.

'To his untutored mind, the waters forcing this new outlet were a sign that the guardian spirit protecting the local people's rights was asserting itself. To appease this spirit, but determined not to reopen the well, he moved down to the present site and started to dig. In due course water began to bubble up through the underlying rock and, miraculously, the inrush in the chimney corner disappeared. The water spirit was obviously satisfied that water was once again made available to the people. This "act of contrition" resulted in local immortality for Mr Higgins.'

The parish is crossed by many green lanes which makes the area popular with walkers. By one of the green lanes is the 'Holy Thorn' which is said to have originated from the Holy Thorn at Glastonbury. Botanically the tree is a variety of the common hawthorn *Crataegus monogyna var.* biflora. Special services used to be held around the tree at midnight on Twelfth Night when it was supposed to burst into blossom. The *Hereford Times* reported that in 1951 about 150 people assembled for the service.

LITTLE COWARNE

Little Cowarne is a hilly parish of barely 700 acres bordered on the east by the Lodon, with spectacular views of the Malverns and Black Mountains from the higher ground, and a scattered population of about 90. There are four medium-sized farms, several smaller holdings and many houses have an acre or two. There is only one bus a week to Hereford and to Bromyard; the village looks to its neighbour, Pencombe, for school, shop and post office, and for activities such as the Women's Institute, Young Farmers' Club, Brownies and a playgroup. Nevertheless, the parish retains its own identity with its own parochial church council and village events.

The base of the church tower may be Saxon, and if so could have been built by Spirites, a priest at the court of Edward the Confessor, who held Little Cowarne as part of his considerable estates; however, just before the Norman invasion he blotted his scroll and was banished! Each succeeding century saw new work on the fabric. In 1478 the living was combined with Ullingswick, and Little Cowarne might well have lost its own church. It remained open, however, even though a commission set up by Cardinal Wolsey to inquire into rural depopulation reported that there were only four families in the parish.

Little Cowarne, wooden steeple,
Two cracked bells, wicked people.

In spite of the traditional rhyme, there is no record of the church having a steeple. There were, however, two bells in 1553 which may have cracked for they were both recast in the following century. As for the wicked people . . . perhaps they were local witches. The Norman font has two notches at opposite sides of the rim where bolts once locked the cover in place to protect the holy water. Three centuries later, the roof of the church fell in, necessitating an extensive Victorian restoration to the whole building by Frederick Kempson, the architect of Hereford City Museum.

Little Cowarne would have been well known to all the surrounding parishes while the Broxash Hundred Court was in existence. The Hundred of Broxash was an administrative area created by the Normans and a neutral place for the court was chosen at the edge of Broxash Wood in Little Cowarne, no doubt greatly to the benefit of the alehouse of the time. Broxash Hundred stretched from Upper Sapey to Withington, from Much Cowarne to Bodenham, and every parish was required to send two representatives.

Several families have connections with the village going back over a century, but the Abells have farmed the White House since the 1600s when an Edward Abell was a churchwarden, just as his namesake is today. During the Civil War, Scottish soldiers supporting Parliament clanked up the steps of the White House and the leader of the forage party gashed a table with his sword as he demanded food and drink. Little Cowarne and Ullingswick later put in a claim for £22 13s 4d for damage.

At the same period, Humphry Smith, one of the early Quakers, came to live at the Court. A renowned dissenter, Smith left his wife and children in Little Cowarne, and travelled the country preaching and writing. Before his death in Winchester Gaol at the age of 39, he foretold the Great Fire of London and the freezing of the Thames, and became known as the 'Prophet of Herefordshire'.

The appearance of the village must have changed radically in the 50 years before Queen Victoria came to the throne, as the last strips in the three open fields were consolidated into the fields we see today. Several new houses were built and for much of the 19th century Little Cowarne had twice the population it has now. Most people were agricultural labourers, but at the same time, the village was more self-sufficient than nowadays with a mill, and lime and brick kilns. There were blacksmiths, carpenters, a wheelwright, a mason, shoemakers, dressmakers, a shop and a baker. There were two inns and a cider house, and a maypole dance was still being performed at the Three Horse Shoes.

During the First World War 14 men from the village were in uniform and at home a timber company leased the part of Broxash Wood in Little Cowarne and felled the trees. There was a church choir during the 1920s and the granary at the Court was used for village activities until the floor became unsafe. Little Cowarne kept its own grocer's shop until the outbreak of the Second World War and its bakery until 1947. For 40 years the Hodges supplied the surrounding villages with delicious 2lb and 4lb round loaves, cottage loaves and lardy cake; and when the horse and cart visited the hopyards during hop-picking the children would come running for apple cobs (turnovers). In 1947 the parish hall opened and for the next 30 years was used for concerts, whist drives and a summer fete. These have been superseded by a village 'fun evening' of games, rounders, a treasure hunt and an old favourite, pillow fighting astride a hop-pole.

Today most of the agricultural jobs have disappeared, but a variety of new occupations are pursued. A new enterprise at Shortwood has enabled visitors to see a working diary farm, rare breeds of farm animals, cider-making and other activities, thus helping to bridge the gap between town and country.

LITTLE DEWCHURCH

Little Dewchurch is a village six miles from Hereford and seven miles from Ross-on-Wye. All roads to Little Dewchurch are uphill, often through wooded areas. The village being set on high ground commands lovely views of South Herefordshire, and in the distance May Hill on the Gloucestershire border, the Malvern Hills on the Worcestershire border and the Black Mountains on the Welsh border.

Before 1950 the village was very scattered with no mains electricity or water supply. Since the arrival of these amenities in the early 1960s the character of the village has changed considerably with the development of nearly 150 new houses and other older properties being modernised. There are just over 300 on the Register of Electors.

The centre of the village is marked by a village green, bus shelter and new village hall, opened in 1996 at a cost of £150,000. Near the centre is the Plough Inn offering accommodation, bar meals and Sunday lunches.

The small road to the church passes the village school, which caters for children of primary age. The church of St David with its 14th century tower is set in a hollow. The church was rebuilt in 1870, when the architect was Frederick Preedy of London and the reported cost of the restoration was £1,500. Mr Preedy's trademark of an open flower can be seen in various parts around the building. The walled-in churchyard is circular and has a very old preaching cross.

The undulating area of the village is farmed with arable crops, cattle and sheep and has many interesting walks.

LITTLE HEREFORD

People have been passing through Little Hereford for centuries, nowadays usually at high speed on an unrestricted stretch of the A456 which links the A49 Ludlow to Leominster road with Tenbury Wells.

The river Teme flows through Little Hereford, not as might be expected forming any kind of boundary, but dividing the two halves of a strangely-shaped parish. The northern part, which includes Bleathwood and 'Dirty' Middleton (so named because of the state of its lanes in times gone by), is situated on a tongue of land jutting up into Shropshire while, on the other side of the river, Middleton-on-the-Hill and Upton extend the parish into Herefordshire. The Teme brought fame to the village in 1924 when a new concrete road bridge to replace the older brick one was, at 110 feet, the longest such construction in the west of England. Another sizeable watercourse is the Ledwyche Brook which forms the eastern boundary of the parish on its way to join the Teme near the well-known Burford House gardens in the neighbouring village.

During the 12th century civil war, between King Stephen and his cousin the Empress Matilda who claimed to be the rightful heir to the throne of her father King Henry I, Little Hereford's river crossing was convenient to the King and his troops who encamped there. Many travellers on foot have made use of 'the Forty Steps' leading from the Berrington road above and down through a clump of trees to the river. Those steps probably afforded passage to monks and priests from Leominster Priory on their way to duties in the northern part of the diocese. More recently they were well used by rail passengers walking to and from Easton Court station. In the very late 20th century the steps were restored after years of neglect, thanks to Mr Bernard Wilcox, Clerk to the Parish Council, and to the Public Rights of Way Warden, Mr Zvegintzov – better known as Mr Zog – and they are now used by walkers and ramblers.

The massive tower of the 12th century church of St Mary Magdalene bears witness to its one-time role as a fortress and refuge. Chief among the historic features of the church is an unusual rood altar set above the arch of the heavy stone screen separating the nave from the chancel. The reason why it is placed so high is not recorded, but the educated guess is that the Blessed Sacrament may have been reserved there to protect it from the frequent flooding of the river.

Between the church and the river lie grassy mounds, all that now remains of the original fortified manor house of the Delamere family. This was abandoned in the early 16th century when the Danseys

St Mary Magdalene church, Little Hereford

built Bleathwood Manor well away from the river. Easton Court became the manor house when in the early 19th century the present house was built on the site of a much earlier structure of which only the 18th century stables survive. In 1837 the manor became the property of Sir Joseph Bailey, a member of the family of Lord Glenusk, by whom it was sold in 1911 to Colonel Wingfield Cardiff, who set about recovering estate land previously dispersed, which his family still own today.

The 18th century canal-builders brought a section of the ill-fated Leominster to Stourport canal over the river Teme by means of a stone aqueduct. Evidence of the existence of the canal remains in the style of some houses and of names such as 'Locks Cottage'. However, to the total mystification and displeasure of local people the Army blew the aqueduct sky-high during the Second World War, presumably to prevent its strategic use by possible invaders!

As the canal company foundered, the railway stepped in to buy the land and to lay track partly along the line prepared for the waterway. Little Hereford boasted a level-crossing and a station, albeit the latter bore the name Easton Court. Parts of the line can now be walked and the station is now a home.

Other notable buildings in the village include Temple Farm, mentioned in the Domesday Book and containing a long narrow window dating back at least four centuries and a unique herringbone construction of old beams. Nearby is the 18th century Nonconformist chapel, a house now since 1972, and the beautiful oak-beamed Upper House, Middleton which boasts an Elizabethan barn. On the other side of the river lie Nun Upton with its distinctively-shaped gables and the magnificent Upton Court, for generations a working farm.

A famous son of Little Hereford was Robert Hues, a mathematical genius, born in about 1553. He entered Brazenose College, Oxford as a servitor, later going on to Magdalene College as a student. His *Tractus de Globis*, published in 1593, records his circumnavigation of the world with the explorer Cavendish. He died, unmarried, in 1632.

A sad little memorial stone on the wall beside the south porch of the church leaves researchers with more questions than answers. It records the deaths of 16 children, all under the age of five years, who died in the summer of 1870. Research carried out recently by Dr David Maund reveals that the ten families involved were of diverse social status and of different parts of the parish, challenging the theory of a contaminated water source or a virulent epidemic among poor peasants living in insanitary conditions. A further discovery was that the burial register for 1870 shows no burials of children that summer, nor even that year. Quite a mystery!

Let it not be assumed from all this that Little Hereford rests on its history or accepts dormitory status. True, most community amenities have disappeared and the village is left without shop, post office or school, but the eye-catching black and white parish hall is well used by parish residents. Farming is still the most important industry in Little Hereford, but many other professions and trades are centred here too. These include cabinet-making, catering, agricultural engineering, builders, cider and perry making and turkey rearing. There is also a major tree-growing company exporting its saplings world-wide.

LLANGARRON

The village is situated between the towns of Ross-on-Wye and Monmouth, off the A4137. In the year 1610 the spelling was Llangarran; today it is spelt Llangarron or Llangarren and there are two signs at either side of the village depicting this.

The village is delightful; it is enfolded by the hills through which the Garron Brook has carved its meandering way, situated in an agricultural area of arable and dairy farms with sheep grazing the pastures. There are also fruit farms, bringing a delightful show of blossoms in the spring.

In the centre of the village stands the beautiful church of St Deinst which is an ancient building of stone in the Transitional style, consisting of chancel aisle, nave of four bays, north aisle and a western tower in which there are six bells. The interior has a medieval stone altar slab with consecration cross, a 14th century font and early 17th century Jacobean pulpit, 13th century windows and monuments dating back to 1692. The church was enlarged in 1841 and restored in 1900.

A new vicarage has been built in the village of Llangrove which is more central for the vicar today as he has several parishes to serve. The old vicarage was built in 1903 and stands on the outskirts of Llangarron.

There are two known Holy Wells in the parish of Llangarron and one farmhouse is said to stand on the site of the ancient kings of Archenfield's residence.

In Llangarron are many houses of historical interest, including a lovely Elizabethan timber-framed house.

The post office and stores which stands in the centre of the village operates a first class service to the villagers. Butts Garage is close by. A chain-saw specialist has premises near at hand, as has also the agricultural repair shop. A thriving secondhand business is quite noticeable on entering the village.

The school closed in 1973, the children of the village travelling outside for their education, either by bus or car. There is no public house, this, like the school, being now residential property. Just past the church stands the village hall which is used for all village commitments.

One Llangarron lady lived to 100 years and eleven days, dying in 1930. She had ten children and lived in the same cottage for 78 years.

Drinking water originally came from a well but in the Jubilee year of 1887 the Reverend de Ewer managed to get hydrants fitted from springs to convenient places in the village. Later, in 1897, a central tap was placed near to the school.

An old custom meant villagers walked to Old Gore to see the Holy Thorn blossom on the eve of Twelfth Night (6th January). They kept themselves warm by drinking cider or whisky!

LLANGROVE

The village of Llangrove is situated in the south of the county, only four miles from the boundary with Gwent. It lies about eight miles from Ross-on-Wye and 17 miles from Hereford.

Llangrove comes within the parish of Llangarron. The ancient place names of the streams and farms and older houses are a reminder that for centuries the language of the people of this area was Welsh. Even today the prefix 'tre-' (meaning homestead) is used for many house names – Tre-Ken, Tre-Wen, Tre-Duchan.

For years there has been controversy regarding the name of the village. In the 14th and 15th centuries the village was referred to as 'Longegrove', but the early parish registers of Llangarron mention 'Long Grove'. By the 1850s the spelling had changed to Llangrove. In 1862 a local directory referred to 'Llangrove Common'. The parish records from Llangarron (before there was a church at Llangrove) refer to the burial of 'Elizabeth Evans of the Grove'. In fact, the older residents of the village, now departed, always spoke of 'living on the Grove'.

Llangrove is a growing village and much building has taken place in the last few years. Llangrove is not built round a traditional village green and is not a picture-postcard village, but the centre is marked by church, school, shop, telephone box, village hall and what was the blacksmith's shop but is now a garage-cum-workshop where all kinds of agricultural machinery is repaired and welded. The 'local' is the Royal Arms which is about 400 yards away.

The village is sited on high ground and the surrounding countryside is very beautiful. From the north there are perfect views extending to the Malverns and round to May Hill. From the south one can see Symonds Yat and the Doward, round to Welsh Newton Common, then westwards to Garway and the Brecon hills. There is a field on the edge of the village where, from the highest point, on a clear day, one can turn round slowly from north to north again and see all the places mentioned above. It is breathtaking.

The church was built in 1856 and dedicated Christ Church. It is a charming small church, with an altar screen of painted panels, and the east window contains beautiful stained glass. From the outside, on winter evenings when the lights are on in the church, this window looks a jewel of coloured lights. The church was designed by George Frederick Bodley, RAFSA, FRIBA. It is believed that Llangrove was his first design for a church.

Christ Church has not been the only place of worship in Llangrove for there were two Nonconformist churches – Wesleyan and Congregational. Due to lack of support both closed in 1968. The Congregational church remains on its old site in a farmyard, but the Wesleyan chapel has been converted to a dwelling.

The Church of England school was built a few years later than the church and extended in the 1960s to accommodate children from the neighbouring villages of Llangarron, Welsh Newton Common and Llanrothal.

The old village characters are sadly no more. Few now remember Mrs Agnes Lawrence and her daughter Mary. Agnes was left a widow at the age of 28 with four small children and another baby on the way. In those days there was no Welfare State and Agnes had to work very hard to keep herself and her family. This she did while her children were at school and a neighbour looked after her baby son.

She undertook the delivery of the daily and Sunday newspapers in the village and surrounding area. The newspapers had to be collected from a village three miles away and delivered to a very scattered community. She also delivered the mail. For 54 years, come rain, sun, wind or snow, Mrs Lawrence never failed to deliver the mail, still on foot. In later years her daughter Mary helped her, and after her mother's death in 1975 at the age of 86, Mary used to tell of the times during the dreadful winters of 1940 and 1946 when the snow was as high as the hedges, but still she and her mother got the mail and newspapers delivered.

Agnes was also employed as school caretaker and cleaner, and she cleaned the church and rang the bell for 43 years. In 1969 she was awarded the BEM which was presented to her by Colonel J. F. Maclean, the Lord Lieutenant of the County.

LLANWARNE

Llanwarne is a small hamlet midway between Ross and Hereford, just off the A49. It has a population of 247 electors, mostly scattered. At the centre of the hamlet is a war memorial, a ruined church and the 'new church' of 1864. There are no longer any shops or tradesmen's premises and the village school built in 1854 for 60 children was closed in 1957, eventually becoming the village hall for the community.

The name Llanwarne is derived from the Celtic 'church amid the alders'. Such churches had a collection of brethren living as a community and perhaps married, not like the later medieval monastic brotherhoods. The church of Llanwarne is therefore recorded as among the oldest centres of Christianity in the country, with 7th century or even 6th century origins. The present ruined church of St John the Baptist was built in the 13th century, with rebuilding in the 14th century and the addition of the west tower. The lychgate to the south is probably 15th century. It is uncertain whether the pre-Norman churches were on the same site – records in the Llandaff charters give a site description that does not tally with the present surroundings.

Over the centuries the church and churchyard became marshier with floods from the Gamber brook. Many attempts were made to overcome the problem, floors were relaid until they were raised by more than a metre. Carved coffin lids and floor slabs were removed and used to resill windows which were also raised to keep pace with the upward movement. As the base of the tower became more waterlogged, woodwork rotted and when it became impossible to reach the church dryshod the struggle was abandoned. Alterations to the course of the stream had little effect and burials could only be accomplished by weighting the coffins with stones.

In 1864 Christ Church was built on higher ground at a cost of £2,350. The 17th century chest and font were moved to Christ Church, also 16th century Flemish or German glass, now in the south windows of the nave. The fourth bell cast in 1350 was too broken for repair so was moved to beside the font in Christ Church.

Llanwarne is situated in the Wormelow Hundred, part of the ancient Welsh kingdom of Ergyng, later Archenfield, of the 6th century. Wormelow Tump lies at the boundaries of the parishes of Llanwarne, Much Birch and Much Dewchurch and was the meeting place for the Wormelow Hundred and its Court. Today no indication of this tump remains.

To the south-east of the village is Monkton, now a half-timbered farmhouse, originally a chapelry and grange of Llanthony Priory. It was first mentioned in 1336 in connection with the Hoskyns family.

One mile from Llanwarne on the old Monmouth road is Lyston Court, a Hanoverian style mansion. Evidence was found of a 16th century house when a stone mullion and lintel were revealed in an inner wall. The original house, which faced east, was rebuilt in the early 18th century with further considerable alterations around 1870 and 1928. It now looks like a Regency house of c1820. It was never inherited by any important county families but became a dower house of Bryngwyn, the home of the Rankins, before becoming the home of the Davey family who lived there until 1959.

In 1890 Mr James Rankin gave a pair of boots to each of the 60 children at the village school who had made 250 attendances that year, plus twelve books as school prizes. Later, boys were given blue jerseys and girls scarlet cloaks and hoods at Christmas. These customs continued on alternate years until 1914.

Today the people of Llanwarne are either retired, work locally in nearby towns, or are engaged in farming or food production industries. The village centre is today perhaps even more of a backwater with two buses a week. Mains electricity and water did not reach the village until the early 1960s.

LONGTOWN

The village of Longtown lies in the foothills of the Black Mountains, with the long wall of the Hatterrall ridge forming a dramatic backdrop. The parish spans the valleys of the Olchon, Monnow and Escley rivers. It formed part of the ancient land of Ewias and, from Norman times, the Hundred of Ewyas Lacy. Longtown (formerly known as Longa Villa in Ewyas Lacy) became annexed to England in 1536 when the boundary was fixed between England and Wales following the Act of Union.

In 1187 a new motte and bailey castle was built on the spur between the Olchon and Monnow rivers to replace a smaller structure further down the valley which had fallen to Prince Hywal. The ruins of the castle remain today and are open to the public.

The manorial court of Ewyas Lacy met in the castle and dealt with land tenure, the appointment of the constable and town crier and other matters. In the early 19th century, when the castle had fallen into disrepair, the court adjourned to the nearby inn, later known as the Court House. This is now the Longtown Education Centre (an outdoor pursuits centre administered by Northamptonshire County Council). A plaque outside the centre marks the site of the village pound.

Across the road from the Education Centre is a short lane leading to the former market square and the 13th century St Peter's church, largely rebuilt in 1868 and now a private dwelling. St Peter's was latterly a chapel of ease to the parish church of St Clydawg, further down the valley. The market square was the site of the village well. The old main street of the borough ran directly south from the market square. Today only a few people live within the former borough but in its heyday there were probably some 400 inhabitants.

The village green, opposite the castle, was formerly the east bailey of the castle. A village school was built within its precincts in 1868 and for over 100 years the green served as a sports field and

Longtown Castle

playground. When a new school was built further up the road in the 1970s, the green fell into disuse and its banks became very overgrown. It was restored by the Longtown Village Pride Group and was the winning entry in the 1994 county-wide Parish Pride Competition. Beyond the northern perimeter of the green is a restored dipwell.

Outside the entrance to the castle is Broome's Garden (Parish Pride winner 1996). Formerly a cottage garden, worked until the 1920s by William Broome, and until the 1950s as a rural science project by the school, Broome's Garden has been cleared and replanted as a medieval herb garden by the Village Pride Group and is open to the public. In the garden is a seat to the memory of Mrs F.M. Gwillim, who for 40 years taught at the adjacent old school and was a stalwart of Longtown WI.

Longtown's parish church is at Clodock (see separate entry). Salem Baptist chapel is near to the village green and the Methodist chapel is at Lower Maescoed in the east of the parish. The community comes together for united festivals of praise at Easter and in July. The annual Eisteddfod is held in May, the Show in August and the Ewe Sale in September. Longtown still retains its primary school, its well-stocked village stores and post office and one of its public houses (the Crown).

LOWER BULLINGHAM

The village of Lower Bullingham lies just beyond the south-eastern boundaries of Hereford city, stretching from the river Wye in the north to the foot of Dinedor Hill in the south. For several centuries it was part of the estate of the Bodenham family, whose imposing mansion, Rotherwas House, stood near the river in the adjoining parish of Dinedor. It was a typical agricultural estate, consisting of farms, smallholdings and cottages. Earthworks discovered near the village (scheduled as an Ancient Monument) indicated by the number of house platforms that there had once been a medieval settlement of some size.

During the 19th century the Bodenham family, who were devout Catholics, established two Catholic orders in Lower Bullingham. In 1880 they extended an existing house for the Sisters of Charity, an order of St Vincent de Paul, to house two orphanages and a school for 180 children. A few years later, in 1887, they built a splendid red-brick convent, designed by a local architect F.R. Kempson, for the Poor Clares, an enclosed order whose nuns lived confined within the walls of the convent. Regrettably, the convent was demolished in 1996, when the nuns moved to a new home in Much Birch.

Another distinctive house was added to the village in the 1880s. This was St Charles' House, designed by Peter Paul Pugin, a member of the distinguished family of Victorian architects, and was divided into five apartments for the poor of the estate. It was later owned by the Sisters of Charity, but fell into disrepair for many years. It has now been fully restored and turned into private flats.

A former resident remembers that the Wye Inn served a large area – there was no public house at Holme Lacy because the great Liberal family, the Chesterfields, did not believe in drink for the working classes. Nor was there one at Dinedor.

As there was no National school or village hall, meetings were held in the unlicensed rooms at the inn, including inquests on local people. The stable was used as a mortuary for suicides, most of whom drowned themselves upriver.

Christmas time was a great holiday for local people. On Boxing Day, lunch was served around the great kitchen table at the inn – ten at a time. This consisted of cold boiled beef, vegetables, pickled onion, red cabbage, horseradish sauce and one pint of beer. After lunch, the main bar would be cleared except for four spittoons, brightened with blacklead, and new sawdust laid. Four men with mops, or brooms, would dance hobby-horse style, weaving in and out around the spittoons, changing direction until the full sequence was completed. The fiddler was nicknamed 'The Marquis', and he kept his fiddle at the inn and provided music in the bar on Bank Holidays.

Many changes have taken place since the Bodenham estate was broken up and sold in 1912. In the 1930s the mansion was demolished, and the War Office acquired the land adjacent to the road at Rotherwas (locally known as 'the straight mile') for a Royal Ordnance factory. With the onset of the Second World War in 1939, this provided welcome employment in the area, but tragedy too, when a lone German aircraft dropped two bombs on the factory, causing several deaths and many casualties.

When the land was released after the war, it became an industrial area, bringing in its wake a great deal of housing development, so that Lower Bullingham today resembles a suburb of Hereford more than a village. The 17th century manor house is a residential home, and the Sisters of Charity convent remains, occupied by the Marian Fathers, a Polish order, providing accommodation for Polish men. Quite a large community of Polish people had built up in Herefordshire during the war years.

The Wye Inn still serves the local area as the only country inn for some miles.

LUGWARDINE

Lugwardine is a village to the east of Hereford, on the A438 road to Ledbury. Driving out of the city boundary one descends to the ancient Lugg meadows. These retain many of the ancient strips and a meeting is still held at the Crown and Anchor Inn for the commoners. Each year from Lammas (2nd August) to Candlemas (February) the commoners graze their cattle and horses, then the grass is left to grow for haymaking. There is a large variety of plants in the meadows worthy of conservation, particularly the fritillaries. On the left across the meadow you will catch a glimpse of the ancient mansion of Newcourt, seat of the lords of the manor for many years.

Passing over the river Lugg you wind up the hill through the village. Note the village pump, made by Thomas Barber, on your left and on your right you pass Lugwardine Court, now a residential home. In 1865 the house was purchased by Sir Herbert George Denman Croft MP of Croft Castle, a leading figure in the county and a fine cricketer. Sadly, Lugwardine no longer boasts a cricket team. Next you pass the modern Roman Catholic comprehensive school and Middle Court. St Peter's church (key at the vicarage) is of Norman origin. In 1872 F.R. Kempson, the Hereford architect, altered and refurbished the church. Very little has altered since. There is a peal of eight bells which are rung regularly, the earliest bell being 10, recast in 1877.

There are some interesting memorials, including one to William Reed of Newcourt, who died in 1634. William Reed mentions 'my mansion of Newcourt' in a deed of 1579. The Reed family came from Bronsil Castle at Eastnor. William's father, Gabriel, was troubled by a restless spirit and on taking advice was instructed to exorcise it by procuring a bone of the first Lord Beauchamp, a previous owner of Bronsil. Bones were found and taken to the castle, which remained in peace. Mr Reed brought the bones with him to Newcourt. They are now lost, but if the horses get restless at Newcourt, more bones of Lord Beauchamp must be procured – and he died in 1496!

Geologically, the neighbourhood is well provided with good red clay, very suitable for making bricks and tiles. Two cottages, Rose

Cottage and Sweet Briar, were the original offices of the brickyard occupied by William Godwin in 1849. The factory has gone, but many houses in the area have examples of Godwin tiles. He also experimented in making encaustic tiles for church floors, based on medieval designs. Such tiles have been used in more than 300 churches, including the restoration of Hereford and seven other cathedrals.

Old Court farm was the original manorial seat with its medieval earthworks. Turning left down the track you will come to 'the Steppes', a very old thatched house, part of the early village. The new graveyard can be seen across the field, on land purchased from Sir Herbert Croft in 1887.

The pleasing modern housing estate built in the grounds of Wilcroft is a mix of starter homes and executive dwellings. Lugwardine no longer depends on its farming for survival. There is an interesting mix of retired people and residents who commute as far as Birmingham to work.

The village primary school closed in 1989 and as most of the development was at Bartestree it was decided to build the new school there near all the new houses. It is now thriving. In 1990 the Gateway Nursery School opened in the old school taking children from babies to school age and catering for a very wide area.

The old village hall was taken down in 1995 to make way for houses and a new village hall was built on the main road in Bartestree and opened in 1997. There is also an ample green area where children and grown ups enjoy football and cricket. This is a great asset to village life.

On the right of the crossroads, which are the boundary with the parish of Bartestree, is Longworth Hall Hotel, the home of Robert Biddulph Phillips in the 19th century. This gentleman left his extensive library to Belmont Abbey and built the nearby convent.

There were three mills, Longwort Mill, Tidnor Mill and Lugg Mill. The latter can be seen on the Worcester road, at the bridge where the Roman road crosses the river Lugg.

LUSTON

With its fair share of black and white North Herefordshire houses, Luston village lies either side of the Richard's Castle road from Leominster for about a mile. Lying low in attractive hilly country, the village is expanding very rapidly. Overall the farming-based work for the village has ceased.

The village no longer has a shop but a grocery van calls twice a week and serves the surrounding farms and lanes. The Balance Inn has survived many changes of ownership and character. A small field beyond the pub is used as a caravan site in the summer months.

Luston is an odd village in that the church is three quarters of a mile away and the village hall a good half-mile out of the village. There is, however, a very small Methodist chapel centrally placed which provides a more central meeting place for village activity.

The nearby hamlets of Eye, Moreton and Ashton were historically more important than Luston, so records have little of note on Luston itself. Nevertheless, it has old cottages and houses dating back to the 16th century. The oldest farms are the Croase and Bury Farms. The latter was used as the original manor court until 150 years ago. At the turn of the 20th century Luston had a sawmill and a stone cider mill, both now disappeared.

In the 1950s piped water came to Luston and the use of the spring at Holy Well gradually ceased. It took a further 20 years for water to be piped to the nearby hamlets. The Parish Council is at present engaged in cleaning the land around the Holy Well and restoring it.

Today, the original villagers resist the suburban habit of street lighting and so only the newer estates have lighting and pay their rates accordingly. An interest has been taken by newer residents in the local footpaths. Once the labourer's way of getting to work, or children to school, they are now regarded as a leisure-time activity. Footpaths have disappeared under the undergrowth or the plough but recently footpath signs have appeared in the roadside hedges and there are moves to open others up again. Though how to decide which footpath to choose out of three parallel paths across the fields to Berrington Hall, made by three men who so disliked each other they could not bring themselves to walk on the same path, may prove a headache!

A four mile lane within the parish, much used by farming traffic until the Second World War, fell into disuse until in 1970 a Mr Riggall bought Lyddiatts Farm halfway along it. He asked the Highways Authority to make it up. Now a few cottages and two farms benefit from a metalled link. Not often kept up by the Highways Dept, the lane abounds in a backwater atmosphere of wayside flowers, butterflies and leafy over-hanging trees – but the locals refer to it as Riggalls Motorway or the M71!

LYONSHALL

Lyonshall village stands at the centre of one of the largest parishes in Herefordshire (5,000 acres), in the deeply rural and hilly Marches country in the north-west of the county, some three miles east of the small market town of Kington.

The village boasts a fine church of 12th century foundation standing above the main road to Kington (A44). Behind the church is a moat surrounding a motte indicating where Lyonshall Castle (late 11th century) formerly stood. Traces of Offa's Dyke, the old boundary between Mercia and Wales, can be found to the west of the church.

The village is said to have originally clustered around the castle and in 1090 was granted a charter enabling its people to hold a weekly market and annual Michaelmas Fayre. While this brought prosperity in the form of travellers and traders, it also, sadly, brought the 14th century Black Death resulting in the destruction of the village and the death of most of its inhabitants.

The present village grew in the valley a scant half-mile south of the church and some of the architecture of that period still remains, the best example being Penrhos Court to the west, a 14th century house with four cruck beams. During the Victorian period Lyonshall enjoyed a brief renaissance when its church was given a facelift and a new school (now a private residence) was built. Contemporary Lyonshall is not much larger than its Victorian counterpart, the

The Old Forge and former village shop at Lyonshall

population having increased in recent years by housing developments on either side of the A480 Hereford road.

Opposite the church, on the main Kington to Leominster road, a row of cottages known as the Wharf indicate where the horse-drawn tramway passed. Completed in 1820, it fell into disuse about 40 years later but part of the trackbed was used in the 1860s for the Titley Junction to Eardisley railway. Run by the Great Western Railway, it was never a success and after closure during the First World War, it was reopened in 1920 and finally abandoned in 1940. Lyonshall station building still stands as part of a private residence on the road between the church and the village, and beside it a small part-time post office serves the residents, as the village shop and PO closed down in the 1990s. An impressive row of Wellingtonias opposite the former platform is a landmark for miles around.

Agriculture and its subsidiary industries have always dominated the employment in Lyonshall although there was a brickworks here in the 18th century. With the modernisation of farming, many traditional crafts are no longer practised and Lyonshall no longer has a blacksmith, wheelwright, tanner or cobbler. However, with the growth of tourism to remoter areas, a new 'trade' has sprung up with many locals offering bed and breakfast, food and local crafts. The 16th century Royal George is the only survivor of eight pubs once scattered round the parish! A local firm supplies marquees of all kinds for functions throughout the country. As well as catering for all needs of local gardeners, Lyonshall Nurseries supply floral decorations for national events and shows.

As befits a village with a long history, some of the local buildings are haunted. In one period house the ghost of an old woman makes her presence known by emitting the heady aroma of lavender. Another tale is of ghostly footprints on steps leading up to the disused railway station – perhaps going to catch the ghost train!

MADLEY

Madley has much to interest visitors of all ages. If you bring a picnic, there is a spacious recreation field with excellent apparatus for the children to play on. If the day is sunny, the well-kept churchyard is a pleasant place to linger. There are many early inscriptions worth reading or 'collecting' and a stone preaching cross almost as old as the church itself. It is fascinating to think that the yew tree which shelters this cross is at least 500 years old: it was a sapling when Columbus sailed west.

The church itself is described by Nikolaus Pevsner as both interesting and beautiful. It is wonderfully light, and well worth a visit, if only to see the magnificent early stained glass, some of the oldest in England. The east window has a number of exquisitely coloured 13th century roundels, and there are also parts of a 14th century Jesse window. The oldest parts of the building date from early in the 12th century, but additions in the following three centuries have produced a parish church of cathedral-like proportions.

Each July the church provides the main setting for Madley's long-established and important music festival.

A drive up the hill behind the village will afford an impressive view of both the village and the Madley Satellite Earth Station, with its great aerials resembling giant saucers. These provide circuits for telephone, telex, telegram, data and facsimile calls, as well as television links, from and to most countries of the world.

MANSEL LACY

The village dates back to the earliest Norman settlements, and in the 11th century became the property of Roger de Lacy. The Foxley estate, with Mansel Lacy at its heart, later belonged for many years to the Price family. Robert Price (1717–1761) took over from his father in 1743, on his marriage, and started the planting and improvements that so influenced his more famous son, Uvedale Price, one of the founders of the Picturesque Movement. Uvedale was much opposed to professional landscapers and 'preferrered to spaddle about in my own clay'. The landscape of Foxley still reflects the Price vision, and the sport of Foxley is still renowned, for the woods and valleys comprise some of the best natural habitat for game, and have done since the 18th century Price planting. After Uvedale's death the property was sold to the Davenports, a family from the Midlands, in 1855. With over 30 smallholdings, the estate gave much employment to the village.

It was completely self-contained, with laundry, gas-house, estate water, church and wheelwright. The school was first built at Yazor in 1869, but closed after 20 years and a church school was built in the village in 1889. The big house at Foxley has now gone; during the Second World War it was used first by the French Canadians, and then as a hospital by the Americans. Many local people remember those busy times when the shop was in full swing, and the post office, run by the wheelwright, delivered the letters and kept the outlying houses up to date with the news. An obelisk to commemorate the American hospital was erected some years ago on the Foxley estate. After the Americans left, the old house was used for Polish refugees and a row of graves in the churchyard dates from that time.

The shop and post office are now gone and many of the tied cottages are in private hands. The church has been divided to include a community centre with all facilities; this has proved a very practical and successful conversion. The mill has been converted into holiday homes and the granary is now a private house. The ancient meadow by the church is now an SSSI, no longer grazed by Hereford cattle for Mansel Court farm is now a private house with the land sold away. A new development has been built behind the old dovecote.

There is still much to attract in Mansel Lacy – the Old Post Office with its dovecote, the church which has stood for at least 700 years, the winding village lying in a semi circle running down from the woods, and the pleasant Georgian house that is now lived in by the owner of the estate.

MARDEN

Marden is one of the largest civil parishes in Herefordshire; it includes a number of hamlets including Burmarsh, Urdimarsh and Litmarsh. It is situated about a mile east of the main A49 Hereford-Leominster road some six miles north of Hereford.

Marden is the traditional site of the palace of the Kings of Mercia. Once a Royal Manor, Marden is still a thriving agricultural and residential parish with a population of over 1,500. Housing development, which started in 1961, has seen the building of many modern bungalows and houses, mainly in the centre of the village.

Agriculture has seen a change in recent years. Marden was once the home of the famous Vern herd of white-faced Hereford cattle bred by Captain R. S. De Q. Quincey, who had a great influence on the development of the breed. Hopfields, which covered many acres of land throughout the parish, have now gone and with them the happy hop-picking days that once kept the villagers and pickers from the Rhondda Valley, on their annual holidays, busy in the autumn. As well as arable crops such as wheat and oats some orchards still remain, but the biggest development has been that of a large potato and strawberry enterprise on the edge of the village, which gives full and part time work for locals and for a large number of foreign students.

There is a small industrial estate at Burmarsh, and a drinking water bottling plant at Little Berrington. There are several guesthouses in the village catering for visitors who wish to explore the surrounding countryside.

The original village school, a pleasant Victorian building built in 1874, finally closed its doors in April 1994 when the long awaited new school and community hall opened; the school now has over 100 pupils up to the age of eleven years. Education was promoted in Marden in 1610 by the generosity of a wealthy widow, Jane Shelley. She established an educational foundation with the object of assisting the poor and needy children. Students today still benefit from the trust, and the old thatched schoolhouse, now privately owned, can be seen at the Sutton Walls approach to the village.

A new recreational area for the younger children has been provided on the playing field where football and tennis continue to thrive. There is a cricket ground at The Volunteer which together with the New Inn provides skittles and the usual pub games.

The inter-village Eisteddfod once held each year on St Ethelbert's Day no longer takes place, and the old blacksmith's forge is now an attractive private dwelling.

There are three places of worship in the village. A Plymouth

The Old School House, Marden

Brethren chapel, a small stone chapel, once privately owned by Lady (Coutts) Lindsay of Amberley Court, but which now goes with the living of Marden, and the church of St Mary the Virgin. This is an old stone edifice in the Early English style with a square tower and spire. The church is situated on the bank of the river Lugg about a mile from the new centre of the village. The site is rather puzzling to the visitor until they learn that the original church was built over the traditional spot where St Ethelbert was first buried after being murdered by King Offa in AD 794. A Holy Well, which is said to have sprung up at that time, can still be seen in the church today.

The river Lugg forms part of the western boundary of the parish and is well loved by fishermen. It is also the home of a mythical mermaid who is said to be holding down one of the church bells, which accidentally fell into the river.

A walk along the riverbank may be rewarded with sightings of kingfisher, heron, sandpiper or sand martin and even the flowering rush in due season.

On the south border of the village lies the Iron Age hill fort of Sutton Walls, which was occupied until Saxon days. From 1948 until 1951 the site was excavated by Miss Kathleen Kenyon, the distinguished archaeologist, and visited by Sir Mortimer Wheeler. Many interesting artefacts were found at that time and these items can be seen in the Hereford Museum.

The village is very well supplied with shops and services. These include a mini market and post offfice, a family butcher, hairdresser, driving school, sewing service and garage. There is a bus service on six days a week to Hereford. Marden is indeed a pleasant place to live.

MATHON

Mathon is a small village nestling in the valley on the west side of the Malvern Hills, and designated 'a village of natural beauty'.

It is famous for three things – its own variety of 'Mathon Hops' which were propagated and grown at Church Farm; its sand and gravel, some of the finest building material in the area; and the 'Mathon Weed' sometimes called metheurum, which has a daisy-like

Brook House, Mathon

flower with a most unpleasant smell, mostly found in cornfields or on the banks of the sand quarries.

The village has a beautiful 11th century church in its centre, built by the monks of Pershore Abbey and under direct control of the Dean and Chapter at Westminster. In the churchyard by the main door is an ancient stone where people paid their tithe money and hired their labourers. Until just before the Second World War, most of the farms were owned by the Church Commissioners. These had been willed to them by a previous vicar of the parish. The farms were sold off to tenant farmers but the Church Commissioners still own all the mineral rights.

Until the 1940s the village was a thriving community with two public houses, two shops with bakeries and a post office, from which the postmistress, affectionately known as 'Flora', delivered mail on her bicycle for years. There was also a village blacksmith. Of these only one public house has survived. The village school stands by the church, but sadly is now a private dwelling.

The village has a number of beautiful black and white timbered houses, and one of these, Little Southend Farm, had its own friendly ghost – a lady with light tapping footsteps which could be clearly heard from inside the house as she walked past down the lane.

A great character of the past was George Jones, known to everyone as 'Gervey'. How he got this nickname is a mystery. Besides his regular job in the quarries he was grave digger, pig killer sand sheep dipper. The children spent many happy hours on Mathon bridge watching the sheep being ducked in the water. Sometimes, if you were lucky, he would give you a sip of cider from his jar!

In the late 1920s while quarrying for sand a number of Bronze Age vessels were unearthed; these are kept in the Hereford Museum.

Mathon has remained more or less the same for centuries but changes are taking place rapidly now. The largest employer in the village is a thriving commercial nursery which is situated on the outskirts. The second largest was the sand quarries but due partly to increased traffic on the narrow roads these are now closed. Farms are being sold off and land divided, farm buildings and barns converted to dwellings; the first of the five dwellings converted from barns at the Church Farm was occupied in 1991. Horses can be seen trekking over roads and fields, coming from two stables in the village.

The neighbouring village, West Malvern, has now established a Cricket Club in the grounds of Mathon Court and in 1998 the village hall, built by the villagers in 1924, was refurbished with the help of a grant from the 'Malvern Millions'.

MOCCAS

The name Moccas is derived from the Welsh 'moch-rhos', meaning pig's meadow or moor. In fact, pigs played a part in the founding of a settlement here in the late 5th or early 6th century. According to legend, St Dubricius, a monk born at nearby Madley, was instructed by an angel in a vision to go and find a place with a white sow and litter of pigs and to build a monastery there. He found the place 'well wooded and abounding in fish', called it 'Mochros' and stayed for many years. Unfortunately, the settlement appears to have only survived to the end of the 6th century, when it is said to have been laid waste by a combination of Saxon raids and the yellow plague.

The present church, dedicated to St Michael and All Angels and built around 1130, is an almost perfect example of a Norman village church. There is some fine 14th century glass in the windows which, in the nave, still bear scratches made by the masons when setting the original jamb stones. On a visitation to 'Mockas' during Henry VIII's reign, in 1540, the church was described as being very poor, with 'no religious books'. However, even if there had been books, no one in the parish could read!

Not far from the church is the elegant, red-brick Moccas Court, standing in gardens laid out in the style of 'Capability' Brown. It is said that the ghost of a 'grey lady' walks the grounds of the Court, which could be that of Mary Jane Cornewall, who 'lamentably drowned in the river Wye' in 1839, aged 17.

Moccas deer park was made famous by Rev Francis Kilvert's description of its great oak trees: 'I fear those grey old men of Moccas, those grey, gnarled, low-browed, knock-kneed, bowed, bent, huge, strange, long armed, deformed, hunchbacked, mis-shapen oak men that stand waiting century after century . . .' This beautiful, medieval deer park has been designated a Site of Special Scientific Interest for its historical value and rare trees and insects.

In the 1880s, the blacksmith in Moccas was also the innkeeper. There is no inn or smithy today, nor a shop or school, but there is a good village hall, which is well used, considering the size of the community. The Rev Sir George Cornewall built a school in the village in 1873, but sadly this has been closed for many years. It was converted to a house with shop and post office in 1953, but is now a private dwelling.

A great deal of time and care goes into the gardens in Moccas, which is reflected in its having twice won the Best Kept Hamlet competition. A flower show is held annually in the village hall and a church fete in the gardens of different houses.

MONKHIDE

Monkhide is a hamlet of Yarkhill. Running through is the old

Hereford-Gloucester canal with three bridges to cross. The main one is Skew Bridge which is lovely, although you have to go under it to see the beautiful brickwork. Walking along the canal you come to the Old Wharf House where barges unloaded the coal. The stables where the horses were kept overnight have been converted to two houses. During the last few years the Canal Society have been cleaning out the canal and restoring the old tow path.

Newtown, at the crossroads, used to have a toll gate with a toll house. People had to pay a halfpenny to go through. There was also a chapel, a shoemaker, and a cottage for the poor of the village. Now there is a garage, shop and post office, a car sales room, a carpenter's shop and a public house.

MONKLAND

Monkland is a village situated three miles west of Leominster on the Brecon road. The total acreage is 1,101, and the village has a population of approximately 160. There are only a few of the characteristic black and white cottages left now.

Monkland is still primarily an agricultural village, having five farms. Whilst there is no longer a dairy farm here, the farms are mixed, with two still growing hops.

The village is fortunate enough to have a post office, a shop and a public house. It no longer has a school, which was closed in the 1940s, and nowadays the majority of children have to travel to Leominster by coach. The old school building beside the church was later used as a village hall but has now become a private house, and a new village hall has been built near the common.

Just off the main road, the Mousetrap cheese dairy is open to visitors all the year round, with a farm shop and cafe; local and British cheeses are made on the premises.

Whilst Monkland no longer has a vicarage, the church of All Saints is covered by the Diocese of Leominster. The church is a stone building in the Norman and Early English style, which was rebuilt in 1866 under the direction of G.E. Street, RA. The village register dates from 1589, the earlier portions having been destroyed.

Sir Henry Baker was vicar of Monkland from 1851 to 1877, when he died on 12th February. Sir Henry was the chief compiler of *Hymns Ancient and Modern*, one hymn being written for Monkland. Whilst vicar, Sir Henry erected a lychgate. He lived in Hawkesley House, on the western edge of the village, and his grave can be found in the churchyard, close to the porch.

A small cell of Benedictine monks formerly existed here, founded in the reign of William II, subordinate to St Peter's Abbey at Conches in Normandy, and to the priory of Wootton Wawen in Warwickshire.

The village is situated on the river Arrow, and at one time was subject to serious flooding in the area near the bridge. During the early 1960s Monkland was bypassed, and now the major part of the village is free from traffic.

MORDIFORD

The village of Mordiford lies five miles east of Hereford and includes the areas called Checkley and Frome.

The main rivers of the area are the Wye, the Lugg, the Frome and the little river Pentaloe. It is well known that the river Wye was navigable, but until early in the 1980s it had been forgotten that the Lugg was locked and must have been used for transporting goods. This became known because of the investigations of a member of the Woolhope Club into the vegetation in the river, which revealed the location of more than a dozen lock sites between Leominster and Mordiford (including one by Mordiford bridge).

Since the embanking of the river (in the 1970s) the road to Hereford does not flood by the bridge. Mordiford bridge is built over a very ancient crossing point on the river Lugg. The earliest bridge dates from 1352 or even earlier.

The battle of Mordiford bridge occurred during the Civil War when the Scudamores of Holme Lacy fought for the King. Barnabas Scudamore held the bridge against the Scots, but when Leven started a flanking movement he withdrew to Hereford and held it till the King's army came to relieve him.

The Herefords have held the manor of Sufton since Norman days on condition that they present the King with a pair of gilt spurs whenever he crosses Mordiford bridge. There are two manor houses on the estate – Old Sufton dates back to the 15th century and is now restored and lived in once again. The other was built in the 1790s and is beautifully situated in a landscape by Repton.

There has been a mill at Mordiford since Saxon times. In the Domesday Book it is one of the two mills listed at Hope (now Fownhope). It must have been repaired and rebuilt many times. It milled corn and, in later times, certain mixtures for feeding stock. It closed about 1935 but has recently been restored.

During the Second World War slits were made in the walls of the top storey so that the Home Guard could fire at the enemy advancing over the bridge across the Pentaloe!

The water to turn the mill-wheel came first from the brook to the south of the Woolhope road. When this became inadequate the Hereford estate built a second mill-race taking water from the river Pentaloe. This was in use as recently as the late 1960s when, during dry spells, it was turned on to water cattle on one of the village farms.

Water supplies in the village now come mainly from the Welsh Water Authority, but there are areas of Checkley, more remote parts of the village, where houses still rely on wells. In times of water shortage this can be a serious problem and is probably the reason why one can find so many derelict properties in those parts.

The spring at Mordiford called 'the Spout' is appreciated by many local people. It has been tested and found to be clean and clear with a low nitrate count (only 19 parts per million). It has only tiny traces of copper, lead and zinc and is of a hardness good for teeth and bones and heart. It also makes a smashing cup of tea!

There are many tales of the Mordiford Dragon. It used to live in Haugh Wood and would come down to get a man for its dinner. When the village found itself getting short of labourers for the fields the villagers offered a condemned criminal his life if he would kill the dragon. The man hid himself in a cider barrel by the river and when the dragon came to drink he shot it with an arrow through the bunghole. However, he could not get out of the barrel quickly enough and the fumes from the dying dragon killed him! Serpent's Lane – the dragon's way to the river – still exists. There used to be an effigy of the dragon on the west end of the church but the vicar had it removed in 1811, thinking it idolatrous.

There are some interesting things to be seen in the church, including a lady who died at her prayers more than 300 years ago and is still praying – in effigy.

Many of the old occupations continue in the village. Farming still employs some, with the same crops and sheep and cattle, but some of the latter look strange to oldsters used to seeing Herefords and Friesians. Timber is still important though bark is no longer collected for tanning. There is seasonal work on the land, apple picking for cider (though fewer farms now make their own), hop-picking and the highly skilled job of hop-stringing.

The Mordiford Corn Dolly is quite famous, being known to collectors in America. Pictures usually show only the straw dolly, but modern ones often incorporate a small bunch of hops.

MORETON-ON-LUGG

Moreton-on-Lugg is situated about a quarter of a mile east of the main road between Hereford and Leominster and was probably sited where it is because of the river Lugg, away from the flood plains and on fairly flat land.

In centuries gone by, Moreton, it appears, was a largely self-supporting village where life was centred around the Court, which was demolished in the 1950s. The site of what was probably the earliest manor house can still be seen at Church House Farm, which shows clear evidence of having been a moated site.

The village has only grown since the 1950s, now having approximately 333 houses, 200 of those being built since the 1970s. Moreton-on-Lugg has a church, shop and village hall with a variety of activities going on throughout the week. The majority of the working population work in Hereford or surrounding areas.

There has been a church in Moreton for over a thousand years and the present church, dedicated to St Andrew, was restored in 1867. Unlike some Victorian restorations, the work carried out at St Andrew's was successful and has resulted in a church well worth the attention of any visitor. The architect was W. H. Knight of Cheltenham and the cost was largely borne by Thomas Evans of Moreton Court. Ironically, the bells of the restored church were first rung in 1872 as his funeral procession made its slow way from the Court to the family vault.

Another structure of interest close to the village and found on the road to Marden is the bridge over the river Lugg. According to some authorities the bridge dates from the 16th century and was built at a spot where the river merges as one, having split into two flows just upstream. Over the years the bridge has seen much repair and restoration but it is still an object of considerable beauty when viewed from the meadows looking upstream.

It is interesting to note that Moreton's earliest station house, on the Hereford and Shrewsbury Railway, was a hollow oak tree known locally as 'Eve'. This tree had a circumference of some 62 feet and as many as 15 people are said to have taken tea in it at one time.

When the railway was first constructed, it appears that a navvy made his home in the hollow tree which was given a thatched roof, a brick chimney and even a fitted door! When in the course of time, his work locally completed, the navvy moved on, the tree became a store house and lamp room. In 1862 the railway line was leased to the Great Western Railway and the hollow tree became the station house and ticket office for Moreton-on-Lugg station.

MUCH BIRCH

The village is set in rolling hilly country about six miles south of Hereford city, in an area designated as one of great landscape value. From various high points there are wide panoramic views south towards Ross-on-Wye and westward to Wales and the Black Mountains.

Since the 1960s there has been much new building, so that Much Birch now has over 310 households. The pattern of roads, lanes and paths has remained virtually unchanged for 200 years or more with the exception of the A49 trunk road which passes through the village carrying heavy, fast-moving traffic. Fortunately most houses lie well away from the busy highway and are thus spared its noise and fumes.

During the 19th and early 20th centuries villagers plied many different crafts related to agriculture and the immediate needs of the community – blacksmiths, thatchers, masons, wheelwright, cooper, shoemaker, dressmaker, baker, butcher, to name but a few, as well as farm workers and their employers. In 1841 the village even had a self-styled professor of dancing amongst its inhabitants. Nowadays, whilst there are still several families whose forbears were here a century or more ago, there are many retired people and most others seek their livelihood beyond the village boundaries.

Despite these changes, or maybe in part because of them, village life is active and varied. The church is well attended and cared for. It was rebuilt in 1887 on the site of an earlier building, as there have been churches here since the Middle Ages and the parish register records baptisms, marriages and burials from the late 16th century. The village school is modern and the number of its pupils shows no sign of decline. There are two village stores which are also sub-post offices, and there are a memorial hall and a community centre, a garage, two inns and an hotel. There is an excellent medical service working from a modern surgery.

Much of the land remains in agricultural use as grazing for cattle and sheep, or under wheat, barley, maize or potatoes. Many of the orchards which once abounded have disappeared, but there are still several farms including a fruit farm and a mushroom farm. Trees and hedges are plentiful, dividing fields and giving shelter to a variety of birds and small animals, whilst the aptly named Wrigglebrook flows down the valley on its way to join the river Wye at Hoarwithy.

Though the village cannot claim to have been the scene of any great historical events yet it is of great age, for there has been a settlement at the Birches since before the Norman Conquest, and there is an ancient legend that King Arthur's son Anir was buried beneath Wormelow Tump (although others say that it was his nephew, Mordred, see Much Dewchurch entry). A later belief is that Kings Thorn, a part of Much Birch, acquired its name thus – until the time of Charles I it was the custom each year to send to the King a cutting from the Holy Thorn at Glastonbury; a cutting received by

King Charles when he was staying nearby was planted and from this grew several bushes, one of which grows to this day beside a narrow lane in Little Birch.

MUCH COWARNE

Much Cowarne stands on a south-west facing slope of 3,535 acres about nine miles from Hereford towards Bromyard and Worcester.

The traveller through Much Cowarne would be forgiven for not noticing its existence! It is a dispersed village – houses are dotted about in twos or threes all over the whole parish area rather than being clustered around the church. The reason for this is probably due to early Anglo-Saxon settlement patterns where each house was firmly placed on its patch of land, back facing the lane and front door overlooking the fields.

It is thought that Much Cowarne's unusual name comes from the Anglo-Saxon words 'cu' and 'oern', meaning 'cow' and 'house' or 'shed'. From before Domesday, the village thrived and was quite important in the area as in 1255 it was granted a charter to hold a weekly market and annual fair – this went on for about 200 years.

The most famous past inhabitant was Constantine, the wife of Grimbald de Pauncefot who went off to the Crusades and was unfortunate enough to be captured by Saladin. Constantine wanted her husband back but Saladin would only release him for the forfeit of 'a joint of his wyffe'. So she sent for a surgeon from Gloucester Priory who cut off her hand above the wrist and sent it to Saladin who released Grimbald! Grimbald de Pauncefot's stone effigy lies in the church of St Mary the Virgin – of Norman origin and placed right in the geographical centre of the village. Its tower is not known for its beauty because it has nine buttresses put up over the years to hold it together – but the church itself is lovely and when you walk in you can feel and smell the love and care which villagers have lavished on it.

Population size and age structure has changed dramatically over the last hundred years, as it has in most rural villages. In 1881 there were about 600 people living here – now there are just over 400.

Also, in 1881 most of the population were young – the village was a busy place with children everywhere. The whole area must have hummed with activity particularly on market day at Bromyard or Hereford with drovers walking their cattle to market, keeping small herds together with the help of dogs and children.

A superb new school was built in 1858 by the local squire – a large 'very Gothic' construction. The school was so unusual it was also mentioned in a Government report of 1861 as being a good example to other villages. The children, however, came unwillingly to school as there was so much to do at home and on the land. Girls were frequently absent 'minding the baby' of their large families, boys because they worked on the land with their fathers.

The agricultural production was mainly apples for cider and hops for beer with corn, potatoes, hay and cattle-rearing taking second place. All of these had many related trades and virtually every cottage had its own cider press. Today, the village still grows hops, but not many acres are laid to this now – the area is mainly cereal and pasture.

The ruling family of the village, the patriarchal Bournes, sold up and left the village in 1921. They were never replaced and since then there seems to be a social and power void, only partly filled by the Church. Most of their land is now owned by various farmers. However, there are some families who have farmed the area for hundreds of years: the Pudges, the Orgys, the Boulcotts, the Buftons.

The most 'developed' area is on the edge of the parish at Burley Gate, which boasts a main road bus service, post office and shop, a new school, a village hall and many new houses and bungalows.

In spring the village glistens with blossom from the orchards; in summer the hops grow high and heavy with foliage and delicate pale blossom. Some of the old barns have been converted to smart new cottages. Farms have diversified and offer accommodation to the weary city-dweller who comes to our tranquil village for peace and rejuvenation. Straw-work and other rural crafts are taught at The Old School House.

MUCH DEWCHURCH

Much Dewchurch is an extensive farming and fruit growing area, situated on the B4348 road between Ross-on-Wye and Hay-on-Wye.

Legend has it that St David was born here in the year AD 500, and the Norman parish church is named after him. Much Dewchurch has been a Christian parish since Roman times in AD 314. Records show that when the Black Death reached here in the year 1348 no less than three vicars held the parish within that one year.

There are several very old houses in the village, the oldest being Church Farm House, parts of which were built in the 13th century. The vicarage dates from the 14th/15th centuries and is now a private residence. The church house built in the time of Queen Elizabeth I was used for a time as the school house, but that also is now owned privately and the village school has been turned into a private school.

There were two large estates in the parish which at one time employed almost all the population, The Mynde and Bryngwyn, the latter once being part of The Mynde. The Mynde, which is mentioned in records of 1300, has been divided up over the years and the farms sold to tenants. It now consists of 400 acres and has no need of a large staff.

Bryngwyn was the home of Sir James Rankin MP who in 1872 built the Free Library in the City of Hereford and was also the founder of Hereford County College in 1880. This estate was also sold off and there is no need any more for 15 gardeners as the house has been turned into flats, holiday accommodation and an old people's home and there is a small engineering works in the ballroom!

At the entrance to Bryngwyn was Wormelow Tump, a burial mound that was reputed to cover the remains of Mordred, the nephew of King Arthur, who was murdered by his uncle at Gamber Head (three quarters of a mile along the Hereford road towards Monmouth from Wormelow); for an alternative story see Much Birch entry. Legend has it that no one was supposed to have been able to step round or across this mound twice in the same number of paces. Unfortunately the tumulus was removed for road widening in the 19th century.

In Roman times the Bryngwyn road junction was of great importance, and was guarded by Aconbury Camp and Much Dewchurch Camp, the latter on the tump where the river Worm can most easily be crossed. Up until the mid 17th century Welsh was spoken in Much Dewchurch and the river Worm divided the English and Welsh-speaking districts.

The local inn, The Black Swan, is said to be one of the oldest in England (14th century). It sits on the route that led from Hereford to Abergavenny and South Wales and was an important rest house for those on horseback or foot.

Although there is no longer the need for estate gardeners, the local nursery at Allensmore does employ many full and part-time staff.

In recent years several new houses have been built so the village has expanded, but has still managed to maintain the village atmosphere.

MUCH MARCLE & YATTON

Surrounded by apple trees and hops, Much Marcle offers visitors of all ages a warm Herefordshire welcome – and plenty to see and do.

In the churchyard, a hollowed-out yew tree, now thought to be over 1,500 years old, stands guard over the delightful church of St Bartholomew. Begun in the 13th century, this houses a number of interesting monuments which bear witness to the importance of the village during medieval times. In the nave, there is a beautiful alabaster tomb effigy of Lady Blanche Grandison and a rare, larger-than-life wooden effigy of a franklin (county squire), thought to be Walter de Helyon, resident of Hellens. This house, which was re-built in Jacobean times, is open to the public and is rich in history.

The Queen Anne rectory is another lovely village house and although now privately owned, it is possible to enjoy a glimpse of it from the road. Just beyond the church, lying in stately park land, is Homme House, home to the Kyrle family who have been lords of the manor since 1577. Readers of *Kilvert's Diaries* may remember an entertaining account of a Homme House wedding at which Kilvert was best man.

The Church of England primary school was built in 1833. It has been modernised over the years and is, today, a flourishing centre of excellence. The Memorial Hall, built to commemorate those who gave their lives in the First World War, provides a useful centre for village activities – from badminton to amateur dramatics. There is also a village shop and post office, together with three welcoming inns.

Traditional 'black and white' houses and cottages are scattered throughout the area – complete with roses around the door and honeysuckle scrambling over the front gate! A small, yet sympathetically designed group of retirement bungalows has also been built on glebe land.

In 1575, during the reign of Queen Elizabeth I, the landscape underwent a dramatic change when a landslip took place on Marcle Hill. This became known as The Wonder, and is still marked as such on today's Ordnance Survey maps. A lively representation of the landslip can be seen on the signboard of The Slip Tavern.

Oldbury Camp also lies on Marcle Ridge, although little remains of this other than a section of rampart three to four metres high. Follow the signposts to the picnic area here and you'll enjoy stunning views across Ledbury to the Malverns.

Apple orchards, hop-yards and gentle white-faced Hereford cattle make up today's landscape and there are a number of local events that offer an insight into Herefordshire life. The Blossom Trail in early May includes picturesque walks, talks and poetry readings, whilst The Big Apple in October celebrates the season's harvest with orchard walks and cider tastings. The Herefordshire Traction Engine and Vintage Club Rally is held for two days in July, followed by the Much Marcle and Yatton Flower Show at the end of August – a tradition that is now over 100 years old and which may owe its existence to the first Marcle Fayre, for which a charter was granted in 1270.

Cider production continues to play an important part in village life too. Farmers have made cider for their own use for centuries and about 100 years ago, Mr Henry Weston, who had recently bought The Bounds, decided to supplement his farming income by making cider on a commercial basis. He was probably spurred on by Mr C. W.

Radcliffe Cooke of Hellens. As the MP for Hereford, he consistently advocated the commercial development of this West Country drink. From such small beginnings the independent company has expanded its cider and perry production and employs a significant number of local people. Today, you can take a tour of Westons cider works (large parties by appointment), visit the on-site cider shop and even 'try before you buy'. The recently opened Scrumpy House Restaurant also uses fresh local produce including, of course, apples and pears.

To the north-west of the village lie the two hamlets of Rushall and Kynaston. In Rushall stands Hall Court, a typical Elizabethan house. On the opposite side of the road is the site of its predecessor, probably a moated medieval castle. The artefacts found during an exploratory dig are housed in the Hartlebury Museum and include a beautiful pendant.

Yatton is a separate parish but, although the benefices are united, the civil administration lies within the jurisdiction of How Caple. In the grounds of Chapel Farm stands a 12th century chapel of ease, now redundant, of the same age as Kilpeck. In the tympanum above the south doorway is a Tree of Life, a good example of a carving of the period. The 'new' church of All Saints was built by William Roberts of Chepstow in 1841. It houses a beautiful 16th century screen brought from the earlier church. The village also has several interesting farmhouses, including Deans Place which dates from the late 16th century.

MUNSLEY

Munsley has no nucleus of houses surrounding the church or pub. It is a parish of about 1,482 acres adjoining Ashperton on one side and Bosbury the other. It is four miles north-west of Ledbury and was mentioned in the Domesday Book. The population in 1931 was 188.

The church of St Bartholomew is supposed to date from about AD 830. When it was being restored in 1863, some very ancient gravestones bearing pre-Christian crosses were discovered. On one wall is an ancient inscribed stone which was deciphered by Rev L. G.

Hunt and Professor L. A. Waddell CB to read 'HAMLET XHETI' or Hamlet the Jute with the date AD 362. This is believed to be a fragment of the sarcophagus of the original Hamlet, Prince of Denmark, of Shakespeare's play. There is also a curious oak chest, about 800 years old, bound with iron and carved out of the solid tree. So strong is it that it now provides another useful service. The bellringer has to stand on it to reach the rope to ring the bell!

Part of Munsley belonged to the Canon Frome estate. In the 1930s when Mrs Hopton renovated The Royal Oak she renamed it as it is known today, the Hopton Arms. A little way down from this pub was a cottage whose tiny front garden, not more than 8 ft wide, became known nationally and internationally. It was featured in the *Sunday Times Supplement,* in American magazines, as well as being shown on television. The farm worker who lived there is a very gifted topiarist. A horse complete with jockey, a lion, a few birds and a basket of flowers were some of the shapes into which he cut his trees.

Unfortunately, the very cold icy winds of an early 1980s winter killed most of them. He has now moved house, but he still practises his art in Munsley churchyard, shaping one of the trees into an angel.

Until the 1960s the Verzons was a farm. During the Second World War, the house was used as an RAF billet. After the airmen left and the farm was sold, the new owner had the house made into three flats. After that, the land was sold off, some of the buildings made into houses and the farmhouse became a pub. Most of the seats in the bar were made out of old iron tractor seats and were very uncomfortable! Now it has become the Verzons Hotel and Bistro.

Munsley's only shop, selling fruit, vegetables, plants and some garden equipment, is at Little Verzons Garden Centre. For all other commodities a trip to town is necessary. Before hop-picking became mechanised and many more workers were needed, each farm stocked up a temporary shop to sell necessities such as bread, milk, etc to the hop-pickers.

NEWTON & ST MARGARETS

Newton and St Margarets are two separate and delightful adjoining parishes – parishes rather than villages, each being sparsely populated in a dispersed pattern of farms and homesteads. The parishes are located in the attractive upland foothills of the Black Mountains, 15 miles south-west of Hereford. To add to their natural isolation the parishes are bounded to the east by the steep well-wooded slopes of the Golden Valley, impenetrable except for two or three minor lanes which wind their way through. The population of Newton is 108 and St Margarets 110.

St John's church, Newton was built in 1844 by the efforts of one man, a yeoman farmer, John Powell, who thought the parish church at Clodock too far away for the people of Newton. At his death John Powell was buried in a place of honour close to the east wall. His story is told in a booklet obtainable at Newton church.

Near the church is a small schoolroom with adjoining stable for the horses of visiting vicars. Over the years this room has had many changes of use and nowadays is mostly used as a meeting room by the local WI. The Methodist chapel at Newton was built in 1832 and has regular services and a Sunday school.

The late Mrs Mary Shaw of The Oaks, Newton was the only parishioner to receive Maundy Money, distributed by her Majesty Queen Elizabeth II, at Hereford Cathedral in 1976.

The ancient church of St Margaret's stands on a hill overlooking much of the two parishes and giving splendid views of the Black Mountains. It is known for its beautiful carved oak 16th century rood screen which is considered one of the glories of the county. In 1989 the church was decorated with the colourful addition of over 50 needleworked kneelers, many of the kneelers being made to commemorate events and anniversaries within families and the parishes.

The churchyard is rich with a flora of wild flowers and grasses which provide much interest to visiting botanists. This varied growth is encouraged and sustained by the traditional hand scything of a succulent haycrop.

Among the many leaning gravestones is one to an old midwife of the parish, Harriet Powell, who died aged 77 on 17th May 1910 and whose proud boast is recorded on the inscription that she attended 526 births and never lost a mother.

Until recently the only tavern for the two parishes was the Sun Inn adjacent to the church but with changing ownership it is now a private house.

One past parishioner who reached fame in pre-war years was Robert Cole, a long distance runner. As a young man he ran against Guvussi at Powderall, Scotland. Robert Cole died in 1966 but he is still remembered as a runner and also for his eccentricity of keeping his racing cycle hanging on the living room wall in later years.

OCLE PYCHARD & BURLEY GATE

The parish of Ocle Pychard, in which Burley Gate is situated, was once bounded on one side by the old Hereford & Worcester Canal. Ocle (or Acle) means oak (derived from the Saxon), and Pychard comes from Roger Pichard, who is mentioned in the Book of Fees of Henry III.

The parish church of St James is built of the local sandstone and the oldest parts are in the Early English style and date from the 13th century. The stone font is said to be of Saxon origin. The three bells are of great antiquity. The treble dates from 1600, the second was cast in 1639 by John Finch of Hereford and the tenor is a medieval head group bell cast in Worcester around 1410.

The largest house in the parish, the owner of which was formerly called the lord of the manor, is Ocle Court, situated on an eminence near the church. The front of the house was rebuilt in Georgian times in stone and the back, which is half-timbered, is probably Tudor and is a listed building. It may well have been moated as a large pond is still to be found to the rear of the property. Other notable properties include Lyvers Ocle which is built on the site of a monastic house and said to be connected by a tunnel to Monkton and the White House, parts of which are 14th century.

There are several farms in the parish. The chief crops grown are hops, grain and apples. The rather picturesque old hop kilns are still to be seen but no longer serve any useful purpose.

Burley Gate is situated at the junctions of the busy A417, Leominster to Gloucester road and the A465, Hereford to Bromyard road. The once dangerous crossroad has now been replaced by a traffic island. With the main local amenities now concentrated here, Burley Gate has become the nucleus of the parish.

The village hall was once Ocle Pychard school and was purpose-built in 1892, by Mrs Higgins who resided at Thinghill Court. Mrs Higgins later had the post office and stores built. It was designed especially and in 1950 was one of the largest rural shops in the county. The police station was originally built next door to the post office, again at Mrs Higgins' instigation. It became a private dwelling in 1939 when a new police house was built on the A465.

A house and stable were built for the local postman, who started his deliveries from where the telephone exchange now stands. Other notable properties include the Burley Gate Inn, a half-timbered listed building which was once a cider house and known as Griffith Farm House, and the Old Blacksmith's Shop. This must once have been a hive of industry for apart from the usual blacksmith's trade the family were the local carpenters, wheelwrights and undertakers.

Electricity only came to the area as recently as 1956 and the mains water still more recently in around 1965. Until then residents had to rely on boreholes and wind pumps with many properties having their own storage tanks. As the area is situated 100 metres above sea level and rather exposed, wind power was readily available. This also gives the additional benefit of spectacular views across to the Black Mountains which at times are further enhanced by glorious sunsets.

ORCOP

'Orcop God Help Us' so the saying goes, and several stories surround this. The most plausible seems to be that in the tiny 13th century church, nestled in a quiet corner of this scattered village, there used to be four bells, each representing one word of 'Oh God Help Us'. The church, which was drastically restored by the Victorians in 1860, now has five bells, the fifth being installed in 1907.

Another story surrounding the saying revolves around an old farmer who used to walk every week into town, a good twelve miles. When asked where he came from he would reply 'Orcop God Help Us' on bad days or 'Orcop God Bless Us' on good days.

Orcop is a very scattered village without any true village centre – this could be the reason why so many say 'Orcop where do you think'. However, the village at one time had five public houses – The Sun, The Globe, The Brewsters Arms, The Fountain and the New Inn. Sadly only one, The Fountain, remains.

Unfortunately we also lost our famous Holy Thorn during the gales in January 1980. The Holy Thorn was situated at The Stars, Little Hill. It was said to blossom on the old Christmas Eve (January 6th) and that cattle used to kneel down around it.

If there is a centre of the village it must be the village hall where most organisations meet and events take place.

We all enjoy the beautiful space and scenery in Orcop during the summer but when it comes to winter – well – 'Orcop God Help Us'.

PARKWAY

Parkway is a small hamlet situated south of Ledbury on the A417 road to the M50 motorway and Gloucester. It is sparsely populated with no church, school or public house and is chiefly a farming community, the only commercial building being a garage and filling station. Before 1967, just on the corner of the road to Woolpits, there was a small timber and builder's yard, on the site of which a house now stands. A Memorial Hall for the 1939–1945 war was built in 1947, the use of which has declined to virtually nothing in recent years.

PEMBRIDGE

Pembridge lies in the heart of 'the land that Time forgot'. Straddling the A44 halfway between Leominster and Kington, it is still

The Old Belfry, Pembridge

charmingly picturesque, the main street lined with black and white houses, many of which are medieval in origin.

Many of these ancient buildings have survived because, although Pembridge was an important maket town in Tudor times, it gradually declined to the extent that its inhabitants were too poor to build new houses; the old ones still stand, providing our heritage.

At the centre of the village, on the crossroads, stands an old coaching inn called the New Inn. It was new in 1311 after the old one had burned down! It was here that the treaty is thought to have been signed after the Battle of Mortimer's Cross in 1461. In the square behind the inn is the old Market Hall, where the original 'mark stone' can be seen, the place where people gathered to exchange goods and from which the word 'market' derives.

Steps up from the square lead to the churchyard and the 14th century church, which is surprisingly large for a village of around 800 people, although this is explained by the importance of the town at the time it was built. Near the church stands the pride of Pembridge: the separate bell tower, a unique three-storey pagoda-like structure of stone and timber, supported on the inside by massive roughly-hewn beams, now known to date back to the year 1115. There are bullet holes in the door, said to date from the Civil War. There is also said to be an underground passage leading from the church to the cellars of the adjacent Court House, which stands on the site of an ancient castle (probably wooden, and pre-Conquest), and parts of the moat which divide it from the church can still be clearly seen.

Pembridge is built on a bank rising from the fast-flowing river Arrow, a tributary of the Lugg, so nearly every house in the village has one or more steps leading up to its door – hence it is sometimes known as 'the village of steps'. From the crossroads, Bridge Street leads down to the river which still tends to flood in winter. The three-arched bridge is mildly hump-backed, built of well weathered grey stone, and leads to the village green, a stretch of meadowland beside the water.

At one time there were 15 pubs in Pembridge parish, but now there are only two, the New Inn and the ancient Red Lion. In recent years the Greyhound in East Street became the Pembridge Inn, then a visitor centre, before once more going on the market; during this phase, a public car park and loos were built behind it – after at least half a century of discussion on where they should be put!

In 1992 the building which had served as the village hall for over a century was finally demolished, and a house built on the site. The new village hall was erected on the outskirts of the village, with all mod cons, its spaciousness and comfort greatly appreciated by all those who use it.

Pembridge also has a garage, a carpet shop, a hairdresser, and a number of antiques and crafts shops. The Old Steppes (the rectory until 1777) supplies newspapers, groceries and wines and spirits, while the 'top shop' in the Square sells groceries and houses the post office. The names of many of the houses reflect the trades originally carried on therein – The Old Wheelwrights, The Forge, Woodsmith's Cottage, and even The Old Bike Shop. There are two rows of almshouses, timber-framed 17th and 18th century cottages which are occupied by elderly residents of the parish. A Voluntary Assisted Church of England primary school celebrated its centenary in 1966, and continues to flourish. Dunkerton's excellent cider is brewed about a mile from the centre of the village, and is proving a great attraction to tourists, while Pembridge Terracotta exports hand-thrown flower pots of all shapes and sizes to Japan, the United States and elsewhere.

There are two major annual events which bring visitors flocking to the village – the Horticultural Show and Trotting Races in July, and the Art Market and Craft Fair in September, when over 400 paintings by local artists are on sale in the school hall, and the old Market Hall comes to life again with craftsmen and women demonstrating their skills and selling their wares. The Pitfield Show also attracts horse lovers from near and far. The May Fair has been coming to Pembridge since the Middle Ages, but times change and it last came in 1996. Originally a hiring fair held in the village streets, in later years it was held on the village green beside the river. It would be hard to hold a fair in the streets nowadays – the old coach road to Aberystwyth was very different from the modern A44 which it became!

PENCOMBE

Perhaps Pencombe is elusive but it does not hide itself away. It lies at a crossroads in the north-eastern uplands, near Bromyard, and is signposted from each point of the compass. Mysteriously, the distance is always three miles, as if these were territorial waters. You may sense that, in its origins in wilder times, perhaps as a stockyard, Pencombe was not intended to be taken by surprise.

The village is tucked into a small, enclosed valley below a range of satellite farms posted like sentries along a broad ridge of high ground. Most are still working farms bearing today the local names adopted by their tenants after the Norman Conquest, who held them in return for military service to the lord of the manor. The population of the outlying farms is about half that of the village alone and together the parish forms a socially united and supportive community.

Mr Lawrence, the wheelwright, has no successor but the inn which he ran and named after his craft in the mid 1800s remains his memorial. There were other pubs too, such as The Huntsman's Tavern and the Flying Horse but then the population was larger than today and the work probably thirstier. Today, much of the housing is modern, replacing older or ruined cottages, but much also survives from the 17th and later centuries.

During the 19th century the lords of the manor, only the third family to succeed to this position since Domesday, were the Arkwrights of Hampton Court. Successive members provided a generally benevolent squirearchy and from 1861 George Arkwright, great-grandson of Sir Richard the textile magnate, was rector of Pencombe. Then followed a frenzy of building in the village which must have had the impact of a city centre development. Within four years, the Norman church had been razed and completely rebuilt in what was called the Continental style and a fine new school had appeared on the next-door site. At the same time, the rector having married into a family of some grandeur, the decaying rectory was rebuilt on a generous scale. The laying of the foundation stone alone involved the consumption of 36 gallons of cider at a cost of 9d per gallon! Unfortunately, rectors with private means became scarce as the years passed and the house rapidly became a white elephant. It now has a new lease of life as a retirement home.

The new church has lost most of its original monuments except for a memorial to an unexpectedly bold adventurer. Young Richard Jordan of New House Farm had lived all his 19 years in Pencombe and we can only wonder what drew him to join an expedition to unknown Central Africa 20 years before Livingstone.

The school has served the village well and continues to provide as agreeable a background to learning as could be wished. As luck will have it, the playground adjoins the churchyard in which grows an ancient cypress of mangrove-like habit. These tangled limbs have been polished by generations of children squirming through, over and round them. Just across the road was the blacksmith's forge which, within living memory, provided a haven for any child with a pie to be heated for his school dinner on a winter's day.

Below the forge runs a brook, vital to the village in the past but so familiar as never to have been given a name. It is fed by several springs along its course, at one of which a stone reservoir has been

Pencombe village

built. This was the Washing Pool, with stone slabs for washboards and constantly overflowing water to ensure thorough rinsing. The days are not long passed when neither mains water nor electricity had reached the village so that, for most people, the spring supplied water to be carried or pumped for every household use. To this day, many cups of tea are made with a strict prohibition on the use of any but spring water.

The Washing Pool was no doubt a social centre in its time but what water ceremony can have given rise to the rhyme, said to have been chanted to taunt the children of Pencombe by their rivals from other villages, that this was the place where they:

> 'Put the pig on the wall to watch the band go by
> And thatch the river to keep the ducks dry'.

PETERCHURCH

Peterchurch lies twelve miles west of Hereford in the heart of the Golden Valley, in some of the most beautiful countryside in all England. All approach roads offer spectacular views of mountains, woodland, verdant pastures and rippling streams. However, if the village itself does not have good looks, it certainly has character.

The village possessed a stone church over 1,200 years ago when Hereford Cathedral was still wattle and daub. This church was rebuilt by the Normans in 1130 and, recognising the craftsmanship of a particular mason, they employed him to carve the archways at Peterchurch. Unfortunately Hugh Fitz Norman tempted the mason away to work at Kilpeck. This resulted in the beautifully carved doorway at Kilpeck and the Peterchurch carvings left unfinished.

The villagers decided to erect a tower on the west end of the church to protect the women and children from the marauding Welshmen from the nearby hills. It was built at the end of the 13th century with walls seven feet thick at the base. The only access was by ladder to the first floor which could be hauled up when they were safely installed. The walls of the tower were made strong enough to support a spire and one was duly built in 1320, but it fell into disrepair and had to be taken down in 1949.

There is pride in the fact that the new 186 foot spire is one of the tallest in England – and is made of fibreglass. It was erected in 1972 in three prefabricated sections, each crane-lifted into place.

Further resourcefulness was shown when the village needed a new hall. Negotiations took place and an agreement was eventually made with the County Council. In 1978 this resulted in the building of a fine spacious hall, to accommodate 300 people, on a joint-use basis with the county primary school. This arrangement was one of the first of its kind in the county.

Another first for the village – it can proudly boast its own television mast. This was due to the tenacity of a former rector who was incensed by the extremely poor reception experienced in the valley.

PETERSTOW

The parish of Peterstow is situated on either side of the A49 Ross-Hereford road, two and a half miles from Ross.

The population is about 300, but is now increasing as new

developments are taking place, which is rather detracting from the rural atmosphere of the village. Very few of the inhabitants now have any connections with farming, as the five or six farms which once comprised the parish have mostly been amalgamated with other farms and the farmhouses either sold or let to non-agricultural families. There are two or three fruit farms in the parish, growing apples, pears, and soft fruit, some of the finest in the world.

The Romans started iron smelting south-west of the common, and there is still black soil on a few fields showing where this took place.

The rectory, which is a handsome house adjacent to the church, was built by Rev Dr Jebb, who was instituted in 1843 and was rector for 40 years. It was sold in 1952 when Peterstow was joined with Bridstow and the new joint rectory is situated between the two parishes.

There is a village shop and post office, a very useful and busy place. Years ago the village supported four alehouses, but only one, the Yew Tree, is still in being, while the Red Lion is more of a restaurant. One of the vanished inns was called The Rising Sun, and legend has it that in the 19th century a murder took place there.

The church of St Peter was originally built in the reign of King Harold, and some portions of this building still survive. At that time Peterstow was in the Welsh diocese of Llandaff. There is a list of rectors of the parish from 1060 to the present time. Probably in the 12th century, a larger Norman church replaced the original Saxon church, and through the centuries many alterations have taken place. There is a charming Norman window in the north wall of the chancel and a mainly Norman chancel arch.

In the 19th century the church was greatly restored by Sir George Gilbert Scott, in the time of Dr Jebb. The church was reopened for worship in 1866 with great ceremony.

There is a small hall in the village, administered by the church. It was built in about 1874 as a Methodist chapel, but in 1924, owing to small congregations, the building was sold to the rector and churchwardens as trustees, and in them is vested the management of the building.

The Church of England school was built over 100 years ago. The

Governors of Guys Hospital, as lords of the manor, gave a portion of land bordering the common to the Rev Dr Jebb for this purpose in 1844. There are a few old photographs in existence of the schoolchildren, at the turn of the century, having sewing lessons outside on the common, and another of the children dancing round the maypole. The school continued to function until the early 1970s when sadly it was closed as there were so few children to attend. The school was then sold and it has been converted into a private house.

Peterstow is fortunate in that it has retained over the centuries its ancient common land. The local authority (Parish Council) now supervises the Common Rights. These grazing rights are still held by some commoners. Up until 1940 Mr Jimmy Link could be seen leaning heavily on his stout stick guarding his small flock of sheep and returning home with them each evening. On cold spring days he would shelter under an impressive horse chestnut tree standing in the centre of the common.

At the north-west corner of the common is the site of a Gospel Bush which must once have been the stopping place in the rogationtide ceremony of beating the bounds and blessing the crops, when a halt was made for reading the Gospel. Near to this site stands the village well with pump still standing and from which villagers could be seen returning home across the common with wooden shoulder-yoke supporting two filled pails. In 1959 mains water was piped to the village.

PRESTON

Though technically just over the official boundary line, Preston is included here as its WI belongs to the Herefordshire Federation. The village has changed but little since Roman legions made and marched along the undeviating road from Newent through Preston to join the Trumpet Road and on through Herefordshire to Stretton Grandison.

Its name is derived from 'prest', meaning priest, and 'ton' meaning home or farm, and it is just that to this day; farms and homes with Preston church as the pivot of the community without the aid of a pub.

The impressive Elizabethan Preston Court belonged (with the church) to the Abbot of St Peter's Abbey, Gloucester, until the Dissolution of the Monasteries when it was granted to the Bishop of Gloucester. Thereafter the manor of Preston was leased to various prestigious gentlemen holding important posts until just after the Second World War when it was bought by a farmer from the Ecclesiastical Commissioners.

Agriculture has been, and is now, the way of life and sustenance of the district. The vicars too had to farm to live and had glebe land of some 40 acres which belonged to the parish church.

Ploughing matches are held annually at different farms in rotation and as in bygone days the ploughing teams show off their prowess in the straight furrow. The ladies confine their attention to keen competition in cookery, handwork and wine making.

Preston villagers, with the adjoining hamlets of Oldfields, Leddington and Hallwood Green, have been working the heavy loam soil for centuries on their dairy and arable farms and with sheep, pigs and fine Friesian herds. Those cider apple orchards and perry pears in particular contribute much appreciated liquid refreshment, vying with the neighbouring hop fields.

PRESTON-ON-WYE

Preston-on-Wye is a village on the south bank of the Wye. It is mentioned in the Domesday Book, when it was an important settlement. It was surrounded by woodlands, none of which now remain. Over the years it decreased in importance, till now it is a small community tucked away between the two roads from Hereford to Hay, one of five parishes in the Wyeside Group. The village includes Bycross, Hainstone, Bellamore and Ploughfield, the latter now being the centre and main part.

Only the church, the court and a few houses remain of the original Preston, half a mile from Ploughfield. Nearby is the site of the old mill which was burnt down during the Second World War, but was used until that time. The brook is bordered by alder trees; these were cut every ten years by the 'cloggers' until the 1940s. They came with their tents and camped while they cut down the trees and shaped the wood into clogs.

The inhabitants live in about 80 houses scattered over several miles. There is a mixture of old and new in the architecture. The largest house, Preston Court, was a farmhouse till recently, but has now passed into private hands. It is in part 16th century, and Lower Bellamore is a listed 17th century farmhouse. There are several cruck houses and old buildings. Mixed with them now are new houses and bungalows, including two small estates, one perpetuating the old name of Ploughfield and the other, Old Thatch Close, named after the original pub which was situated on that site. The vicarage, renamed Pope Place, is now a private house and studio.

Though many people travel to work in Hereford and other places, there is a wealth of talent and enterprise working from homes and small premises in the village. The Yew Tree Inn has been updated and enlarged but continues to keep its 'old world' atmosphere. It holds the post office two mornings a week and runs a thriving petanque club. The farms are medium-sized family farms, employing very little outside labour allied to agriculture. There are four small local businesses.

The church at Preston has a Norman doorway, showing the age of the settlement, and a refurbished belfry with new and recast bells, rung regularly by enthusiasts. Stone to build this and the other riverside churches nearby was brought up the river from Capler on barges. These were winched up the Monnington falls just below Bycross with a windlass. The river was much used for such traffic in the old days, but now only canoes and rafts are seen on it. The annual raft race from Hay to Chepstow passes through. There is salmon and coarse fishing.

Bycross got its name from the ferry which was still used in living memory. The old ferry cottage, now raised up to prevent floods entering the building and thoroughly modernised, still commands splendid views of the river in all its moods and is a vantage point for watching swans and many other water birds. The old ford two miles down stream, opposite Byford, was a regular crossing place until

Sollers Bridge was built in the 1890s and even now, when the river is low, canoeists have to get out and push in the middle of the river.

Two chapels both in Ploughfield, are well attended, the Methodist being one of a group of chapels in the surrounding area. A sports club, mainly used for tennis and junior football, is a fairly new and popular facility but the centre of the community is the village hall, opened in 1957.

PRESTON WYNNE

Startling events, great houses, famed inhabitants – Preston Wynne has none of these. And if you follow the signpost from the A465 Hereford-Bromyard road you are likely to find yourself in the next parish within minutes. For both Preston Wynne and its neighbour Felton (which lie neatly defined between two easterly tributaries of the river Lugg) are no more than hamlets, each only one and a half miles across. The scene is of small hedged fields rarely over 300 feet above sea level sloping unevenly to the south, with scattered farms and cottages. In Preston Wynne they are in three groups: Upper Town, Lower Town and Preston Marsh.

The first documented appearance of the village is in the 1086 Domesday Book. Here it is listed as part of the land held by the canons of Hereford. Only five villagers and one female slave are recorded; today's population is about 150.

Nothing can be traced back to this time. The present modest stone church dates only from 1727, though the church plate (a chalice and cover paten of silver of 1576) implies an earlier building. More significant are the bumps and hollows in the pasture where this isolated church stands. They indicate a deserted medieval village. A question which only excavation could help answer is: was this Lower Town (now shrunk to a farm and a bungalow) the original Preston Wynne, since transferred to better-drained land at Upper Town?

For it is here that the village's most prestigious medieval timber-framed building stands. Court Farm consists of a 14th century barn-like hall with cross wings at either end. Three centuries later it was 'modernised' by division into two storeys and a rebuilding of the cross wings. The original hall roof includes some remarkable curved braces – there is no doubt that Court Farm was the home of a substantial landowner.

Rosemaund Farm (in Preston Wynne postal area though in Felton parish) has put Preston Wynne on the agricultural map. Just after the Second World War it was purchased by the Ministry of Agriculture to be one of a dozen Experimental Husbandry Farms (EHFs) in England and Wales. Here on its 176 hectares – the site also of a Meteorological Office weather recording station – systems aimed at profitable cereal and hop production and stock rearing and finishing are carried out on a farm scale. This is the only EHF still experimenting with hops, and it has recently set up trials to rear deer as a farm animal in lowland conditions.

Traditional building materials have given way to factory produced barns, doors and windows; though there is much sympathetic restoration. The vicarage, the school (still sporting its tiled motto: 'We teach them for Heaven') and the shop no longer fulfil their purpose. The Frenchman's Inn is just a memory with stones to mark its site. There are new houses and bungalows, and no longer do all villagers get their living from the land. But rural continuity is a very strong force and no doubt Preston Wynne's past inhabitants would still be able to find their way around their old village.

PUDLESTON

Pudleston is a scattered rural parish lying to the north-east of Leominster between the A44 Leominster to Bromyard road and the A4112 Leominster to Tenbury road. It is approached from the Leominster end along country lanes with beautiful views on all sides, looking forward to farmland and woods and back to the Border hills and Welsh mountains. It is an area of outstanding natural beauty.

Pudleston has no real village centre or the traditional public house, but the church of St Peter stands in the centre of the parish at the junction to Bockleton and Tenbury. The oldest portion of the church is the belfry tower with its short stumpy spire and old quaint sundials. The western door of the tower is of the 12th century. The drystone or weather moulding is perfectly plain. At the entrance to the church is a fine cedar tree shading a horse-mounting stone, still used by horse riders today. The west end of the church overlooks the well wooded domain of Pudleston Court, and also overlooks two of the oldest oak trees in the county, known as 'Adam' and 'Eve'. A new graveyard was added to the existing one in 1981 which is well maintained. Many ancient gravestones have been removed from the old churchyard.

Pudleston Court, once the home of the local squire, is now a boarding school for boys, owned by the Education Authority. It was built between 1845 and 1850 with stone taken from a local quarry by private railway. At the beginning of the Second World War, it became a convalescent hospital for the RAF. Two bombs were dropped close by during the war – but they both fell in the woods.

The industry is chiefly farming, with family farms who do not employ full time labour. The Bulmer estate, who farm quite a large area of the parish, are the only ones to employ labour. The Bulmer family live at the Old Rectory. A few years ago every farm employed some labour, but the work is now done by contractors. Some cottage industries have sprung up recently.

As Pudleston is between 500 feet and 600 feet above sea level, the winters can be very severe, with snow drifting up to 20 feet in the narrow lanes. Inhabitants can be cut off for some time, so they make sure they stock up their deep-freezers. Years ago, the drifts had to be dug out by hand and food had to be fetched on foot from Leominster. In 1963 the parish was cut off for six weeks. In the summer, however, the view from the highest point – The Bines – is breathtaking. Five counties can be seen from there.

There is quite a history of Roman occupation in this area. Just over the border of the parish is a Roman camp known as 'Bache Camp'. Many Roman roads leading to and from the camp, are still visible today. Close by is a field named 'Battle Acre' where it is believed a battle took place in Roman times.

Pudleston has changed considerably in recent years, with the closure of the post office and shop in 1977, which now means a journey to Leominster for supplies. The school which was built in 1874, was closed in 1982 after much protesting. There has been no bus service here since 1983. The redundant Victorian school has been converted into an excellent community centre.

PUTLEY

Putley was once described in a newspaper report of the late 1920s as a 'most immoral parish'. This came about at a session of Ledbury Revision Court when the then owner of Putley Court described Putley to the Revising Barrister as 'the most immoral parish he had ever been in although he had been all over the world', and he claimed that there was no crime they did not commit there.

Further enquiries into this affair revealed that the owner of Putley Court had been a heavy-handed squire, stopping up footpaths, locking gates and so forth, generally limiting the parishioners' access to places previously always accessible. As a result the parishioners retaliated by breaking locks, taking gates off hinges and generally asserting their rights.

He was in marked contrast to the previous squire Mr John Riley, who had resided at Putley Court from 1872 until 1922. By all accounts he appears to have been a highly respected squire, who took a great deal of interest in his estate and home farm. Many people residing in Putley today still talk about the Riley influence and many families are still here whose parents or grandparents worked for the estate. His home farm appears to have been a fine example of a traditional mixed farm, and he kept Longhorn cattle and Tamworth pigs (both rare breeds today). He was an authority on fruit-growing and a pioneer of modern marketing of fruit: grading, packing and co-operative selling.

A lasting reminder of John Riley is the village hall. Erected in his honour in 1927 by donations from his children it has served the village well. In order to protect the hall, the village post office was built on as part of the extension and a proper village store, able to supply peoples' immediate needs, was incorporated. This means the village shopkeeper/subpostmaster also acts as hall caretaker and it all adds up to an efficient system.

Among the most regular activities in the village hall are 'Putley

Ceilidhs'. These ceilidhs, famed throughout the folk fraternity of the county, are held once a month at the beginning of the month from November, which is the Harvest Supper Ceilidh, to April, the All Fools Ceilidh.

In the face of high house prices Putley is perhaps fortunate in having many young families. However, the breadwinners of these families are less likely to be involved in the traditional occupation of the area, farming. Originally an area of fruit orchards and hop-yards, both of these have declined. Decline in demand for traditional varieties of hops and the spread of vertimicillium wilt have caused the decrease in the number of hop-yards. Similarly the apple and pear orchards have decreased in number as a look at an old map would reveal. The traditional orchards of standard trees are now only found in hidden corners, most existing orchards consisting of trees on modern dwarfing root-stocks. Among soft fruits, fields of blackcurrants are to be found. In Roman times vines were probably grown around Putley, and today one or two people are experimenting again.

Now, however, much land is used for arable crops, rape, potatoes; or for sheep fattening, or spring lamb production, mild winters enabling early lambing to take place, even before Christmas. Suckler herds are also popular with farmers. The older residents delight in describing how they worked the land 40 or 50 years ago, and comment how much easier it is today with modern machinery.

Ross-on-Wye

The name probably comes from the Welsh 'Rhos' meaning a moor or plain, and could refer to the flat land of the riverside, or the stretch of land below Chase Hill, the striking backdrop to Ross on the summit of which is the site of an ancient Celtic camp. In 1931 the official name of Ross was changed to Ross-on-Wye, but it had probably been in common use much earlier.

The earliest reference to Ross is in a document of 1016 when it was presented to the Bishopric of Hereford. In 1138 King Stephen granted to the Bishop of Hereford a market on Thursday each week to be held in

Ross-on-Wye from the bypass

his manor of Ross. These days a flourishing market is also held on Saturdays.

The red sandstone Market Hall at the centre of Ross-on-Wye was built in 1670, and several of its 16 pillars were strengthened in 1997. Its upper storey, accessed by stairs or lift is now in use as a free-entrance Heritage Centre, and its museum houses archaeological finds from the surrounding district as well as an audio-video telling the history of Ross and its environs.

Ross has been fortunate in having several benefactors in the past, chief of whom was John Kyrle who was born in 1637, the same year that an outbreak of plague killed 315 people in the town. A plague cross stands in St Mary's churchyard as a memorial to those unfortunates. During Kyrle's long life of 87 years he financed many projects in Ross, but probably his most lasting memorial is The Prospect, a walled public garden at the rear of the church, from where there is a splendid view over the magnificent Horseshoe Bend of the river Wye and on to the Welsh mountains. His splendid timbered house, now an art gallery, still stands opposite the Market Hall.

Tourism started early in this picturesquely situated little place. The Royal Hotel, commanding fine views of the Wye, was built in 1837 and Queen Victoria stayed there the following year. Many celebrities, including Charles Dickens, have stayed there since.

The past ten years or so have seen many changes in Ross. New housing estates have been built on the perimeters of the town to provide for the increasing numbers of people who wish to settle here, and the population has increased from 7,700 in 1990 to 10,000 in 1998.

The new Ross Community Hospital was opened in 1997 so that minor physical complaints can be treated there instead of patients having to make the 15 mile journey to Hereford County Hospital.

In March 1988 a new library opened in Cantilupe Road with a room dedicated to Dennis Potter, the playwright who lived in the town for many years until his death in 1995. A large community hall called the Larruperz Centre opened in 1990 and is in contant use by numerous societies.

A new pedestrian precinct in the Crofts incorporates several small shops. In the late 1980s a precinct called The Maltings was built on the site of an old brewery. A spacious Antiques Centre opened in 1997 in what used to be the United Reformed church in Gloucester Road. Since the arrival of the two supermarkets in the 1980s many of the small shops have catered for specialised needs, whether in wholefoods or food for the spirit, as in bookshops and artshops. The town is also now more pedestrian-friendly with wide pavements, seats and floral displays. These changes should allow more opportunity for 'standing and staring' at the variety of buildings that line the principal streets of the town – mediaeval, Tudor, Georgian, Victorian and Edwardian, right up to the present day.

Some visitors might wish to time their visit to coincide with the Ross-on-Wye Festival, a popular attraction in late August. A large marquee is erected at the riverside in which to stage performances ranging from pop to classical music, folk-dancing, ballet, drama and poetry-readings.

Many sports take place in and around Ross. Ross Rowing Club stages a Regatta each summer that attracts competitors from all over the country. Swimmers are catered for in the local swimming pool, while golfers have a choice of the old-established Ross Golf Club or the more recent South Herefordshire Golf Club, both about five miles from the town.

Apart from work in the service industries in Ross, local people are employed in four trading estates incorporating factories and trading outlets. There is also a large nationally-advertised discount warehouse selling a great variety of branded clothing situated on the dual carriageway to the north of the town.

St Weonards

The village of St Weonards lies in the south-west corner of Herefordshire, with part of its boundary less than a mile from the Welsh border. The A466 Hereford to Monmouth road runs through the middle from north to south, and it is along this road that the church, school, post office stores and village hall are grouped.

A large man-made mound or tump stands in the middle of the village. This contains a prehistoric burial which was excavated in 1855.

The church is dedicated to St Weonard (or St Gwenaeth) a little known Welsh saint believed to have been a local hermit and woodcutter. This building originates from the 13th century and its tower can be seen against the skyline for many miles. Points of interest include a dug-out chest made from a single tree trunk which is now located in the Mynors chapel, two carved chairs and the altar rail dating from the 17th century, a mutilated coffin lid from the 13th century showing the chalice and a book of a priest, and the font, the bowl of which dates from the 15th century.

About half a mile away in the valley below the high road lies Treago Castle. It was built by Richard Mynors, a prominent administrator in South Wales in the last quarter of the 15th century, who was also Sheriff of Herefordshire in 1500.1t is of interest to note that the same family has held possession of the estate from the 15th century to the present day. Clearly seen from the road at nearby Treago Farm, set in the gable end of a barn, is a sundial dated 1664.

The present post office was originally an inn, The Treago Arms.

When the licence was removed the parishioners retaliated by burning the barns at nearby Pen-y-Gate. It then became a butcher's shop, becoming a post office in 1918. A former postmistress Mrs E. M. Williams, who worked the manual telephone exchange until it went automatic in 1954, was awarded the BEM in the same year. The medal was presented by her family to St Weonards primary school and now hangs in the school hall.

St Weonards is basically an agricultural area but due to more mechanised farming the majority of young people are seeking employment further afield. Life for the parishioners became decidedly easier when mains water was brought to the village in 1952. Previously one tap near the village green was the full extent of the public supply. A further step forward came in 1958 with the coming of electricity, this was a tremendous advance from the candle and the oil lamp.

The old school, which was built in 1846, was closed in 1975 and has now been converted into three dwellings. The new school was opened in 1976 and provides primary education for a large catchment area. A new housing estate and vicarage was built on a site adjacent to the new school. In 1981 a further improvement came to the village when a new hall was built, and this supports a thriving social community.

There are many legends in this area. One story goes that a man was carrying a stolen sheep across his shoulders tied with a rope around his neck. He leaned against a large stone to rest, lodging the sheep on top. The struggling sheep apparently slipped off the stone, and strangled the man. He was found dead next morning but the sheep was still alive. This stone is still to be seen on the side of the road south of the village.

Another story is told that a pig with a saddle on its back appears at midnight at a nearby crossroads. This could have originated from an over-indulgence in locally made cider!

SALTMARSHE

The Saltmarshe estate north of Bromyard, once owned by the Earls of Essex, was purchased by William Higginson in 1799. By 1840 the estate covered land in eight different parishes. Saltmarshe Castle was built in the 1840s on the site of the old Saltmarshe House by Edmund Higginson. In 1871 the estate passed to his nephew William Barneby, then to William Theodore Barneby whose only son Christopher was killed in action in Burma in March 1944. A nephew, Thomas Barneby, inherited in 1946 and sold the estate in 1953. Most of the properties were purchased by the sitting tenants.

The castle was demolished by the new owners; only the kitchen area, the coach house and some barns remained. There was great opposition from people in the area, but nothing could be done to save the castle as it was not an ancient monument, nor at that time considered to be of great historical interest as it was only 100 years old.

The Coronation celebrations in 1937 were held at Saltmarshe Castle. In 1946 Saltmarshe & District WI was founded by Mrs Barneby, and Saltmarshe Young Farmers Club in 1948. Both held their meetings there.

Near the castle, Littlebridge, a large house believed to have been built as the agent's house, included the estate offices with the sawmills and timber-yard nearby.

Saltmarshe is now a caravan park with its own clubhouse situated in a pleasant woodland area.

SHOBDON

Protected to the north by a forested hill and to the south by marshland and the river Arrow, Shobdon has developed from the Domesday village of Scepedune, along both sides of a mile long stretch of road two miles from Mortimer's Cross, westwards towards the Welsh border and Presteigne. It also encompasses Easthampton, Uphampton and Ledicot.

Shobdon has always been difficult to find and rumour has it that even the Devil gave up. Having decided to destroy the church, boasted about by the pious and contented villagers, he loaded a shovel with earth and set off. Near the village, he met the local shoemaker who, in fright, dropped his sackful of shoes saying that he too was looking for the village and had worn out the shoes in so doing. The Devil, in disgust, dropped the earth off his shovel and vanished. Thus it is that on approaching the village from the east, the mound behind the village war memorial is sometimes known as 'The Devil's Shovelful'.

The church lies several hundred yards off the main road up a delightful, tree-lined avenue which passes between two large, landscaped lakes. Built on the site of the old Norman church, for the second Viscount Bateman in 1756, it is in the style known as Strawberry Hill Gothic. It was fully repaired and redecorated in 1971 and has a most unusual blue and white interior. Beyond the church rises a quarter mile long avenue of turf, flanked by young trees, leading to the Norman chancel arches, re-erected there when the old church was demolished. They are at the highest point in the village and command a panoramic view of distant hills and an area abounding in lakes and trees.

Like many other villages occupied mainly by agricultural workers, poverty and poor facilities were prevalent in 'the good old days', and caused the population to drop in the 1930s. It was at this time that Shobdon was shocked by three suicides and an axe murder!

After these traumas, the village took on a new lease of life in 1940 when a wartime aerodrome was built. The land proved too marshy for the use of heavy bombers and so only one runway was completed. It was used extensively for the No 5 RAF Gliding School and was a main training area for the Normandy and Arnhem landings.

After the war, the sites previously used for service quarters were at first occupied by squatters but in 1956, when the land was de-requisitioned, a council estate was started and other areas were bought by private developers. A private holiday caravan site, using some of the old concrete sites for hard standing, has also developed round what is the largest natural lake in Herefordshire. The airfield itself has developed into a leisure centre for flying, gliding, parachuting and microlighting, and has a small caravan site and spectator facilities. The perimeter of the airfield is occupied by several light industries and these, together with others developed close by, have brought many jobs to the area.

In 1957 Colonel Uvedale Corbett bought what was left of the old Shobdon Court, together with its 700 acres of parkland. Originally built in the early 1700s most of it was demolished in 1933, to leave a smaller gentleman's residence. Before this was restored, the main rooms were used as a chicken hatchery until a new hatchery was built and Sun Valley Poultry Limited formed in 1960. There have been many changes to Sun Valley since then but it remains a main source of employment. More jobs were also provided by the development of land for the growing of soft fruits, especially blackcurrants.

By 1983, there was a need for further housing development. A number of sheltered council bungalows were erected, together with shared ownership starter homes and other private detached houses on one site. Another small private estate of converted barns, assorted houses and bungalows has been completed behind the site of the old village hall. This latter building, which catered for 510 villagers for the celebrations at King George V's Coronation, was demolished in 1987 and the area of the village green extended.

Although the village no longer boasts a blacksmith, a cobbler, a tanner, a pig sticker and a baker, it still has a splendid Grade II listed pub called The Bateman Arms, two shops, one of which now doubles as the post office, a hairdresser's, a garage and car showroom. The butcher, the baker, the milkgirl, the mobile shop and the mobile library call and there is a bus service to Leominster. What more can one ask?

Easthampton is approximately one mile north-east of the village of Shobdon and is a hamlet of nine houses. More recently two larger modern houses have been built plus some farm building conversions and four bungalows. It was also part of the Bateman estate and was part of the original 'sell off' which took place in the early 1920s.

Uphampton is another hamlet in the parish of Shobdon just north of Shobdon Arches. At the centre is Uphampton Farm lying on a plateau at 650 feet above sea level but rising to 1,080 feet on Shobdon Hill. In the 18th century and the first part of the 19th century activity centred around Lord Bateman's estate workshops, blacksmith and carpentry and the farm was not very significant. In 1861 Lord Bateman commissioned a Model Farm which included a fully mechanised farm building capable of employing all the farm staff in the winter. Today much of the farm is forested, the rest being arable.

STANFORD BISHOP

Stanford Bishop parish lies to the south of Bromyard in rolling countryside. The main road to Malvern, once a turnpike, runs through the middle, passing the inn, the village hall, the old rectory and Stanford Court. The Norman church stands on the highest point near the centre of the parish in a large circular churchyard which is thought to indicate a pre-Christian use as a holy place. It is thought that a medieval village existed between the church and the Court. Beyond the Court in those days was Wofferwood Common which was not enclosed until 1862. Once a railway ran through the north of the parish and in earlier times salt routes from Droitwich crossed the district.

The main occupation is farming, with pasture and orchards and crops of corn, hops and blackcurrants. There are ten farms, as there were at the time of the tithe settlement in 1838. At that time the meadows around the river Frome were still divided into strips which were allocated to nine farms, two of which were outside the parish. The parish is well wooded but in the 19th century there were more trees, indicated by the frequent use of the terms coppice and ash beds in the tithe apportionment.

There are just over 40 houses scattered throughout the parish. Six of these, listed as of architectural interest, are farmhouses built in the 17th and 18th centuries, either timber-framed or built of stone. Rumney barn is an interesting stone building standing in a field well away from houses. Over the door on the south was once written 'School for Girls, endowed by Phineas Jackson, Vicar, AD MDCCXXXI'. On the west side there is still a faint inscription: 'This school was rebuilt with the assistance of the National Society AD MDCCCXXI'.

The church of St James stands alone surrounded by pasture, hops and blackcurrants, with a fine view over the countryside. It has a 12th century nave, a 13th century west tower, a 14th century chancel and a 19th century porch. It was restored in 1867 and 1885. The south door is modern but has its 13th century strap-hinges. The most interesting thing about the church is its chair.

In 1846, James Johnston, a medical student, came to Herefordshire on a walking holiday in the course of which he looked at Stanford Bishop church. He noted the many large yews, one of which was hollowed out. As it rained he spent some time inside the church, saw the remains of a fire in the bottom of the tower and an old wooden seat. Forty years later he visited the church again. He found it had been repaired, the inside tidied and there was a vestry in the tower, but the seat was nowhere. The sexton, whom he had had to fetch as the church was locked, told him that the masons who had been working on the church had found it cold and had made fires. Fearing that the old chair would be burnt he had removed it and put it in his garden. Dr Johnston went to see it, decided it was really very old so he bought it and had it sent to his home in Birmingham. He also noticed that the largest yew which had been hollow had gone. He was told it had been cut down as it had become a regular lodging for tramps and vagabonds. The sexton said he had seen as many as ten of them sleeping in it and sometimes they would light a fire inside and cook their food.

Dr Johnston then did some research on his chair and became convinced that it was the chair that St Augustine had sat on when he met the Welsh bishops in AD 603.

He kept the chair and wrote a book about it called *The Finding of St Augustine's Chair*, published in 1898. When he died the chair was given to Canterbury Museum. In 1943 Canterbury was badly bombed and it was suggested that the chair would be safer in Stanford Bishop and it was returned to the church. The county history society examined the chair and decided it was not old enough to have existed in AD 603 and that the meeting probably did not take place at Stanford Bishop at all. But it is a nice story and the chair has still a place of honour in the church.

STAPLETON

Stapleton is in the extreme north-west corner of the county. A handsome 17th century rubble bridge with three cutwaters crosses the river Lugg into Presteigne, Powys and from this bridge Stapleton Castle ruins can be seen, standing boldly on their natural motte about half a mile away. Of the original 13th century castle nothing remains. Belonging to the Say family, this formed one of a continuous chain between England and Wales. The ownership passed first to the Mortimers and eventually in 1706 to the Harleys. The old castle has a splendid crop of lurid legends, covering kidnapping, murder and revenge, also of high chivalry, exciting the imagination. It is also reputed to be haunted.

Near the castle are several very old cottages, some 13th or 14th century. The main body of the village follows the road from the bridge and here there is a pottery. At one time, this corner of Herefordshire had several makers of domestic pottery but as the special clay ran out, so the trade disappeared.

This is a quiet backwater, where the Lugg flows through lush meadows before entering the gorge at Kinsham and where the strife and upheavals of the Civil War seem remote and incongruous.

STAUNTON-ON-ARROW

Staunton is a very ancient village, set in a beautiful river valley surrounded by hills, woods and orchards. There is a nucleus around the church and castle mound although there is no school now and the post office opens for only a few hours each week. A lot of Staunton villagers live in small hamlets, or in scattered farms and cottages within the parish. It is only about five miles away from the border with Wales, and many local families originated in the Welsh hill-country.

In the Ice Age the melting glaciers dropped some of the soil and rocks that were carried along with them, leaving very distinctive little hummocks, which you can see near Mowley Woods, and which were once thought to be burial mounds. There was an Iron Age hill fort on top of Wapley Hill (supposedly belonging to Caractacus and his people), and the remains are still clearly to be seen, including a well on top of the hill which has never been known to dry up.

In Norman times there was a motte and bailey fort, probably a wooden structure, on the mound where the Dane-elder grows, behind the church. There are many very old farms in the parish, the oldest probably being cruck built Highland Farm on the slopes of Wapley Hill. The handsome black and white Old Court Farm was built around the 15th century, and was originally two buildings with a cider press, working until comparatively recently.

There is a very strong sense of continuity with the past, as all around are old houses, large and small, the remains of old water systems, mills and tan-houses; and the fields still bear their ancient names like 'The Medlands', 'Costard Close', 'Quarry Fields' and 'Spanish Ways' etc.

Formerly, almost everyone worked on the farms, or in the traditional trades and occupations of a farming area where corn, cattle, hops and sheep, plus, of course, cider, were important products. Now, as in many villages, there is a much wider range of occupations.

They certainly were a tough lot in the village in past times. In the influenza epidemic of 1893, nearly every house in the village was affected. There was no doctor in Pembridge, and a local man walked six miles in deep snow to Presteigne, and six miles back, to fetch medicine for everyone. Mrs Morris, the schoolteacher from 1874–1895, had children constantly absent because they were working in the fields or doing other manual work. Jabez Preece, at the age of eleven, worked singling turnips from 6.30 am to 6.00 pm for one shilling a day. There are many entries in the school log-book referring to children with no shoes; and one lady remembers running round and round the farm kitchen, as a child, to get warm one cold winter!

STAUNTON-ON-WYE

Staunton-on-Wye is situated about two miles from the river Wye, but is so called to distinguish it from Staunton-on-Arrow. It lies behind the main Hereford to Brecon road and is almost two miles from one end to the other. The village's scattered dwellings date back 400 years. They now have all amenities, electricity having been brought to the village in 1953. The 300 people on the electoral roll enjoy two pubs – The Portway and The New Inn, a church and a chapel, a doctor's surgery, an excellent village shop with delicatessen and bread baked daily, a busy village school and a newly refurbished village hall.

The church stands at one end, and the climb up the steep path is well worth while for the reward is a spectacular view to the south – from Hay Bluff to the distant hills of Gloucestershire. In May the sight of the apple blossom in the orchards towards Monnington is one to savour and store in one's memory. A Norman doorway with capitals indicates it is 12th century, while the tower has no buttresses – possibly it was a watch tower to warn of the marauding Welsh!

The rambling red brick building on the main road was built with bricks made at Handmore Cross as part of a legacy to Staunton from George Jarvis, who died in 1793. He was a local boy who made good as a currier, was prominent in his Livery Company and became a Freeman of the City of London. It is recalled that in the 1940s schoolchildren were given clothes and boots by the Jarvis Charity while the older people grew produce on the Tobacco Plot to sell for their 'baccy money'.

Although Staunton lacks a focal meeting point it manages to offer a variety of social activities. The annual summer fete and Harvest Festival are popular events in the seasonal calendar.

STOKE EDITH & TARRINGTON

'Lusty Tarrington, lively Stoke, beggars at Weston, thieves at Woolhope', so goes the ancient rhyme. Tarrington and Stoke Edith, however, lie in beautiful countryside midway between Hereford and Ledbury surrounded by hop-yards, apple orchards and white faced Hereford cattle.

The Stoke Edith estate was bought in 1670 by Thomas Foley of Worcester, a wealthy ironmaster, whose son Paul was Speaker of the House of Commons 1690–1694. Passing down the family, the estate eventually came to Lady Emily Foley, a daughter of the 3rd Duke of Montrose. She died on 1st January 1900 leaving no heir so the estate went to her nephew, Paul Foley of Stourbridge. The Foleys still live at Stoke Edith, but despite one of the most up to date private fire brigades possible, the mansion was destroyed by a disastrous fire in 1927. Local resident Mrs Weaver tells of the only day she played truant from school to watch the Ledbury and Hereford Fire Brigades struggling to deal with the blaze and rescue the treasures. The water in the ponds was frozen and the estate fire engine hoses were also frozen, making it impossible to use them. The headmaster, realising where his pupils were, went to round them up to bring them back to school for lessons. The house was rebuilt in 1936 but the interior was left unfurnished and it was finally demolished in 1957.

Legend has it that when the original church was being built at Stoke Edith, St Edith herself carried the water to mix the mortar, but owing to the distance she had to walk she became exhausted and the water then miraculously appeared out of the ground. St Edith's Well as it was called still exists today, although Lady Emily Foley had it covered to discourage people from trying its supposed healing properties.

Tarrington church has a chancel and nave built in the second half of the 12th century although much of it has been rebuilt. There is also a legend attached to this church, namely that you can make acquaintance with the Devil by walking seven times round the church and saying the Lord's Prayer backwards, then, if you peep through the keyhole of the door the Devil will appear. There is no record of this happening!

In 1644 the Royalist vicar, John Praulph of Tarrington, on being challenged by Parliamentary soldiers proclaimed he was for 'God and King' and was instantly shot near St Edith's Well at Stoke Edith. A record of his death is to be found in the register at Tarrington church.

The GWR line was built in 1856, the railway running through

Stoke Edith estate. One condition was that the Foley family could halt the train if they wished at the Stoke Edith station, a tradition that continued until the 1960s when Beeching axed the railways and Stoke Edith station was demolished. The last train stopped in 1962.

According to Mr David Hodges, in the past the parish of Tarrington had three bakers, five general grocery shops, two blacksmiths, one wheelwright and two cobblers. The Tarrington village post office has been in various houses in the village, starting at Drury Cottage, and then the Laurels but moving to the Old Post House on the main road. It is now situated at Swan Stores at the top of the village, the only shop in existence in the area. Mrs Edith Evans was postmistress for over 50 years and also played the organ in both churches. Miss Elsie Hill delivered the post around the district for many years and people remember her for her generosity when as children they looked forward to her visit on Christmas morning dressed as Santa Claus, bringing each of them a chocolate and an orange.

Tarrington school was built in 1874 by Lady Emily Foley, who was very keen that the local children should receive a good education. In 1881 farmers paid 4d, tradesmen 3d and agricultural workers 2d for their children to attend the school, which was thriving in those days, there being over 100 pupils on the register. Unfortunately the school has now closed owing to the lack of pupils. When Lady Emily Foley was alive the girls of Tarrington school received a red cloak at Christmas and the boys all received a pair of boots.

Tarrington was very proud of John Gwillam, foreman at Foley Farms, when in 1960 he brought home the World Ploughing Championship from Rome. There were celebrations to mark the event in the village.

STOKE LACY

Stoke Lacy lies four miles south-west of Bromyard and ten miles north-east of Hereford on the busy A465 road. This straggling village drops down into the valley of the river Lodon. There is a nucleus of houses around the cider works and another near the church but many Stoke Lacy villagers live in scattered farms, smallholdings and cottages within the parish. The village is a mixture of old and new. Several black and white timbered properties date back to the 15th century and many of the other houses are built of warm red brick.

The parish church of St Peter and St Paul stands at the bottom of the valley opposite Nether Court and forms the focal point of the Conservation Area created in 1993. The church is Grade II listed and occupies a slightly elevated site. It was rebuilt in the 19th century, although retaining its chancel arch which dates back to Norman times. The peal of six bells often rings out around the village.

Up on the hill at the north end of the village is Symonds Cider Works. Started in 1727, it was no accident that the factory was located in Stoke Lacy as industry grows around its raw material and it was widely recognised that the village's old red sandstone soil with is inherent fertility was ideal for fruit growing. In fact there has been a resurgence of apple growing with new orchards taking over from hop growing.

The land is well farmed, adding beauty to the landscape. Farming ranges from sheep and cattle to cereals, hops and cider apples. In the old orchards mistletoe berries hang from the trees in abundance in the autumn. The Woodland Trust is set to create a varied broad-leaved woodland on a nine acre site at the southern end of Stoke Lacy. This will provide a community woodland of native trees and a habitat for wild life.

The village is also the birthplace of Mr Morgan, whose three-wheeled cars were well known before the Second World War. The Morgan family lived in the old Rectory for more than 60 years, Rev Henry George Morgan being rector for half a century.

There was at least one mill in the parish for hundreds of years, in fact the Domesday Book contains a reference to the mill at Stoke Lacy. However, the last one ceased operation in the l940s.

At one time the village could boast not only a flour mill, but also a garage, butcher's shop and general store/post office and public house. All that remains now is The Plough public house which provides local cider and other refreshments and a part-time post office. However, there has been a regeneration of business with the development of six industrial units at the north end of the village and the opening of a children's nursery. The village hall was once the school, built in 1876, enlarged in 1894 and closed in the mid 1960s. A new village hall is planned as a millennium project.

STOKE PRIOR

The name Stoke Prior comes from a cell or monastery belonging to the Prior of Leominster. It is situated three miles south of Leominster and eleven miles north of Hereford. In the 15th century, after the Welsh war of independence, Owen Glendower gave Stoke Prior to one of his faithful followers, Rhys ap Griffith.

The church is dedicated to St Luke. It was entirely rebuilt in 1863 in the Decorated style, on the site of a Norman edifice. The embattled west tower contains five bells, the oldest of which is pre-Reformation and was made at the Worcester foundry in 1460. The huge stained glass east window is a memorial to Thomas Bryan in 1864, the MP for Leominster. A tombstone of the first burial in the churchyard is to Elizabeth Howl in 1331.

There are three historic houses in the village. The Priory is thought to be of medieval origin, and to have been used as a monk's cell. Paradise Walk, to the north of the building, still exists. The Great House has a cross wing at the west end and the south gable has the original dentilled barge boards. The dovecote, south-east of the house, is reputed to be 17th century, with 470 nest holes in 13 tiers, and the strap-hinges on the doorway are of the same date.

The third is the Bury Farm. In 1841, a Mr Waland, the owner, offered the farm of 223 acres, exclusive of timber, to John Arkwright of Hampton Court for 12,000 guineas! At one time this farm was charged with payment of trug wheat (a twelfth part of a horse wagon of corn) to the vicar of Leominster for officiating at the chapels of ease at Stoke Prior and Docklow. This claim, unknown elsewhere in England, was passed to the incumbent when separate parishes were formed in the 17th century.

The population in 1861 was 348, but it had declined to 230 in 1988. The occupations, 100 years ago, suggest that the village was self supporting. There were farmers, hop-growers, gardeners, wheelwrights, blacksmiths, millers, tailors, plumbers, glaziers, grocer, butcher, postmistress and shoemaker. Today, the inhabitants are farmers, builders, bank employees, people working in surrounding towns and senior citizens.

At the eastern end of the village, a Roman settlement was found at Blackwardine. Here, coins, shards, skeletons and a kiln were uncovered during the construction of the railway in 1881.

Headlines in 1891 reported a hoard of seven silver vessels discovered in a rabbit hole behind the Slough Farm. It was declared Treasure Trove and obtained by the Victoria & Albert Museum in 1893. The Crown awarded £25 to each of the discoverers. These vessels were thought to have been hidden during the Civil War, when Sir William Waller took Leominster in 1643 and left it in the command of the famous Col John Birch, but the true facts have never been known.

The football club is thriving and the ten-strong bell-ringing team is very active. There were two public houses in the village, but only one remains. It was refurbished in 1985 and the brewers supplied one free pint of beer daily to our oldest inhabitant, then in his late eighties, for his long and loyal custom. Unfortunately, he died in the summer of 1988.

The school was opened in 1879 with 80 pupils. Today, children attend from the surrounding villages and there are about 60 on roll. It was the custom for the children to dance around the maypole on May Day, dressed in traditional costume.

STRETTON GRANDISON

Stretton Grandison is situated eight miles east of Hereford on the A417 with a population of about 250 people. It is in the fertile Frome valley which is renowned for its hops, cider fruit and arable farming.

It is a small village of mainly black and white half-timbered buildings and farmhouses almost surrounding the old stone-built church. The old road through was of Roman origin, hence the name 'Stretton', but in latter years the road has been widened and constructed to take present day traffic; this, with some more modern buildings, has somewhat hidden the character of the old village. 'Grandison', was the family name of the local nobility whose home was a castle in olden times in Ashperton, the adjoining parish.

The church of St Lawrence is the focal point of the village, dating from the 12th century although it was generally rebuilt during the 14th century. The south porch was added in the 17th century and the north vestry during the late 1800s. The six bells made in Loughborough and installed originally in 1868 were rehung in a steel frame in 1953. The clock, made in Derby, was fitted in the south of the tower in 1912.

The original vicarage is now a rest home for the elderly. The village school was closed in the mid 1960s and converted into flats for the elderly of the parish.

On a by-road from the A417 to the A4103 one can pass through Homend Park with some fine trees. Homend House used to be the 'big house' and employed many of the villagers. Now it is divided into three homes with the stables, cow shed and outbuildings making more homes.

SUTTON ST NICHOLAS

The village of Sutton St Nicholas was originally the separate parishes of Sutton St Michael and Sutton St Nicholas, remaining so with a separate Poor Rate. Finally the union of the benefices was recommended with one parsonage, and under one patron – the Bishop of Hereford.

On approaching St Michael's church the beautiful view over fields to the Welsh hills is in keeping with this tiny peaceful church that belonged to the preceptory of Dinmore, having been mentioned in the Domesday Book. The east window is Norman, a single round-headed light with a similar one in the north wall re-cut and widened. Also Norman is the round font with four half-lions at the base. The cover is modern. The nave door is 14th century, and the lady of the 17th century, Elizabeth Cotton, is sculptured on the ledge of her wall monument.

Leaving the church the land rises to Sutton Walls, an area of 30 acres once occupied by King Ethelbert and where he was thought to have been murdered in AD 794. Buried first at Marden, he was moved to Hereford where the Norman cathedral was dedicated to him. Excavations at Sutton Walls in 1948 showed relics proving the varied industries of that time. To the west is Freene's Court with only traces of the moat left.

St Nicholas' church is 12th century with a square tower. Little remains of the original church, only the single-light windows in the north wall, and the font that is also 12th century with a round bowl made from Withington sandstone. The bowl was broken during the Civil War and the damaged part clamped-in with two pieces of iron. The altar table and two decker pulpit are 17th century. In front of the pulpit the remains of the clerk's desk can be seen.

There is the Sutton County primary school and also a play school nearby. There is a daily bus service to and from Hereford, and many commute to Hereford for school and employment. There is a village shop, post office, and the Golden Cross Inn.

The Freenes, Walwyns, Lingens, Unetts and Aldridge families willed monies for the poor from as early as 1704, and these charities are still being distributed.

Near the Hereford road stands the Wergins Stone, about 5 ft high, with a recess probably for offerings. It is said it was moved by the Devil one night, and then moved back the next.

TEDSTONE DELAMERE

Tedstone Delamere is a picturesque parish in a lovely part of Herefordshire on the border with Worcestershire. It is approximately four miles from Bromyard just off the B4203 road.

The main residence, Tedstone Court, now has new owners. It was the Bellville family home from 1908 to 1996. Mrs N. C. Bellville MBE regularly opened the Court gardens for charities and other functions.

The church of St James stands in a field directly below the Court with exceptional views over the Teme valley across to the Malvern Hills, Bredon Hill and the Cotswolds. In spring the churchyard is a mass of snowdrops and daffodils.

In the church the old Norman font, the carved oak chancel screen and the wrought iron frame in the porch, which used to hold the parson's hour-glass, are well worth seeing. By the porch is an old churchyard cross which has the original square-built plinth of AD 614, the upper part bearing the date 1629. It was altered to support a sundial in 1768, and restored in 1856. The old cross is said to be on the spot where prayer meetings were held before the church was built, and is now classified as an ancient monument.

The last resident rector, who lived in the old rectory (now Delamere House) until 1937, was the Rev F. Williams. He was a great character. While preaching a sermon one Sunday his sleeve caught fire on a nearby candle. Not noticing this he continued until a voice from the back of the church said, 'Beg pardon, sir, Parson's alight.'

St Agnes Well or the Holy Well in the field below the old rectory never dries up. However, no record of its history can be found.

The parish is divided by Sapey Brook, a beautiful area of dingles and woodland, with derelict cottages called Box's, Whitehall, Quay Head, and Paradise, where snowdrops grow in profusion in the old garden amongst the bushes. The other side of the parish over the brook belongs to the Whitbourne estate and some of the properties have been sold off.

Ladywood school, commonly called Woodend school, long since closed, was built by Mr and Mrs E. B. Evans of Whitbourne Hall and administered by them. Every Monday morning two children had to walk about two miles there and back across country to Whitbourne Hall to fetch a very large jar of jam and another preserve for the children, which had to last them the week.

Most of the farms in Tedstone Delamere have old black and white houses – Pixhill, Tipton Hall, Winley and, across the brook, Tidbatch which is on the old salt road from Droitwich, Woodhall Woodend and Lea Ley, with an old house called Primrose nearby. Today the cottages have been modernised, some have been restored and other old buildings have been converted to residential use. The Clifton-on Teme Hunt have their kennels on the site of the old brickworks.

Though times have changed, life still carries on at an unhurried pace in this peaceful part of Herefordshire.

TEDSTONE WAFRE

Tedstone Wafre is three miles north of Bromyard on the western side of the B4203 road from Bromyard to Stourport on Severn. This road for about a mile northwards is locally known as the High Lane.

The parish had three farms, The Court, Cutnell and The Green. Like many farms today, the farm buildings at The Green have been converted to residential use and Cutnell is now a private dwelling.

In the 13th to 15th centuries the Mortimers were lords of Tedstone Wafre, and prior to this the parish belonged to the Wafre family. It was part of the Saltmarshe estate until 1953 when the estate was sold. From the sale, land was reserved for a village hall for the parish of Tedstone Wafre, and subsequently the Saltmarshe & District Hall was built.

Prior to the hall being built functions were held at High Lane school, later known as Tedstone Wafre school. Local people well remember a concert held there. As a singer, a local farmer, completed the first three lines of *Bless this House*, and the floor gave way. It did not break up but sank with the stove in which there was a good fire, about three feet into the cellar where there was a considerable amount of water. Fortunately no one was hurt. Tedstone Wafre school was closed in 1962 and the pupils transferred to Brockhampton Primary School on Bromyard Downs.

The parish church of St James, built in 1870 near to the ruins of a very old church, was closed in 1970 and is now a private house.

There is no longer a post office, and the nearest public house, The Gate Hangs Well, is on the Worcestershire side of the High Lane in the parish of Harpley.

In 1953, Dr J.K.S. St Joseph of Cambridge University discovered an old Roman marching fort in the northern part of the parish. Subsequent excavations by members of the Hereford Archaeological Group found Roman pottery, fragments of a bowl, which could be dated to the 2nd century AD.

TITLEY

Titley lies in a sheltered, verdant position in the Arrow valley, 500 feet above sea level on Offa's Dyke and close to the river. About 150 adult parishioners occupy some 50 dwellings spread over an area interlaced by old drovers' roads. The village, base since 1895 of the Radnorshire and West Herefordshire Hunt and kennels, has changed little in recent years, its architecture ranging from Tudor to Georgian and Victorian, with a few modern properties.

Trains of the local railway once stopped at Titley Halt and Titley station, whence passengers could travel to London without once alighting. But nearby railways died in the Beeching era and public transport is now limited to a once-weekly bus service to Kington. In recent years the village school and shop have also closed, the only remaining community buildings being the church, village hall, post office and inn. Of three earlier inns, the Stagg, Half Moon and Balance, the last two survive as private dwellings, the Stagg Inn alone functions as a hostelry, reopened in 1961 after a century's closure. Titley is still a farming community, but with a variety of professional members, artisans and newcomers retired from elsewhere.

Earliest traces of habitation comprise implements from the Mesolithic period (10,000 to 8,000 BC) and tools, flints and scrapers from early and mid Bronze Age barrows, now lost to the plough, at Priory Leasow and Oatcroft. A later settlement was built in about AD 784 on Offa's Dyke fortification against the marauding Welsh.

From early Norman times alien priories were established. One of them, a cell to the Benedictine abbey at Tiron in La Beauce, France, was founded in Titley around the church's present site. It was dedicated to St Tirella, to whom a small chapel was raised to the north. Nothing now remains of the priory except a privately owned 14th century holy water stoup, timbers thought to be incorporated in the recently restored timber-framed house behind the churchyard, and a spring-fed pool, later piped to a roadside drinking well in 1864 by Lady Elizabeth Hastings of Eywood, the waters of which were attributed curative powers. Unfortunately this water has recently been tested and is unfit for human consumption.

After farming the land as tenants for generations, the Greenly family purchased the manor house, lands and advowson in 1861. The present Titley Court was built by them between 1875 and 1885, incorporating parts of an older house to produce the building of mixed architectural styles in which a member of the family lives today.

Earliest recorded education was in a tiny cottage dame school, now a private dwelling near to the Balance Farm. This was replaced in 1826 by a schoolhouse, built, with the aid of a National School Society grant, to the memory of Lady Coffin Greenly. This school was closed in 1962.

Eywood Mansion, built in the late 17th century by the Honourable Edward Harley, later Auditor of the Imprest to Queen Anne, was enhanced and enlarged by him shortly afterwards. It later became the principal residence of Edward Harley, 5th Earl of Oxford, Earl of Mortimer and Baron of Wigmore, who further comprehensively improved it in 1806. The entire estate was sold in 1954. The mansion was later demolished but associated buildings are now private dwellings.

Another notable building is the mixed Tudor-Georgian house, originally built by Reginald Boddington Esq, which later became the vicarage and ultimately The Old Vicarage.

There have been at least five churches in Titley. The first disappeared in the 13th century when the Black Death devastated the area. Nothing is known about the second, but the third was burned down in 1406 during a battle of the Owen Glendower campaigns. According to churchwardens' reports, the fourth church fell into disrepair before 1761, when it was rebuilt at a cost of £220. The present church dates from 1868 and its fine silver plate from 1569.

Surprisingly, the churchyard contains the newly-restored grave of Lazar Meszaros, the Hungarian general who in the mid 1800s led his country's armies against the oppressive Francis Ferdinand of Austria. The liberated Hungary, however, fell to an invading Russian army and Meszaros, then Minister of National Defence, fled first to Turkey and thence via England, France and Guernsey to exile in the USA. In

October 1858, en route to Switzerland, he visited Eywood, the home of Lady Langdale whose daughter had married his old friend Count Teleki. On arrival he was gravely ill and he died on 16th November, being interred in Lady Langdale's plot in the churchyard. Repeated attempts were made by the Hungarian government to have the general's remains returned to Hungary. However, exiled Hungarians worldwide saw a parallel between the Russian invasions of 1849 and 1956 and successfully resisted efforts at repatriation. In 1991 the general's remains were returned to a free Hungary and were buried with full military honours in the town of his birth, Baja.

There is an excellent new village hall in Titley made possible by local effort and fund-raising and with the help of grants.

TUPSLEY

Before the Second World War Tupsley was a small community. St Paul's church and the school were at the centre of village life. Most things were connected with the church – fetes, country dancing, socials, tennis, garden parties and jumble sales were all held on the vicarage lawn. The schoolchildren marched to the Castle Green on Empire Day to sing *Land of Hope and Glory*.

Down the road at the Manor, Lady Hopton lived. She rode a horse side-saddle and all the boys raised their caps to her. Nearby, the Rose and Crown was kept by Mr Chave who was well-known for charming warts off hands.

There were six farms and a smallholding near the Rose and Crown. Pigs were kept on the smallholding, much of their food coming from scraps collected from the houses in Tupsley. Milk was delivered from the farms, carried on floats drawn by horses. The milk was in churns and was measured out into the householders' containers. Probert's nurseries provided tomatoes for the Tupsley residents.

Near the war memorial (Tupsley Cross) there was the Alice Ottley Children's Home at Ivy House. The children attended Tupsley school where they were identifiable by their clothes – jumpers for the boys, instead of shirts, and plain white pinafores for the girls. Mr Croome was the headmaster and the children were able to walk to school along footpaths crossing fields where houses now stand.

There were also footpaths leading to the Lugg Meadows where many people enjoyed walking. Just before the war there was great excitement when Amy Johnson landed her small plane on the Lugg Meadows. Other leisure activities for Tupsley residents were provided by Ellis' riding school at the stables (Uplands) in Folly Lane and by the tennis courts at The Three Counties Club (now Carter Grove).

Work was provided by the laundry in Ledbury Road (where Highgrove Bank houses were built), while the kitchen providing school meals was in Ledbury Road (the site of the Cathedrals estate). The Isolation Hospital was situated in Gorsty Lane, where children afflicted with scarlet fever would spend some time.

After the war Tupsley expanded rapidly as new estates were built where once it had been farmland. Only one farm remains. Tupsley is no longer a village but part of the City of Hereford. Tupsley school became known as St Paul's and doubled in size and another primary school was provided to serve the parish. A secondary school was built in the 1950s adjacent to St Paul's primary school. The Bishop of Hereford's Bluecoat School is now a large comprehensive. Further educational opportunities are provided by the sixth form and technical colleges in Folly Lane. A second church – the United Reformed church – was established in the 1960s to serve the community. The post office and a few small shops continue to provide a service for Tupsley residents.

TURNASTONE

Turnastone is situated in the Golden Valley about eleven miles southwest of Hereford and is one of the smallest parishes in the county, covering roughly 530 acres, with a population of 29. The parish is partly bounded by the river Dore which was said to have been the border between England and Wales in Saxon times.

The parish church, dedicated to St Mary Magdalene, is of late 12th century origin. The nave and chancel have a handsome wagon-form roof dating from the early 16th century, and the pulpit is a simple example of Jacobean work. The church was restored in 1884 when the south porch was rebuilt, the chancel and nave reseated and refloored and a stained glass window added to the east end – at a total cost of £450.

The village shop, which was once the post office, has two famous petrol pumps which are visited by vintage car clubs and other motoring enthusiasts. Recently the Fire Authority wanted them to be shut down because of their age and their proximity to the road, but an appeal by the owner and a petition signed by hundreds of residents in the Golden Valley resulted in a stay of execution. The pumps continue to dispense petrol – still in gallons!

TYBERTON

In the 18th century Tyberton consisted of a manor house, a church, and three farms with cottages belonging to the lord of the manor. Blacksmiths, carpenters, woodmen, gardeners and servants, all working for the manor and drawn from the village, made it a completely self-sufficient community.

Today, it is quite a different picture. The manor house built in 1728 by John Wood of Bath was dismantled in 1950–51, and a bungalow is now erected on its foundations. However, the servants' quarters remain and are being converted into four new dwellings.

The 18th century church of St Mary is very much the centre of the village. Designed by the same John Wood, it is unique with a brick exterior and curved wooden reredos. Its five bells, having recently been fitted with new ropes, are regularly rung.

The village consists of 34 houses, six of which are new and three barns have been converted. The population is approximately 80, of whom only eight are children who travel by bus or car to local schools.

The farmland and surrounding woodlands, having changed hands many times, are now owned by the Prudential Insurance Company, three farms having been amalgamated into two. These dairy farms only employ three people and only five properties are occupied by farming folk. Many cottages have been sold or let and the majority of the inhabitants commute to work or run their own small businesses.

Tyberton Lakes, quite a local feature, have recently been cleaned and landscaped.

ULLINGSWICK

The small village of Ullingswick is situated in undulating countryside between Bromyard and Hereford near the A465. The village was an Anglo-Saxon settlement and the name means the village or dairy of Willa's people.

Domesday Book records the village but there is no mention of a church. The present structure dates from the 12th century. Several small round-headed windows date from this period. Much needed restoration work was undertaken in the 19th century when a new rectory was also built opposite on the site of an earlier one. A vestry was added more recently, using materials brought from the ruined church at Avenbury. Inside the church the most notable feature is a painted wall memorial to John Hill of Lower Court who died in the late 16th century.

John Hill's family were responsible for much of the building of Lower Court, a half-timbered farmhouse situated just down the lane from the church. The building dates from the 15th to the 17th centuries and has a fine Jacobean overmantel. Upper Court, adjacent to the church, is by contrast built of stone and dates from the 16th and 17th centuries. There are many picturesque, half-timbered cottages and farmhouses in the parish, many of which are listed buildings. At the end of the village furthest from the church and known as 'Upper Town' is The Steppes, a fine half-timbered 17th century house formerly a farmhouse and now a small private hotel. However, several stone built properties can also be found along the lanes, adding to the charm and character of the area.

One notable structure in the parish is 'The Camp' adjacent to the main A417. This was built to house Land Army girls during the Second World War but found a different use as a POW camp for Italian soldiers who were set to work in the nearby farms. Some of the

POWs worked at Lower Court where a searchlight and a machine gun post were placed. The Nissen hut where they slept still stands. No record exists of any POW escaping!

One man who also didn't escape has provided the village with a claim to history. Unfortunately a young maid from a local farm was killed on her way home after visiting a local cider house to purchase candles. The man who was found guilty of unlawfully killing her was the last man to be hanged in public in Hereford. A tablet recording the event hangs in the local tavern, The Three Crowns.

The village, which like so many others was once as self-sufficient as possible, no longer has its own blacksmith, the clog bottom maker has long since given up using the local trees and no hops are now grown in the parish. Electricity came to the village in the late 1950s along with mains water and the old wind pumps and storage tanks are no longer used. The village school closed in the 1970s and the schoolhouse is now a private home, the village hall is no longer used and the village shop has closed. These services are now provided by nearby Burley Gate. However, the village, which still has a post office,

Ullingswick village

continues to thrive with older properties being renovated and new bungalows being built. Old cider orchards still exist and, along with perry pears and damsons, provide a colourful spring. Many former lanes are now footpaths and bridlepaths, providing pleasant walking along gently undulating countryside which abounds with wild life.

Upper Sapey

Upper Sapey, situated on the north-east border of Herefordshire with Wolferlow on the western side, has two concentrations of dwellings, the larger one by the church and the other at Sapey Common.

The church of St Michael stands at the end of Church Lane. It is a small church dating back to pre-Norman times. In the rear of the church there is a fine carved stone arch which was the original chancel arch, but was moved and replaced by a Norman arch. The pulpit, lectern and clergy's desk are very old and beautifully carved, as is the 13th century font. The pulpit is inscribed with the words 'Blessed are they that heare the worde of God and keepe it'.

Church Cottage beside the church gates was once dame school, and later the post office, which is now in 1 Lockhill Council Houses in Church Lane. A considerable number of attractive new dwellings have been built on land at Church Farm and Brook Farm, greatly extending the village. Upper Sapey Golf Course and club house, constructed and built on Church Farm land, is very popular with local people and visitors.

The only public house is the Baiting House, so called because drovers and hauliers used to stop for their 'bait', as it was on the route from Wales to the Midlands. It is believed to be the only public house in the country with that name.

At a parish meeting in 1953 a proposal was adopted to build a village hall on land given by Sir Francis Winnington. An estimate for £1,250 was accepted, and the hall named The Edith Silcock Memorial Hall, 'in appreciation of services to the parish of the late headmistress', was officially opened by Sir Francis Winnington in 1956. It is extensively used and Sapey Cricket Club have their ground there.

The village school was closed in 1969, the classroom divided into two flats and with the school house let to elderly people of the parish. All three dwellings were demolished about three years ago and new ones built on the site.

The Sapey Brook rises in the north-west of the parish and flows in a southerly direction through the village to some lovely dingles in Lower Sapey (Worcestershire) and Tedstone Delamere, then winds its way through Whitbourne where it flows into the river Teme.

UPTON BISHOP

Upton Bishop is surrounded by extensive and beautiful views to the Brecon Beacons, Malverns, Cotswolds, May Hill and the Forest of Dean. Situated four miles north-east of Ross-on-Wye, it is considered to be a healthy location with rather a cold and bracing climate. The village is very scattered and divided into the areas of Tanhouse, Fishpools, The Crews, Crow Hill and Phocle Green.

The Reverend Francis Havergal was vicar from 1874 until his death in 1890. He was a historian, musician and scholar and brought his own organ to the church, which was later removed by his family after his death. He is particularly known for his book on Hereford Cathedral and for his records on Upton Bishop. He was a contemporary of the Reverend Kilvert and is well remembered for his generosity to the poor in the parish.

The church of St John the Baptist is built in the Norman style with a west tower, nave, chancel and south aisle. The present building dates from 1180 and reached its present stage in about 1400. The font is of particular interest and this is over 600 years old, having been cut out of a solid block of Forest of Dean stone. The 116 steps up the tower take you to magnificent views of the surrounding countryside. The parish chest dates from 1703 and has three padlocks, one key for the vicar and the other two for the churchwardens. The chest could only be opened when all three were present. It is interesting to read the list of vicars commencing from 1180, and to note that Thomas Smyth was actually murdered in the church. The vestry was built in memory of the Reverend Havergal's sister, Frances Ridley Havergal, the famous hymn writer who lived with her brother in the village for a short time.

Each parish was required to have a workhouse and Upton Bishop's was built at The Crews in the early 1800s, although no records now remain. The parish room was built in 1897 on land donated by the Reverend Andrew Pope. Many activities and events have been held there including a working men's club which was opened every night of the week at a cost of three shillings per annum. Before the County Library came around in 1928 there was a library in the parish room which cost one shilling per year.

It took many years to get a telegraph office but in 1910 it actually began to operate. The telephone also took some time to arrive and it is said that a farmer at Mulhampton rigged up wires and poles to speak to his cowman a quarter of a mile away. The shop, baker, post office and butcher sadly are no more, but we still have a farrier, builders, pottery, fine craftsman and a vintage car restorer.

The first school was in a small thatched cottage near the manor house, until money was donated to buy land at Church End meadow in 1845. This remained open until July 1972. Children on the west side of the parish went to school at cottages at Bamfords until 1874 when the school was moved to Gayton, and this subsequently closed in 1950.

The Lord Wellington situated at Crow Hill has been refurbished and renamed the Moody Cow but it still retains the atmosphere of a village pub. Two new housing developments have been built, The Pastures and Spring Meadow. The whole aspect of farming has changed, as Phocle Farm and cottages have been sold but one of the original owners has purchased the land and the herd of Hereford cattle at Phocle are still winning prizes. Fruit farms selling soft fruit to supermarkets have replaced arable fields and at Castle Farm many varieties of herbs are grown. A potato store has been built at Phocle Green, and up the 'new road' a crop specialist has set up business. The Vineyard at The Beeches is now producing its own wine and young children of pre-school age have the advantage of attending the Red House Nursery in the wonderful rural setting of The Old Vicarage. Wobage Farm has a much visited craft centre, where pottery, furniture and jewellery are made.

When it became apparent that the Victorian Parish Room was beyond economic repair, and following the decision of the parishioners to build a new village hall and community centre, the committee of UB.2000 was formed and a 4.5 acre site purchased from Felhampton Farm. It is hoped to build the new hall with the help of money from the lottery, the Rural Development Commission, Southern Marches Partnership and other grant-giving bodies and our own fund-raising.

The ebb and flow of village life continues where we say goodbye to old friends and welcome our new villagers who no doubt will take up the challenge of living in a vibrant community and enter into the spirit and fun of the village.

Vowchurch

There are several houses round the church including the 16th century Old Vicarage, but Vowchurch Common is the biggest residential area in the village, with a further 50 to 60 properties. The exterior of the parish church which is dedicated to St Bartholomew is described as Gothic. It has retained its rectangular form since the 14th century.

The Old School House is now privately owned. There is a well-used village hall and a Saturday morning market is held there every week during the summer months. Most of the work locally is agriculturally based and there is a garage repair business.

Walford

About two miles out of Ross on the B4234 road to Coleford lies the historic village of Walford – deriving its name from Wales-ford, where the old turnpike road from Ross crossed the river into Wales about half a mile upstream from Kerne Bridge.

Walford village itself is strung out over about a mile, from Coughton at one end to the extensive sawmills at the other. The latter together with the public house/restaurant and garage in the main section of the village are still thriving, but the post office/store closed in 1995. Centrally lies the old stone church of St Michael and All Angels, which was dedicated to St Leonard until the major restoration in 1887 and is well worth a visit. The earliest part of the nave was built about 1100, making this church one of the oldest in the county of Herefordshire. The de Walford family held the knight's fee of Walford and the north aisle of the church formed their private chapel.

The old railway embankment runs along the west side of the churchyard, from where there are very good views of Goodrich Castle. When the castle was besieged during the Civil War, Oliver Cromwell is said to have stayed in one of the historic houses of the neighbourhood, Walford Court, situated opposite the church. The other old houses are Old Hill Court, Hill Court itself, and Wythall and Lower Wythall. In recent years considerable restoration work has been carried out at Wythall, part of which dates back to 1400, and the house is occasionally open to the public.

Gradually, over the last few years, as older residents have died or moved away, their cottages and land have been bought, largely by incomers, and the houses renovated. The farming land is mostly worked by or on behalf of a few large farmers and is now mainly arable; cereals, potatoes and onions in particular being grown. The number of people keeping horses for riding has increased considerably, and the network of bridleways is well used, as are the footpaths, which include parts of the Wye Valley Walk. A nature reserve, owned by the Herefordshire Nature (Wildlife) Trust, has been established within the parish and this was recently augmented by the adjoining 'Parish Field'.

Three housing developments have taken place since 1985: the house and grounds of a hotel being developed at Coughton, part of a field opposite the sawmills, and the site of an engineering yard on the Hill Court road. The sheltered housing complex at Fowbridge has also been extended. The primary school, with its extensive playing field purchased with aid from the Robert Pashley Trust, is well attended and has an energetic Parent Teacher Association, and the Pashley Memorial Hall at the other end of the village hosts pre-school and toddler groups as well as other social activities.

WELLINGTON

Wellington is a linear village, at right angles to the Hereford to Leominster (A49) road. On the north side, the Wellington Brook runs parallel to the long street, with Dinmore Hill providing a wooded backdrop. At the junction with the A49 stands Bridge House, formerly a coaching inn of early Georgian times. The blacksmith's forge opposite was dismantled during road widening, and has been rebuilt at Avoncroft Museum at Bromsgrove, in north Worcestershire. Next door to where it stood are the almshouses founded by Sir Herbert Perrott in 1682, rebuilt in 1887, Queen Victoria's Jubilee year.

Originally the way into the village was north of Bridge House along the causeway by the side of the brook past Bridge Farm, a 17th century black and white farmhouse, to join the lane which is crossed at the ford. This latter leads to Wellington Court, a handsome square brick building which was the birthplace of Benjamin Tomkins the younger in 1745, whose family originated the Hereford breed of cattle. One of the newest housing developments now clusters round Bridge Farm.

The church is mainly Norman. The school, also taking children from Moreton and Lyde, and village hall are opposite with playing fields (bowls, tennis, football, cricket) behind. The many black and white cottages now have modern houses between them – and in many cases behind them also, being built on the orchards belonging to each cottage. Stocks House is a tall Victorian replacement for an older farm burned down in the 1860s, but the octagonal dovecote of earlier property remains. There is an inn, shop and post office, chapel and garden centre, and at the western end of the street, the mill has been converted into small houses. The population of Wellington remained stable for over 100 years, but with considerable new development, now houses over 600 people. The children go on to secondary school in Hereford and many adults also work there, but some are still employed on the local farms and by building firms.

There are three small hamlets surrounding the village. Auberrow has about 30 houses and a gypsy site. Wellington Marsh on the main road used to house the village policeman, and has the Old Comrade Inn (previously the New Inn) and 30 houses. Burghope is north of the village at the foot of Dinmore Hill, with 15 houses, a farm and an organic farm shop. It also contains Burghope Court, a timber-framed house added to in the early 18th century.

All that remains of Burghope House is one gatepost. It appears that in 1740 it was owned by John Goodere who had no children and, being on bad terms with his brother, threatened to disinherit him in favour of his nephew John Foote of Truro. This so alarmed Samuel Goodere, a sea captain, that he arranged for his elder brother's murder aboard his ship in 1741. The unscrupulous deed was immediately discovered and the captain, who had succeeded on his brother's death, was tried at Bristol and executed in April 1741. The house later passed to a Mr Turberville who sold it as the house had acquired the reputation for being haunted as a result of the murder. There are more details and a poem on the subject in the County Archives Office.

There was a tanning pool on the Wellington Brook, and old lime kiln remains are up in the woods. In 1988 a Roman villa was discovered when a new gravel pit was opened by the railway line, between Wellington and Marden. Dinmore Manor, with its woods

Rose Cottage, Wellington

and farmland, lies up a secluded valley between Wellington and Burghope and contains a chapel of the Knights of St John of Jerusalem, a house with some medieval parts and a 20th century hall and cloisters round a rock garden, and has superb views across the Lugg valley towards the Malvern Hills. The house and gardens are open to the public.

WEOBLEY

Weobley, the jewel of Herefordshire, is so called because there is no prettier village. The many black and white houses stand all down the main streets as they have stood for between 400 and 600 years. Many a tale they could tell if they could speak. There is an old saying:

Poor Weobley, proud people,
Low Church and High Steeple.

Until about 45 years ago a well known saying was, 'I'm going to Weobley to see the tide come in'. This was an allusion to the overflow of a brook passing across the road in Bell Square. Local children loved to play in this area, paddling across the road and going home to tea with soaking wet shoes, to the consternation of their mothers. At certain times of flooding the menfolk would carry the women in their long dresses over the water because the floodwater would gush under the doorways in the square. Villagers would push the tide back with brooms. Since then the stream has been piped under the road.

In Weobley churchyard stands an old memorial cross, and the saying goes that if one walks backwards seven times around each tier of steps, one then sees the Devil. This feat has been completed many times in the past but no one has yet admitted seeing him.

Between the World Wars and prior to the National Health Service, Weobley possessed a poor law institution and a private lodging house for gentlemen of the road. The workhouse was run by a master and became a permanent residence for some. A night's shelter and food could be obtained by breaking stones for the road to the required size. The lodging house on the other hand charged one shilling per night for a camp bed and a blanket in a communal room. These two buildings still stand today, one as a private house and the other has been turned into flats. The lodging house brought many amusing and colourful characters to the village. There was Sid who turned up every night at the local inn with ferrets in his trouser pockets, and old Joe who sharpened knives for 2d – the fact that your knives wouldn't cut paper when he'd finished didn't bother him if he had earned enough for a pint of cider or some snuff.

Weobley has expanded dramatically. Two large housing estates fringe the old village. The council built one in the 1950s and private companies the other in the 1970s. Both estates have approximately 100 houses thereby considerably increasing the population. Since 1990 there have been three new developments of about 20 houses each, one in Kington Road, one next to the Unicorn and one next the Hopelands Village Hall. There has consequently been a great increase in traffic, and the village is in danger of being overwhelmed by the motor car.

A new primary school has been built, to replace the wooden structure built in 1934. It opened in 1998, and boasts a new boiler which will burn straw. The grocer has been taken over by Londis, and is a very successful mini-market, making trips to the town almost unnecessary. The village, in fact, is regaining its old prosperity, with butcher, grocer, draper, post office, newsagent, furniture maker, gift shop, two garages, agricultural engineer, garden shop and a picture framer. Tourists are well provided for with several establishments offering bed and breakfast and three public houses and two restaurants with accommodation.

Add to this the enduring charm of the many timber-framed buildings, and well laid out small museum and a twice-weekly library, and it will be seen that Weobley is a favoured place. The many local societies – Gardening, History, Drama, the Guides, Brownies and Scouts – three well-attended places of worship and, of course, the WI make sure that the spirit and the mind are as well catered for as the body.

WESTHIDE

Westhide is one of the few peaceful and unspoiled villages in the county, having altered very little during the 20th century. It lies between Withington and Ocle Pychard, the connecting road being narrow and winding. In the 1991 census the population was 69.

Farming remains the only industry. There are lovely woods in the area. The church, dedicated to St Bartholomew, has a short unbuttressed 12th century west tower with a pyramid roof. In early spring masses of snowdrops and primroses can be seen in the churchyard.

The village has no vicarage, post office, village shop or school. The latter closed in 1884 when the children were transferred to Withington school. In 1885 it was decided that all children not resident in Withington were to pay 3d per week for schooling. If they attended 175 days or more, 1d per week would be refunded!

WESTON BEGGARD

Weston Beggard is a village of the byways with old farms and cottages scattered between two busy roads from Hereford, the river Frome flowing by one side and Shucknall Hill rising on the other.

A narrow lane winds to the church with a 14th century tower neighboured by white capped oasthouses (hops are grown in the village), an old black and white building which is said to have once been a vicarage and a tiny black and white cottage. The churchyard has two survivals from Stuart times – one is a tiny brass sundial of 1649 set on the base of the medieval cross and the other is a shapely yew planted in the memorable year of 1688 when the seven bishops defied James II and the King fled for his life. Most of the old work in the church is 14th century but the restored doorway with a head at each side is Norman, and the graceful painted chancel arch with a carved bracket on each side is over 700 years old.

Shucknall Hill, with its water spout on the side of the road, was the source of water for cottages on the hill and at one time a local man carried the water by yoke to cottagers for a halfpenny a bucket. However, if you gave him a whole penny for the water he promptly turned it down – he had to have his halfpennies.

The road leading from the spout to the chapel on the hill was built by cottagers living on the hill. They raised the money and men, women and children all helped to build the road. The spout today is still used mainly by travelling families but there are people from afar who won't use any other water for their winemaking.

WESTON UNDER PENYARD

This Herefordshire village has not received fame as the result of some battle fought nearby, or some famous personality born within its confines, but it has beauty and tranquillity in spite of being astride the main A40 road. It does not possess any large estates although in the 1950s one small estate, partly bungalows for the elderly and private houses, was built.

Besides the building firm of J. Robbins & Sons, it was the numerous farmers in the locality and the gentry in the large manor-type houses who employed most of the menfolk between the two World Wars. Most of the young girls were in service in those large houses, such as the famous Elizabethan Weston House, The Wye, Weston Hall, The Old Rectory, Sandiway and Queen Anne House.

Today the friendly Weston Cross Inn is all that remains of local services, although some may recall the old smithy and the blacksmith, old Mr Rigsby, shoeing the horses.

The parish church still stands out in all its majesty and the nave has a fine arcade of four Norman arches. Of the memorials the most interesting is a brass on the south wall of the nave commemorating Walter Nourse, who died on 7th January 1601, depicting a man kneeling in prayer. The Nourse family lived at Lower Weston – Weston Hall – during the 16th, 17th and 18th centuries and were very generous benefactors of the area.

Adjacent to the Queen Anne House on the Bromsash road leading out of the village is an old building that was reputedly a chapel in the distant past. It hides under the old railway embankment that carried the now disused line from Gloucester to Hereford, built 1840. The last train to go through the village was in 1964. On the other side of the embankment is the Elizabethan cruck cottage of St Mary's, said to have been a House of Correction for Cistercian monks, presumably from Flaxley Abbey.

In the late 1920s workmen digging a trench uncovered the foundation of the Roman wall that surrounded the Roman town of Ariconium, then the largest iron smelting town. The main part of Ariconium lies just within the parish boundary on the elevated plateau between Bromsash and Castle End.

Near the old railway bridge close to St Mary's is a steady flow of water into a trough which no doubt was so placed for the benefit of the work horses of 100 years ago. This water source from a spring on the Ariconium plateau was also the source of private supply for the residents of Weston under Penyard.

On the periphery of the parish are the remains of Eccleswall Castle, which, like Penyard Castle on the other side of the parish, was the home at one time of the Earls of Shrewsbury – the Talbot family.

From Bromsash to Weston Cross, you will pass the ruins of Aske Barn and the pseudo Bollitree Castle. There are fields near Aske Barn with the names of Kill Dane Meadow, Kill Dane Field and Kill Dane Orchard and tradition has it that human bones were found in this locality. Historically, it is a fact that King Ethelred issued an order in 1002 that all Danes living on the periphery of the existing Danish kingdom should be killed. This became known as the Massacre of St Bric's Day.

Bollitree Castle is said to have been the product of some Herefordshire 'Don Juan' who tried to woo his Spanish love of wealth and high-standing. Tradition maintains that he did not succeed. Bollitree House itself is a fine building of historical interest.

The hamlet of Kingstone has its preaching cross whilst Ryeford has its 1731 Baptist chapel and pre-1731 baptistry in the grounds of Ryeford Villa as evidence of yesteryear. The Dancing Green is a hamlet hidden among the trees with a history of dancing round the maypole, and outdoor religious meetings in the clearings. Kettle Bottom with its hidden-away houses, unseen from any road, has only footpaths except when you ford the brook. The name Kettle Bottom may have a link with the preacher in those days, Rev Kettle, who lived in the locality.

There is a solitary grave with headstone in Hoovers Lane. It is in the grounds of a property that was part of the Quaker settlement at New House Farm, Pontshill, created about 1800.

The old village hall has gone. It came from Hyde Park after the 1914–18 war. It was an old army hut and it served the village very well for a number of years. The village is now using a lovely new hall built on the recreation ground.

Many years ago W.G. Grace played cricket against Weston and the newspaper report is still held in the village today.

WHITCHURCH

The village of Whitchurch is situated on the river Wye. The A40 dual carriageway built in 1966 divides the village, leaving the shops and the pub on one side and the church and school on the other.

An interesting feature of the village square is the old clock tower next to the butcher's. The clock tower was erected in 1867 by the sole surviving sister of the Panting family, in memory of her brother and sisters. This is now maintained by the Parish Council.

Near the square is the local pub, The Crown Inn, which in days past was visited by many a stage coach. Three houses next to the pub, Portland Guest House, White Roses and The Cedars, were once the asylum. Opposite The Cedars is the Catholic church.

Approaching the village from Monmouth one can see the Memorial Hall which is very well used by all the village organisations. Opposite the village hall is the Gallery Restaurant which used to be the village reading room. Nearby is the old village forge and the mill house, opposite which is the village post office. The post office also sells groceries but the greatest asset is its bakery. To have freshly baked bread in a village is a delight.

Crossing from the shops side of the dual carriageway to the right is Crocker's Ash where the Romans smelted iron. Following this road one reaches the Little Doward, the Great Doward and back down to Symonds Yat West. To the left is the fire station which is manned by volunteers. Around the roundabout is the village school, originally built in 1858 but replaced in 1981. The new school has retained the old school bell which makes a most attractive feature.

Just past the school is the Wye Valley Visitors Centre. This is a pleasant area of gardens which has a tea room and houses the World of Butterflies and craft workshops. A bridge leads from here to the Jubilee Maze. This was built by the Heyes brothers, Edward and Lindsay, during the Queen's Silver Jubilee year. Along the road past the maze one comes to St Dubricius' church. This is situated on the river bank and was once reached by boat. It is one of the oldest churches in the Deanery of Ross and Archenfield, dating back to the 13th century. There is a rare tulip tree in the churchyard and a most interesting spacious vault belonging to the Gwillim family, who lived at the manor, now the Old Court Hotel.

Situated next to the maze is the leisure park which has amusement arcades and a bird park. Boat trips are available from here up and down the river.

Towards Symonds Yat is the Paddocks Hotel, once known as the 'Washings' and then the Ferrie Inn. A ferry operated by a boatman and a rope runs from here to Symonds Yat East. There is another ferry further along the river past the Wye Rapids Hotel.

On the Doward there is a most interesting and extensive Heritage Museum where one can see old farm machinery and kitchen implements.

The great fortification which crowns the Little Doward has been described as a Roman camp, but it is much older. It may have been one of the strongholds of Caractacus, and of the Silures who inhabited the area prior to and during the Roman occupation. Many Roman relics have been found.

Evidence of former inhabitants goes back to prehistoric times. When King Arthur's Cave was excavated in 1870 it was found to have been a hyena den and the bones of prey were found in great numbers, including those of the lion, woolly rhinoceros, mammoth, reindeer and many others.

WHITNEY-ON-WYE

Whitney-on-Wye is situated on the A438, 16 miles from Hereford and four miles from Hay-on-Wye. The name 'de Whitney' was assumed by Eustace, son of Turstin the Fleming, a companion of William the Conqueror, who was given possession of the land as mentioned in the Domesday Book.

The life of the village, both past and present, has been dominated by the river Wye, the meaning of the name Whitney being 'white water' as the river is subject to sudden and destructive floods. The remains of Whitney Castle, which was built to guard the Welsh border, were washed away by floods. So, too, were the three stone toll bridges across the river to Clifford. The present bridge, part timber, part stone, dates from 1802, and traffic crossing it still has to pay a toll in the old tradition. During the holiday season groups of canoeists can be seen at the bridge 'putting-in' their canoes for a trip either up or down the river. Angling for salmon is also an attraction on this stretch of water.

The church of St Peter and St Paul was built in 1740 to replace an earlier one which was threatened with destruction by the flooding of the river Wye when it changed course in 1735. The land adjacent to the road floods in extreme conditions several times a year, causing property damage. This is being dealt with by a flood relief scheme which hopefully will cure the problem. In the same year, 1735, the rectory was also threatened and this was replaced by Wardour House at the end of the church drive which was later used for the rector's curate. East of the church is West Hills, the former rectory built in 1846.

A large neo-Tudor house is visible on high land to the right, from the main road. It was built between 1898–1902 for the Hope family, still lords of the manor. The red brick building further along the main road on the left was the Whitney Court pumphouse, last used in 1976. Opposite this is the former Whitney school. Beyond it, a gated track on the left once led to Whitney station and if you continue to walk under the former railway line, on the left can be seen the power house with its large chimney stack. This provided power to the Whitney Court estate.

Today farming is the major local occupation, the farmers mainly being tenants of the Whitney Court estate. There are many stone houses in the vicinity which were used for the farm workers and are now privately owned and restored. The cutting of timber is still carried out in Whitney Wood which now houses a large sawmill dealing in native timber. There used to be a quarry and kiln and shards of pots in a distinctive honey-colour can still be found today.

Whitney is on the old drovers' road and there is an old inn, now a private dwelling, where the drovers rested, complete with the blacksmith's cottage. The Boat Inn now offers meals and accommodation. The main road has been straightened to eliminate a bad bend, thus virtually cutting the original village in half.

WIGMORE

Wigmore is an attractive and ancient village situated in the hills on the A4110, in the north of the county.

The church of St James stands on higher ground away from the main street. Its nave is early Norman and there is 13th to 15th century work to be seen, although the church was restored in 1864. Just to the west of the church is Wigmore Castle, one of the largest of those built along the Welsh border and which was mentioned in the Domesday Book. It was held by Ralph de Mortimer and remained in that family till the 15th century. After the Battle of Mortimer's Cross the castle passed to the Crown. In the 16th century it was held on a lease from Queen Elizabeth by the Harley family of Brampton Bryan who bought it in 1601. During the Civil War the family deliberately slighted the castle in 1643 rather than let it fall into Royalist hands.

To the north is Wigmore Abbey, founded in the 12th century by Hugh Mortimer. The abbey church was the Mortimers' burial place, though little remains, but it appears to have been situated just off Barnet Lane on the western side of the path still known as Jacob's Ladder.

The market hall stood on the Pavement in the triangular market place in front of the Old Oak Inn. It is shown on the old tithe map of 1840 but it is not on a map of 1871. Probably it was demolished in

1848. One of the old village pounds, in which stray cattle were impounded and released on payment of a fine, still remains on the main road north of and below the church. By 1304 there was a weekly market on Wednesdays and an annual fair.

Wigmore was one of the first areas in the county to have an Enclosure Act. This is dated 1772 and the enclosure was of the common on the moor and in the woods. The plots on the moor can still be traced with the drains dividing them and flowing into the Great Drain and so into the Teme, while in Barnet Wood and Woodhampton Wood the earth banks dividing the plots still exist.

There is also more recent history in Wigmore, which was one of the eleven places in the county to have a police station under the 1839 Act. The Court House and Police Station were built in 1848 for a Superintendent, with the court and cells adjoining the house. The Petty Sessions Court closed on 31st March 1971, and then was used as the County Library for a time until 1977 when the whole building became a private house.

At one time there were three chapels and now there are none. In September 1853, the Primitive Methodists purchased for £95 the Independent Chapel which had been built in 1847. This became Chapel Cottage in Castle Street which was lived in until the death of Mrs Preece when it was sold to the next door owners of Steppes House. A new chapel was built in 1863 on the A4110 which in 1983 was sold and converted into a house. The Wesleyans had a chapel near the Cross of the Tree on Deerfold where memorials can be seen in the burial ground. The Primitive Methodists in 1864 built a chapel at Crookmullen. It closed and in 1976 was sold and since has been converted into a house.

The first known school was founded by the will of William Allen, yeoman, dated 5th May 1659, who left a house for 'one honest maid or single woman therein that can teach children to sewe and reade and shee to have the same rent free as long as shee behaveth herselfe well' and to be paid 20s yearly. This building which still stands to the east of the church was replaced by the stone-built school to the west which opened on 16th October 1860. In January 1968 this school was replaced by a modern one alongside the High School. The old school and schoolmaster's house reverted to the descendants of the giver of the land who sold it to a private individual.

In 1801 the population was 362 and by 1841 had increased to 506, since when there has been a decline. Between 1961 and 1988 approximately 50 dwellings have been built and their occupants integrated into the community. The village still has two public houses, a shop, a garage, a village hall and its two schools. Now a new development of 106 dwellings and twelve industrial workshops is under way.

WINFORTON

Winforton is situated on the A438, 15 miles from Hereford. The village is overshadowed to the south by the steep, dark height of Merbach Mountain.

The church of St Michael and All Angels dates from the 12th century, although there may have been a church on that site from the 9th century. There was a hermitage on an island of the river Wye, begun by St Cynidr, which is now in ruins and little of which remains as the river has changed course at this point. The site, when the river is in flood, is surrounded by water, giving a small island called Hermitage.

If when leaving the church, you turn right and go through a small wicket gate, you will then see the former Winforton school on the right. Further along the track is Pennys, the first of many black and white half-timbered houses in Winforton. Next to it is the 12th century black and white Cross Farm, now divided into Cross House and Cross Cottage. As the track joins the main road there is the remains of the medieval preaching cross.

On the opposite side of the road is the old parish hall (now privately owned). This was once the malthouse for the Winforton House estate and during the Second World War was used for storing pictures for the National Gallery. Winforton House is Georgian and set behind and to the right of two former labourers' cottages. Along the main road on the left can be seen Winforton Old Court farmhouse with its fine barns and further along is Winforton Court, once owned by Roger Mortimer, Earl of March. Traces of a chapel (used by a later

Catholic owner) have been found in the rafters. The Court House was visited on several occasions by Judge Jeffreys. The cell where the prisoners were kept is still there. There is a new development of several houses built in the old black and white style.

Between these buildings is Baker's Lane which leads to the river Wye. The tale is that a baker with his horse and cart used the lane to cross the river by a ford to Clock Mills on the other side, to deliver his bread. Legend has it that the baker, horse and cart were swept away during a time when the river was in flood!

Opposite the preaching cross is the Sun Inn and to the right of it is a road leading to Winforton Common where there are a number of houses, some old and some modern. Several of the latter are bungalows which were used as laboratories by Professor Merton, who worked with Barnes Wallis, testing the famous 'bouncing bomb' during the Second World War.

Winforton has a light industry, using the old garage site, dealing in mail-orders for fishermen.

WITHINGTON

The earliest written record of Withington is in the Domesday Book of 1086. The 1991 census showed that Withington had a population of 1,038; since then a factory manufacturing timber-framed houses has closed down, and approximately 60 new houses have been built on that site. It is estimated that the present population is around 1,118. Agriculture was the main industry but fewer men are now employed on the farms. Many small farms have disappeared, the land having been taken over by larger farms and the farmhouses becoming desirable residences.

In a large area of Thinghill Court Farm specimen young trees are grown. In 1988, 25 young beech trees were planted in the Savill Garden, Windsor Great Park. In September 1998, an avenue of 58 lime trees was planted at the Three Counties Showground in memory of Mr Lyn Downes MBE, a former chief executive of the Three Counties Agricultural Society – one tree for each year of his life. Mr James Hawkins, of Wyevale Hawkins Trees, helped to hand select these trees. Trees have also been ordered to be planted around the Millennium Dome in London, thus a large quantity of Withington village soil will be transported to the capital.

There have been many changes during the past decade. A large grocery cash-and-carry stores, a post office and the tile works have closed down. Tiles had been made at Withington since 1848. Encaustic floor tiles from earlier years have been used in many cathedrals, including Worcester where there can be seen a floor depicting all the seasons. In 1857 these tiles were used for restoration work in Hereford Cathedral. In the final years glazed decorative wall tiles were produced.

The village now has one public house – the Cross Keys – one post office, one garage dealing with repairs, maintenance etc, and one with a large car sales department, a mechanical engineering business, a blacksmith's shop, a custom-made furniture workshop and a retail shop which sells chiefly pinewood furniture. The former tile works site has been modernised and some ten or so smart business units have been built and occupied by various traders. There are also two market gardens.

The memorial to the fallen of the two World Wars stands in the centre of the village and a plaque in the church which is a few yards away and dedicated to St Peter. The early 14th century octagonal spire is a good landmark to lead one to Withington. The church tower is late 13th century and in the south wall of the nave is a piscina of the same period. In the churchyard is an original preaching cross of the 14th or 15th century. Half a mile south is Whitestone Baptist chapel erected in 1821.

Education in Withington was made possible by a bequest of Mrs Elizabeth Byworth in 1636. Records show there was a school in Stallenge used from 1732 to 1870. The next school was built in 1872. When this school closed in 1984 a service of thanksgiving was held in St Peter's church which was filled with many ex-pupils. A new school was opened in Lock Road on 6th September 1984.

In 1983, 24 houses were listed as ancient and historical monuments, among them Eau Withington Court which lies west of the village. Parts date from the late 17th century. A small building west of the house has the date 1682. Thinghill Grange, a mile north-west, is a 14th century hall house. In recent years several old listed barns and granaries have been converted into private dwellings.

A hop field was situated near the bottom of Nunnington Pitch belonging to the then Eau Withington Court Farm. It was here that the last hops were picked by hand in Herefordshire.

John Phillips, 1676–1709, lived at Withington Court. He wrote the poem *Cyder* and other verses. He has a memorial in Poet's Corner, Westminster Abbey.

WOLFERLOW

Before the Norman Conquest, Aluric the Sheriff held Wolferlow and at the date of the Domesday survey it was in the possession of Roger de Lacy and later the Mortimers. Some of the parish became part of the Saltmarshe estate until 1953 when the properties were sold. In the north of the parish there was a walled deer park, and the area, now farmland, is still known as Wolferlow Park.

Wolferlow is situated on the north-east border of Herefordshire, and is mainly a farming community. The 12th century church of St Andrew is built by the site of the old medieval village, and on the north side of the church is a long mound thought to be a medieval burial ground. In the north wall of the chancel there is a 14th century effigy of a woman, possibly Joan, widow of Peter de Genevile. Unfortunately her nose is missing, it is believed to have been broken off by Cromwell's soldiers! Two of the bells bear the dates 1611 and 1725.

The Rectory used to be the last call on the postman's round. The letterbox which has since been moved, was there, and by the roadside was a postman's hut – a wooden hut in which the postman rested and had his lunch before starting back, in those days on foot, on his collection round some four miles back to Whitbourne. Nowadays the mail is delivered by van from Upper Sapey.

At the junction of the road to the church and the road to Stoke Bliss, locally known as Wolferlow Lane, is an old pound which used to hold stray cattle and sheep for their owners in years gone by.

On the western side of the parish the land slopes steeply, dropping off some 300 feet to Underley, the home of the late Sir Archer Baldwin. He was MP for the Leominster Division from 1945 to 1959 and one of the co-founders of the local firm of auctioneers Russell, Baldwin & Bright.

Wolferlow Court is the oldest farmhouse in the parish and has on the first floor a room panelled in original 17th century oak panelling. The Edwards family have lived there for nearly 100 years.

WOOLHOPE

The village of Woolhope, perched on a south-east slope, amid wooded ridges and fertile valleys, is situated in a triangle between Hereford, Ross-on-Wye and Ledbury. The distinctive topography of the surrounding area is the result of the wearing down over 150 million years ago of an uplifted pear-shaped dome to expose older Silurian limestones and shales, with an abundance of fossilised remains including crinoids, corals and bryozoa. Graptolites have also been recorded in the area. The Woolhope Club, a well known naturalists' Field Club set up in 1851, takes its name from the Woolhope Dome.

The name Woolhope was recorded in 1234 as Wulvivehope, the 'hope' being Anglo-Saxon for valley. Wulviva was the sister of Godiva (of Coventry fame) and these two sisters gave the manor to Hereford Cathedral in the 11th century.

Woolhope is sometimes called the 'walled village', as solid stone walls surround the houses instead of hedges. The parish of Woolhope extends to some 4,414 acres and the population of 397 live in the village and in farmhouses, houses and cottages scattered around this very rural area. The village has one of the tiniest village greens in the area, which is centrally situated. This well kept green has an oak tree planted to commemorate the ending of the First World War.

At the centre of the village stands the church built firstly in the 11th century from sandstone, and now dedicated to St George but originally dedicated to St Mary. The church is almost hidden away behind a very large old yew tree and a procession of lime trees. The entrance to the churchyard is through a 17th century lychgate known locally as 'The Skallenge', originally a resting place for coffins en route to church. The 13th century tower, recently restored, houses a peal of six bells. The north side of the arcade is 14th century and the south side is modern. There are several notable stained glass windows in the church. In the north wall Godiva is riding her horse through the streets of Coventry, and again below she is seen patting a dog and cat and her sister Wulviva has a dog and some rabbits at her feet. At the east end is a very beautiful stained glass window depicting the incidents in the life of Jesus. This window is in memory of Mr H.P. Mildmay, MP for the County of Hereford. Just outside the church door are some crosses carved in the wall. They were said to have been carved by men going to fight in the Crusades. It was the practice to put a second horizontal bar on the cross when coming back safely. There are no horizontal bars!

There are several notable houses in the area, one of which is Wessington Court, a 19th century neo-Gothic mansion with an impressive gateway and lodge. Also of interest are black and white houses and farmhouses, namely, The Croose, Sapness, Terrace Hall, The Yare, Bent Orchard and Lower Buckenhill (showing the date 1592). In the village is an unusual projecting corner-stone mounted on the wall of the Stonehouse. It is said that the stone was cast in a chamber pot with the pot having to be broken afterwards. Also at the Stonehouse is a set of mounting steps, formed in brick.

The parish has two public houses, namely the Butchers Arms – a 600 year old inn which was orginally three cottages – and the Crown Inn in the centre of the village. The second set of mounting steps are at the Crown Inn, plus in the Crown garden wall can be seen a ring. Presumably this was to tie the horse to whilst visiting the inn for refreshment – not as some locals would have it, to tie the boat up to, as Woolhope stands 600 feet above sea level!

Included in Woolhope parish is the 35 acre Broadmoor Common owned by Herefordshire Council and designated in 1986 as a Nature Reserve. There are ancient grazing rights attached to the common and rights of six parishioners were acknowledged under the Commons Registration Act of 1965. It is reputed that a colony of dwarfs once lived on the common and several older residents remember a wedding of one of the dwarfs. Also remembered is the wedding of a 90 year old lady and her 82 year old lodger, with the bridesmaid being a present resident's grandmother! Both the weddings took place at St George's church.

Berryfield (owned by the Parish Council) is said to have been the burial place of victims of the plague. It is now, however, used by members of the local tennis, football and cricket clubs for recreation, and also hosts the local annual Church Fete and Dog Show. The field is also a public open space.

Part of Woolhope is designated as an Area of Outstanding Natural Beauty. There are two Sites of Special Scientific Interest and with the river Wye, four Herefordshire Trust Sites and Haugh Woods all nearby, it is an ideal area to walk and ride. Woolhope is wonderful for natural history, bird watching and more recently glow-worm watching (by night). The area abounds in spring with daffodils and bluebells. In secluded places there is a profusion of cowslips and primroses.

Regrettably, Woolhope lost its school in 1959, and its shop in 1988. The post office still survives, opening its doors in the Parish Hall on two half-days a week.

WORMBRIDGE

Wormbridge is situated on either side of the A465 Hereford to Abergavenny road about eight miles from Hereford.

The early history of Wormbridge is that it was a possession of the Knights Hospitallers of St John of Jerusalem centred on their Commandery of Dinmore. The list of Dinmore possessions includes Wormbridge, Church, Manor and 200 acres of land. This part military, part religious order grew to have a position of very great privilege and power throughout the country. One of their privileges was the granting of sanctuary.

An interesting case concerning Wormbridge is on record. In the year 1485, William Bongam of Garway, labourer, was imprisoned for burglary at the house of Isabel Cutta of Penbleyth, from whom he had stolen goods worth £3, a horse and six shillings in money. He pleaded guilty, but stated that he had taken refuge in a house at Wormelow-brugge, a possession of the Knights Hospitallers, from which he had been forcibly removed by Roger Bodenham, Sheriff of the County. He demanded to be restored to the said house. John Stokes of the Hospital of St John said, 'that the house in question was a parcel of the preceptory of Dynmore and that from time immemorial the Hospitallers have always had and still possess this privilege, to wit, that any man or woman coming to any house belonging to them to take refuge after felony committed, and demanding this privilege, shall have safety and protection for their life without disturbance from any Officer of the King of England or any other person'. The jury found that the house belonged to the Hospital and the Hospitallers claimed their privilege.

At the Dissolution of the Monasteries the Wormbridge property was sold. Through marriage it became the property of a branch of the Clive family of Clive in Salop. All that remains of the great house that stood opposite the church at that time is part of the laundry which now serves as the village school.

Although considerably rebuilt in Victorian times, the church of Wormbridge is still entered through the Norman door. The church has some lovely medieval glass and fine carved wood furnishings.

WORMSLEY

The land around Wormsley has been cultivated since the 12th century. In about 1200, a priory of canons of the Rule of St Augustine and Order of St Victor was founded, the canons choosing to erect their priory near a farmhouse which still retains the name, The Grange. There was a chapel, a mill and a fishpond nearby. The old water channels, originally fed by Sap well, an unfailing spring below Court Farm, can still be seen.

In the early years of the priory many gifts of land were given for its upkeep, and it soon became a thriving medieval hamlet, the monks farming mostly sheep on the rich grass fields that lay around them.

Standing in the grounds of Court Farm, the parochial church of St Mary was used by the monks to hold mass for their workforce when they visited them once a month to give orders for the following month's work. There are still remains of sites of mud huts and small dwellings scattered all over the hills of Wormsley, but the more substantial buildings were built during 1555 – these being Upper House Farm and Court House Farm.

A large area of this beautiful countryside is now occupied by the Herefordshire Golf Club, but otherwise the hamlet is much as it has been these past 700 years. People are still tilling the land and are basically farmers, though the little fields are now large and intensively farmed, with up-to-date modern machinery. The Grange is still a farmhouse, Court House Farm now farms all the land around the hills of Wormsley, and Upper House Farm is now a private dwelling.

St Mary's church was made redundant in 1972, but the Churches Conservation Trust spent much on its restoration and it is cared for by them and the parishioners. Wormsley Grange was the birthplace, and St Mary's church the final resting place, of two brothers who later lived at Downton Castle and became known to the world. They were grandsons of the iron founder Richard Knight. The elder, Richard Payne Knight (1750–1824), a poet, archaeologist and collector, is particularly identified with the Picturesque movement. The younger, Thomas Andrew Knight (1759–1838), was a renowned horticulturist who carried out pioneering experimental work on the growth of fruit trees. The inscriptions on their tombs are unfortunately in Latin!

YARKHILL

Yarkhill is a village on the Hereford–Worcester road. The church has a medieval tower with battered gargoyles and the porch still has timbers from the 14th century in its roof. One of these is a boss carved in foliage and ring interlaced with one another. Inside is an old stoup. The doorway into the nave is 13th century and the nave still has the black and white roof from medieval days. The font with a fluted bowl is more than 700 years old and in the churchyard is a splendid yew tree with a trunk 20 feet round.

Flowing close by is the river Frome. The village hall is more than a hundred years old as it was once the village school. Adjoining it is the old school house with a lovely old lime tree and close by used to stand the blacksmith's shop.

YARPOLE

Yarpole lies in the shadow of Croft Ambrey, the 390 BC hill fort and settlement. The Romans in transit laid Watling Street to the north and later the Normans displaced Edwin the Saxon Earl and built Croft Castle, still today occupied by the Croft family but owned by the National Trust. From its mention in Domesday, Yarpole remained a farming village until a small housing estate was discreetly developed in the 1960s. Its peaceful history has been disrupted only by the Battle of Mortimer's Cross in 1461. The group parish embraces some 540 acres of common land and woodland including Fishpool Valley and fishponds, designated a Site of Special Scientific Interest and managed by the National Trust and Forestry Commission.

St Leonard's church with its unusual 13th century detached bell tower and fine yew trees is central to the area. For many years it was unsafe to ring the three bells as once they were, twice each Sunday,

The Gate House at Yarpole

by Charles Chamberlain, so fondly remembered today for his stalwart support of church and village affairs. Happily, in 1997 the three bells were rehung following repairs and refurbishment of the frame and are now rung again each Sunday.

Of the original manor only its medieval gatehouse remains and that has reputedly been used as a gaol, an illicit Quaker meeting house and more recently a bakehouse. If the walls could speak what a story they could tell. The central and older part of the village was designated a conservation area in 1984.

The village is a mix of retired folk, farmers, and families with children of varying ages. They are served by one well-stocked shop, post office and home bakery. The Bell Inn offers a cheery welcome and like other timber-framed buildings in the village is noted for its 17th century traditional style. There is a real sense of community and many functions are held in the village hall.

A son of Yarpole was Thomas Johnes the younger, who grew up at Croft and is remembered in literature for his translations of the chronicles of Joinville, Froissart, Monstrelet and de la Brocquiere. Thomas Knight of the famous 'Ironbridge family' and friend of Sir Joseph Banks, the dominating president of the Royal Society, was closely associated with the village. He is remembered for his experiments with the grafting and cultivating of new varieties of fruit, particularly apple trees.

INDEX